J Randall Koetting
April 2007
AERA
Chicago

THEORY
FOR
EDUCATION

theory4

A book series from
ROUTLEDGE

Theory for Religious Studies
William E. Deal and Timothy K. Beal

Theory for Art History
Jae Emerling

THEORY
FOR
EDUCATION

Greg Dimitriadis and George Kamberelis

Routledge
Taylor & Francis Group
New York   London

2006

Routledge is an imprint of the
Taylor & Francis Group, an informa business

Published in 2006 by
Routledge
Taylor & Francis Group
270 Madison Avenue
New York, NY 10016

Published in Great Britain by
Routledge
Taylor & Francis Group
2 Park Square
Milton Park, Abingdon
Oxon OX14 4RN

© 2006 by Taylor & Francis Group, LLC
Routledge is an imprint of Taylor & Francis Group

Printed in the United States of America on acid-free paper
10 9 8 7 6 5 4 3 2 1

International Standard Book Number-10: 0-415-97418-6 (Hardcover) 0-415-97419-4 (Softcover)
International Standard Book Number-13: 978-0-415-97418-9 (Hardcover) 978-0-415-97419-6 (Softcover)
Library of Congress Card Number 2005028172

Library of Congress Cataloging-in-Publication Data

Dimitriadis, Greg, 1969-
   Theory for education / Greg Dimitriadis and George Kamberelis.
       p. cm. -- (Theory 4)
   Includes bibliographical references.
   ISBN 0-415-97418-6 (hb : alk. paper) -- ISBN 0-415-97419-4 (pb : alk. paper)
   1. Education--Philosophy--History. 2. Educators--Biography. I. Kamberelis, George. II. Title.
III. Series.

LB17.D55 2006
370.1--dc22   2005028172

Taylor & Francis Group
is the Academic Division of Informa plc.

Visit the Taylor & Francis Web site at
http://www.taylorandfrancis.com

and the Routledge Web site at
http://www.routledge-ny.com

CONTENTS

INTRODUCTION   vii

PREDECESSORS   1

1. John DEWEY   3
2. Sigmund FREUD   17
3. Karl MARX   29
4. Ferdinand de SAUSSURE   37

THE THEORISTS   45

5. Mikhail BAKHTIN   47
6. Basil BERNSTEIN   59
7. Pierre BOURDIEU   65
8. Jerome BRUNER   75
9. Judith BUTLER   81
10. Gilles DELEUZE and Félix GUATTARI   87
11. Jacques DERRIDA   101
12. Michel FOUCAULT   111
13. Paulo FREIRE   119
14. Clifford GEERTZ   125
15. Antonio GRAMSCI   131
16. Stuart HALL   137
17. Bell HOOKS   145
18. Jacques LACAN   151
19. Jean PIAGET   167
20. Edward W. SAID   179
21. Gayatri Chakravorty SPIVAK   185
22. Lev Semenovich VYGOTSKY   191
23. Raymond WILLIAMS   201

INTRODUCTION

Education is a field largely dedicated to practice. Because students are often training for a specific professional task—becoming a teacher—it has long been considered an "applied" area of inquiry. It should come as little surprise, then, that students (and faculty) are often reluctant to engage with theory. In the immediacies of practice, theory is often seen as a luxury, unnecessarily distracting from the real task at hand. This, however, is a profoundly limiting way to look at theory. Theories are abstract sets of assumptions and assertions used to interpret and sometimes to explain psychological, social, cultural, and historical processes. Theories are tools to help us think about things in new ways. Good theories are useful.

From the outset, then, we disagree with those who draw sharp distinctions between theory and practice in education. We see the distinction between theory and practice—between so-called pure and applied kinds of knowledge—as false and debilitating. Maintaining such a distinction hinders educators in many respects. It marginalizes the work of teachers and other practitioners, assuming that it is simply about implementing a set of disconnected strategies to teach a prescribed curriculum. It also marginalizes the work of theorists, assuming that their concerns are disconnected from real-world pressures, constraints, and struggles.

In addition, this distinction does not serve those interested in educational research. Here, we face the danger of what C. Wright Mills called "abstracted empiricism"—disconnected studies that take on individual empirical questions without regard to a larger "research imaginary." Theory helps us see our research as part of a bigger project, as in dialogue with a more expansive set of issues with social and political implications. Good theory is useful on every front. As Stuart Hall and Lawrence Grossberg (among others) have argued, we take "detours" through theory. We do not theorize for the sake of theorizing. We theorize to help us understand some phenomenon or process in a new way. Theory gives us a set of glasses to help us see the world differently—glasses we can put on and take off. Critical reflection on education allows us to meet our everyday conceptual and practical challenges in new and creative ways.

Theory for Education provides a short introduction to the work of key contemporary theorists, teasing out their implications for education. We focus on those who advance recent "post" currents—postmodernism, poststructuralism, and postcolonialism. Although we do focus on some earlier theorists who did their work during the early part of the twentieth century, they are thinkers whose work has increasingly resonated over time (e.g., Bakhtin, Vygotsky, and Gramsci). Theorists of the "post" are diverse in their insights and interests, yet all are concerned with critiquing the idea of a single, grand narrative that explains all human history and struggle. All resist the idea that there is one "story" to tell that explains everything. There are, to echo Lyotard, lots of different, smaller stories to tell.

Most of the work discussed here comes from outside the field of education. Indeed, that field has always existed in a subordinate relationship with more traditional disciplines. Education departments are home to concentrations such as English education, mathematics education, sociology of education, and history of education. In each case, the concentration has defined its own particular trajectory in the field of education, complete with its own journals, book series, and conferences. Yet these concentrations largely rely on the ongoing dialogue begun and sustained by the more traditional disciplines, so looking outside the field is nothing new for scholars in education. More broadly, however, we look to open up an even more expansive dialogue with the important insights being generated by contemporary theorists outside the field. We want to see where such connections can take us.

Genesis

Of course, any undertaking like this will be partially selective.[1] The goal has been to introduce figures we feel are necessary for students to know and understand if they are to be conversant with contemporary concerns and currents. Toward this end, we have included four key predecessors and twenty-two key theorists. We have endeavored to provide a concise and clear introduction to these individuals, including their biographies, their major contributions to their respective disciplines, and their key constructs. In addition, we have underscored their particular relevance for the field of education, including their own work on education, how others in education have used them, and the ways their work might be appropriated for future theorizing, research, and practice. The predecessors are John Dewey, Sigmund

Freud, Karl Marx, and Ferdinand de Saussure. The theorists are Mikhail Bakhtin, Basil Bernstein, Pierre Bourdieu, Jerome Bruner, Judith Butler, Gilles Deleuze and Félix Guattari, Jacques Derrida, Paulo Freire, Michel Foucault, Clifford Geertz, Antonio Gramsci, Stuart Hall, bell hooks, Jacques Lacan, Jean Piaget, Edward Said, Gayatri Chakravorty Spivak, Lev Vygotsky, and Raymond Williams.

In many respects, we had to approach this less as a coherent, overarching narrative and more as a series of puzzle pieces. We had to decide which pieces of the puzzle were most important and how they might fit with one another. This book is thus distinct from our recent book *On Qualitative Inquiry* (2005), though it shares similar concerns. In the previous book we discuss the ways in which different theoretical orientations inform approaches to research, particularly in education. We offer, to that end, four historically and temporally situated ways of reading the world: objectivism, interpretivism, skepticism, and defamiliarization. Each embodies a different set of assumptions about the world, knowledge, the human subject, language, and meaning. Each can be read through and against contemporary theoretical movements. In the present book, we have taken a different approach, choosing to foreground the work of particular scholars and theorists, and highlighting their own trajectories as well as the ways people have picked up their ideas and moved with them. We mean this book to be read as overlapping "lines of flight."

How to Use This Book

This book can be read from cover to cover. It can also be read selectively to find information on a particular theorist. Readers can also trace how ideas unfolded across the work of different theorists at different moments—for example, the moves in Marxism from Karl Marx to Antonio Gramsci to Stuart Hall. Readers can identify key themes and see how they evolved, and also see how individuals picked up these ideas and used them to inform educational theory and practice.

Each chapter begins with a list of "key concepts" critical to understanding the work of these important theorists. They are "road maps" to understanding the entries as followed. They are set in **boldface** type when they first appear in the text. We then provide biographical information about each theorist as well as a narrative that discusses his or her individual contributions.

We end each entry with a list of suggested readings. This includes important work by and about each theorist, as well as pieces particularly relevant for education. In some cases, we have included work that does not explicitly reference the figure in question but draws on their ideas in relevant or generative ways. We have marked key introductory texts with an asterisk (*).

The goal of this book is to "open up" the field of education to a wider range of ideas, to make these ideas more accessible. We think it will be useful to teacher educators, allowing them to reflect on their practice in new and perhaps surprising ways. We also think it will be useful to researchers, leading them to think about their objects of study in new ways. In both cases, we hope that *Theory for Education* will provide a "detour" through theory, on the way back to practice. We hope, as well, that this book will lead to reading these theorists in primary form. There is no substitute for that kind of work. We hope this book is a beginning for readers, not an end.

References

Kamberelis, G., and G. Dimitriadis. *On Qualitative Inquiry*. New York: Teachers College Press, 2005.

Note

1. The task at hand here was to rewrite the excellent first volume in Routledge's "Theory 4" series, *Theory for Religious Studies* by William E. Deal and Timothy K. Beal. In some cases, we preserved most of the entry's narrative, only adding remarks, sometimes brief and sometimes longer, about the particular importance of their work for the field of education. This includes the predecessors Sigmund Freud, Karl Marx, and Ferdinand Saussure, and the theorists Mikhail Bakhtin, Pierre Bourdieu, Judith Butler, Gilles Deleuze and Félix Guattari, Jacques Derrida, Michel Foucault, Jacques Lacan, Edward Said, Gayatri Chakravorty Spivak, and Raymond Williams. In some cases, these entries were almost wholly rewritten (e.g., in the case of Bakhtin). In most others, they were revised only to address concerns of those in education. We also added new entries that are key for education: Basil Bernstein, Jerome Bruner, John Dewey, Paulo Freire, Clifford Geertz, Antonio Gramsci, Stuart Hall, bell hooks, Jean Piaget, and Lev Vygotsky.

PREDECESSORS

JOHN DEWEY

Key Concepts

- pragmatic epistemology
- instrumentalism
- inquiry
- pragmatic metaphysics
- pragmatic ethics
- pragmatic aesthetics
- education and experience
- intelligent action
- reflection
- progressive education

John Dewey (1859–1952) was born into a middle-class community in Burlington, Vermont. Burlington at the time included both longtime New Englanders and new immigrants from Ireland and French Quebec. After high school, Dewey went to the University of Vermont, an institution that encouraged intellectual independence in students. Dewey immersed himself in coursework on political, social, and moral philosophy. After graduating from the University of Vermont in 1879, he worked for two years as a high school teacher in Oil City, Pennsylvania. He returned to Vermont in 1881, where he taught high school and continued to study philosophy.

In 1882 Dewey began graduate study in philosophy at Johns Hopkins University. His professors included Charles Sanders Peirce, G. Stanley Hall, and George Sylvester Morris, whose work on Hegel and Kant had a powerful effect on Dewey. Dewey wrote his dissertation on the psychology of Immanuel Kant.

Dewey's first academic position was in the Department of Philosophy at the University of Michigan, where nineteenth-century

British and Continental philosophy, especially German idealism, was a key strength. In 1886 Dewey published two articles in the journal *Mind* that attracted much attention in the academic community. In them he mapped the similarities between philosophy and psychology, arguing that philosophy did not need a special methodology because it was comprehensive psychology, for which viable methodologies already existed. Dewey's first book, *Psychology*, published in 1887, built upon and extended this basic idea. The book was well received by some scholars and was adopted as a textbook at several universities, but it was criticized by G. Stanley Hall and William James.

In the late 1890s, Dewey began moving away from German idealism and toward a new philosophical perspective that would eventually be called pragmatism. He also became very interested in curriculum development at this time. By 1900 he had developed or helped develop twenty-three different education courses at the University of Chicago. He also helped found the university's Laboratory School, which opened in 1896. At the turn of the century, Dewey's program (now called the Department of Education) was considered both the most comprehensive and the most innovative in the country. Eventually Dewey's education scholarship earned him recognition as the preeminent educational philosopher of his time.

Largely because of political differences about the governance of the Laboratory School, Dewey resigned his position at the University of Chicago in 1904. Soon afterward he became a professor at Columbia University, with appointments in both the Philosophy Department and the Teacher's College. Dewey continued to teach and conduct research at Columbia through the 1930s, when he retired completely. The intellectual environment of New York and the Northeast seemed to motivate Dewey, and it was at Columbia that he produced his best-known works. These include such important books of philosophy as *The Influence of Darwin on Philosophy and Other Essays in Contemporary Thought* (1910), *Essays in Experimental Logic* (1916), *Reconstruction in Philosophy* (1920), *Human Nature and Conduct* (1922), *Experience and Nature* (1925), *The Quest for Certainty* (1929), *Logic: The Theory of Inquiry* (1938), and *Knowing and the Known* (1949). Dewey also published major books on education, including *How We Think* (1910) and *Democracy and Education* (1916), which many consider his most important work. Dewey continued to write and speak about philosophical and educational issues until shortly before his death.

Dewey was always fascinated by epistemology or the theory of knowledge and how we come to have knowledge. In his view, traditional epistemologies, whether rationalist or empiricist, drew too sharp a distinction between "mind" and "world," and he set out to construct a new epistemological model, which we might call **pragmatic epistemiology**. In his early work on this problem, represented in articles such as "Is Logic a Dualistic Science?" (1890) and "The Present Position of Logical Theory" (1891), his solution derived directly from Hegelian idealism. He posited that the objective world is not separate from thought but is defined within thought as its objective manifestation. Later, Dewey rejected this solution for several reasons. Hegelian idealism could not accommodate the insights and methods of experimental science that he espoused. In this regard, Dewey was influenced by William James's more naturalistic arguments about epistemology, which cast idealism as superfluous. Dewey also found Darwin's work on the origin of species compelling, especially the attention Darwin paid to the complex relations between organisms and environments. He thus began to think that the development of human knowledge was an adaptive response to the environment, defining environment as "whatever conditions interact with personal needs, desires, purposes, and capacities to create the experience which is had" (Dewey, 1938, p. 44).

Unlike most previous epistemologies, wherein thought was regarded as a primitive of mind, Dewey's posited a genetic epistemology wherein thought was viewed as an effect of the interaction between organism and environment. His thinking here was much like that of his contemporary Jean PIAGET. Dewey also posited that knowledge was fundamentally practical or instrumental—developed to solve problems that human beings encountered in the world. In fact, Dewey used the term "instrumentalism" to refer to his epistemological approach

Dewey outlined what he meant by **instrumentalism** in a seminal essay, "The Reflex Arc Concept in Psychology" (1896). In this essay he argued against behaviorist approaches to psychology and learning because they were grounded in an erroneous mind-body dualism. As an alternative to these approaches, Dewey offered an early version of constructivism. According to this version, the organism interacts with the environment through self-guided activity that coordinates and integrates sensory and motor responses. Knowledge and learning are thus produced through active manipulation of the environment. Crediting William James for having led him to these insights, Dewey continued to refine and elaborate this basic position in many other essays. It became a central element of his particular version of pragmatism. Fundamental to Dewey's pragmatism is the role of **inquiry**.

According to Dewey, inquiry involves three phases: (a) a problematic situation, (b) identification of the parameters of the situation, and (c) reflection upon those parameters and the situation itself with the goal of generating a solution. Dewey emphasized that the uncertainty or perturbation of the problematic situation is not inherently cognitive, but practical and existential. Similarly, the solution to the problematic situation is not fundamentally cognitive, though cognition is clearly involved. Instead, it is practical action, efforts to get things moving or working again. This position stood in sharp contrast to most idealist epistemologies of the day, which both privileged reflection and drew a clear line between reflection and action. Besides being nonidealistic, Dewey's position was antifoundationalist. He claimed fallibilism—the idea that all knowledge is provisional, true only until proven otherwise—as a central element of pragmatism.

Over the years Dewey refined and deepened his instrumentalism by rethinking a number of key tenets of traditional Enlightenment epistemologies through its lens. For example, he argued that the traditional correspondence theory of truth—the idea that we can both *discover* and *represent* the facts of an *a priori* objective reality—only begs the question of what the "correspondence" of representation with reality is. Dewey maintained that any correspondence between representation and brute fact is true only if it is effective in solving real-world problems. This pragmatic theory of truth met with strong opposition, especially among British philosophers of language and logicians such as Bertrand Russell. Dewey became increasingly suspicious of these critiques because they were hopelessly embedded within modernist assumptions, especially the separation of subject and object and the privileging of the former. He later replaced "fallibilism" with the notion of "warranted assertability" as the acid test for the "truth" of ideas generated from successful inquiry. Importantly, this move foreshadowed major epistemological assertions of what has now come to be known as the "qualitative paradigm" in scientific research.

In positing knowledge as an effect of goal-directed activity rather than as an *a priori* psychological or ontological phenomenon, Dewey rendered classical metaphysics obsolete and opened the door for an empirically grounded metaphysics. Dewey introduced his **pragmatic metaphysics** in "The Postulate of Immediate Empiricism" (1905) and "Does Reality Possess Practical Character?" (1908). Importantly, he posited a phenomenological foundation for metaphysics, arguing that things experienced empirically are what they are experienced as. To clarify what he meant by this, Dewey offered the following example.

A person hears a noise in a darkened room. Initially, it is experienced as frightening. After inquiry (for example, turning on the lights and looking around), the noise seems to be caused by a shade tapping against a window and thus is not a reason to be afraid. The inquiry does not change the initial knowledge status of the noise—because it was experienced as scary, it was scary. The point here is that knowledge is constituted in and through our relations with the world. The noise was initially frightening, but this fear was an effect of the inadequacy of then present knowledge to deal effectively with the pragmatic demands of then present circumstances. Further inquiry did not disclose a new reality underlying mere appearance. Instead, it changed the dynamic relations between self and percept, and thus effected a change in reality. It put the initial experience of fear in context, changing its meaning and force.

Dewey's perspective here has important implications for metaphysics. First, it renders unstable and contingent knowledge as valid or legitimate, thus casting doubt on idealist versions of metaphysics (for example, Plato's *eidos* or Kant's pure reason). Second, the fact that knowledge changes with renewed inquiries that lead to more adequate understandings of natural events suggests that our experience of the world at any given time is never entirely wrong. Thus, skepticism with regard to the veracity of perceptual experience is unwarranted. Sensations, hypotheses, ideas, representations, and so on are all potentially valid mediators of knowledge. With successful inquiry, these mediators drop out and disclose things "to the agent in the most naively realistic fashion." Central here is the idea that all modes of experience are valuable and valid in the construction of knowledge. Importantly, these ideas foreshadowed Martin Heidegger's famous articulation of the hermeneutic circle, wherein the foundation of all knowledge is the practical engagement of *Dasein* (being) in the world .

Probably the fullest statement of Dewey's pragmatic metaphysics appears in *Experience and Nature* (1925). In this volume Dewey argued that social relationships are significant not only for developing social theory but also for developing metaphysics, because it is through collective human activity that mind itself emerges. Against the Enlightenment tradition, which viewed mind as a primitive, individual attribute and a precondition for intentional action, Dewey posited a genetic view wherein mind is an effect of collective activity mediated through symbols, especially language. In this regard, his thinking was remarkably similar both to that of the symbolic interactionists such as George Herbert Mead with whom he worked and to that of

Lev VYGOTSKY, a contemporary about whom Dewey probably knew nothing. For all these thinkers, consciousness and knowledge are produced through socially and semiotically mediated activity in the world.

Dewey's theory of inquiry cannot be fully understood without knowing something about his **pragmatic ethics**. He rejected rationalist, interest-based systems of ethics (for example, the social contract of Thomas Hobbes) because he believed that individual thought and action issue from social experience in the first place. He went on to argue that ethical conduct is a matter of guiding human action in ways that satisfy individuals within their social contexts. Dewey's ethics, then, is more gestural than systematic, suggesting a method for approaching ethical conundrums rather than providing specific principles or algorithms to follow. Indeed, he carefully avoided what he regarded as the misguided practices of other moral philosophers who sought one or another version of Kant's categorical imperatives with respect to living a moral life.

According to Dewey, his approach to ethics was essential to democratic forms of life, by which he meant the cultivation of cooperation and public interest that could produce collectives of individuals working to make life better for all through experimentation and inventiveness rather than through subscribing to the same dogma. He went on to argue that for such an ethics to take hold, the development of democratic habits must start in the earliest years of children's socialization through schooling. He considered schooling to be continuous with civil society itself. More important, he imagined schools as sites where students were actively encouraged to pursue their interests in conjunction with other people pursuing their own interests, in cooperative fashion and toward collective goals. Pedagogical activity organized in this way, Dewey believed, is the best preparation for responsible democratic citizenship.

Dewey's *Art as Experience* (1934) is in many ways an odd book, in that it is the one place where he attempted to develop a **pragmatic aesthetics**. Like his epistemological, metaphysical, and ethical theories, his aesthetic theory is both genetic and pragmatic. He argued, for example, that the roots of aesthetic experience lie in commonplace experiences of everyday life. Whenever one experiences a qualitative unity of meanings and values drawn from previous experience and present circumstances, one's experience has a distinct aesthetic quality. Among other things, this perspective ruptures the elitist distinction between "high" and "low" art and culture. The creative work of the artist is not necessarily any more remarkable than certain everyday experiences of ordinary people. The imaginative development of possible solutions to problems, which leads to a satisfying reconstruction of experience, is creative activity. What distinguishes artistic creation from other forms of creation is quantitative, not qualitative. It has to do with the artist's ability to elicit the enjoyment of unified qualitative complexity by marshalling and refining more than just immediate, local, and concrete resources of human life, meaning, and value. The artist concentrates, clarifies, and vivifies these elements in the work of art through emotion—not immediate, raw emotion, but emotion that is highly reflexive and guides the process of creation.

Important here is how Dewey's theory of aesthetics parallels his epistemology, metaphysics, and ethics. All are pragmatic or instrumentalist at both the individual and collective levels. Art, he argued, is a cultural product through which people express what is significant about their lives, as well as their joys, suffering, hopes, and ideals. Producing and consuming art has an affinity with more common human experiences like eating, walking, gardening, or caring for one's family. This affinity accords art a critical democratizing role in relation to prevailing social conditions. When visions of a meaningful, satisfying life are embodied in art but not realized by common people, art functions to question, even condemn, those social conditions. Dewey's ideas here were motivated by the effects of the industrialization of America, which he saw everywhere around him. These effects included engaging workers in nonmeaningful, repetitive, unsatisfying tasks that alienated them from their labor and from which they could derive no sense of accomplishment or personal pride. Dewey insisted that art and everyday life are woven from the same thread for strategic political reasons. When art is seen as separate from real life, transformative, counter-hegemonic potentials are eclipsed or even negated.

Dewey's theory of **education and experience** flowed seamlessly from his pragmatic epistemology, metaphysics, ethics, and aesthetics. For Dewey, the purpose of education is the intellectual, social, emotional, and moral development of the individual within a democratic society. Development along these axes both depends upon and contributes to increasingly democratic and democatizing contexts. Education is thoroughly social, providing individuals with personal investments in "social relationships and control, and the habits of mind which secure social changes without introducing social disorder" (1916/1944, p. 99). Education and experience are cut from the same cloth: "a reconstruction or reorganization of experience which adds to the meaning of experience, and which increases the ability to direct the course of subsequent experience" (1916/1944, p. 74). Education must thus be experienced-based and not externally imposed because "there is an intimate and necessary relation between the processes of actual experience and education" (1938, p. 20). Dewey's insistence on experience as the heart and soul of education is founded on principles of interaction and continuity. Like Piaget, Dewey recognized that experiences build on previous experiences, and he insisted it is the teacher's responsibility to determine the direction in which an experience is heading. In relation to this point, he believed that experiences (and their facilitation or toleration) can be both educative and miseducative. He defined an educative experience as one that broadens one's horizons of experience and knowledge and leads in a constructive direction toward **intelligent action**. Intelligent action involves forward momentum rather than stasis. It is deliberate rather than impulsive. Above all, it is reflective. In contrast, a miseducative experience is one that "arrests and distorts" development. It cultivates a callous, unreflective, self-absorbed disposition. It inclines the individual toward "routine actions" and "narrows [his or her] field, limiting meaning horizons and eclipsing possible solutions to problematic experiences." Miseducative experiences neither suggest nor promote awareness of self, social relationships, and the general sociopolitical ecology in which one lives. They obscure ways in which the actions of individuals can contribute productively to that ecology.

"Inquiry" is the term Dewey most often used in talking about educative experiences. His perspective on the nature and functions of inquiry are perhaps most fully developed in *Essays in Experimental Logic* and *Logic: The Theory of Inquiry* (1953), which posits a continuum of inquiry from nonhuman organisms through human beings. Dewey viewed all forms of inquiry as adaptive responses to environmental conditions for the attainment of organic needs. He called human inquiry "intelligent inquiry," the hallmark of which is mediation by language. Because language is fully symbolic, it allows for the hypothetical testing of adaptive behaviors before their actual implementation in the real world. He went on to argue that logical form, the specialized subject matter of traditional logic, is grounded not in reason but in functional value. Logical form involves managing evidence relevant to a problematic situation that invites inquiry, and controlling the procedures involved in generating multiple hypothetical solutions to that situation. Again, this was a unique perspective on inquiry that defied classic dualisms (for example, subject/object, universal/particular, rationalism/empiricism) and questioned the idea that human reason is the sole foundation of truth. Dewey's formulations about inquiry had considerable impact within the philosophical community and paved the way for future work on theories of logic.

Central to Dewey's perspective on inquiry is his unique understanding of the nature and functions of **reflection**. He defined reflection as an *"active, and careful consideration of any belief or supposed form of knowledge in light of the grounds that support it and the further conclusions toward which it tends"* (1938, p. 9; italics in original). As such, reflection lies at "the heart of intellectual organization and of the disciplined mind" (1938, p. 87). For Dewey, reflection is a kind of thinking "that consists in turning a subject over in the mind and giving it serious and consecutive consideration." It is disciplined yet imaginative thinking. It involves "sustained movement to a common end" (1933, p. 5). Dewey proposed four key criteria for reflection. First, it involves the continual construction of meaning and purpose, moving the learner from one experience to the next with deeper understanding of the connections between and among related experiences and ideas. It helps form the thread of continuity that constitutes the deepening and thickening of understanding. Second, reflection is deliberate, disciplined, and rigorous. Third, reflection is participatory; it happens within communities of committed practice and leads toward the accomplishment of shared goals. Finally, reflection is grounded in attitudes that value and celebrate both personal and collective growth and well-being.

Dewey also posited that reflection, as the most elevated form of inquiry, involves six basic phases: (a) a problematic lived experience, (b) an intuitive or spontaneous interpretation of the experience, (c) defining or naming the specific problems presented by the experience, (d) generating possible explanations for and solutions to these problems, (e) pondering these explanations in order to generate hypotheses for dealing with the problematic situation, and (f) testing these hypotheses to determine their intellectual purchase and pragmatic value (intelligent action). Evidence is paramount in this process. An object or event does not necessarily mean something that it suggests unless one can establish a logical relationship between the two. Learning, for Dewey, was thus "learning to think," and "education consists in the formation of wide-awake, careful, thorough habits of thinking" (1933, p. 78). In this regard, Dewey was critical of schooling in which the connection between process and product is overlooked, and where logically formulated, ready-made information is transmitted to the learner and instruction is delivered in lock-step fashion with the "cut and dried" logic of an adult. In contrast, he valued education in which thinking considered an *art*, and the goal to provide "systematic care to safeguard the processes of thinking so that it is truly reflective" (1933, p. 85).

Dewey proposed a unique way for teachers to cultivate reflective habits of mind in their students, which he referred to with the somewhat odd term "social control." When a teacher acts as "a director of processes of exchange in which all [students have a] share ... [he or she] loses the position of external boss or dictator [and] takes on that of leader of group activities" (1938, p. 59). In other words, the goal of the teacher is to provide opportunities for experiential learning to happen. Teachers and students exist in a dialogic partnership (in BAKHTIN's sense) or perhaps operate in a zone of proximal development (in Vygotsky's terminology). Teachers and students both are learners within a social group or community of practice. The teacher may have more knowledge or experience (at least about some things), but her role is that of a shepherd or facilitator and not an expert and authority figure. Within such a context, learners act cooperatively with teachers and peers to construct their purposes for learning, as well as what and how they learn. Dewey used the metaphor of the map to drive this point home: "The map, a summary, an arranged and orderly view of previous experiences, serves as a guide to future experience; it gives direction; it facilitates control, it economizes effort" but the map "does not take the place of the actual journey" (1902, p. 199).

Perhaps more than any philosopher since Plato (for example, *Meno*, *Republic*), Dewey attended to educational issues in his thinking and writing. Although he did not coin the term "**progressive education**," it is usually attributed to him. Dewey believed that education and social democracy are mutually constitutive. He thought that schools should focus on judgment rather than knowledge, that they should help students learn to live and to work cooperatively with others, and that students should participate in decisions that affect their learning. Yet he was not naive; he realized that schools are often repressive institutions that do not encourage (or even allow) exploration and growth. Armed with these insights, he promoted a number of new schools and school reforms to help make schools sites where students could develop creativity, problem-solving abilities, and open-mindedness; his most notable act was the founding of the University of Chicago's Experimental Laboratory School. Dewey also advocated for the rights and academic freedom of teachers. Finally, more than any other theorist represented in this book, Dewey left a legacy providing the foundations for a broad range of theoretical, pedagogical, and research activities in areas as diverse as curriculum theory, inquiry learning, teacher education, and educational policy.

Further Reading

By Dewey

1902. *The Child and the Curriculum.* Chicago: University of Chicago Press, 1959.

1902. *The School and Society* and *The Child and the Curriculum.* Chicago: University of Chicago Press, 1990.

1910. *The Influence of Darwin on Philosophy: Essays in Contemporary Thought.* New York: P. Smith, 1951.

1915. *The School and Society.* Chicago: University of Chicago Press, 1943.

1916. *Essays in Experimental Logic.* New York: Dover, 1953.

1916. *Democracy and Education: An Introduction to the Philosophy of Education.* New York: Free Press, 1966.

1922. *Human Nature and Conduct: An Introduction to Social Psychology.* Amherst, MA: Prometheus, 2002.

1925. *Experience and Nature.* London: Open Court.

1929. *The Quest for Certainty.* New York: Minton Balch.

1929. *My Pedagogic Creed.* Washington, DC: Progressive Education Association.

1932. *Ethics.* New York: Henry Holt.

1933. *How We Think: A Restatement of the Relation of Reflective Thinking to the Educative Process.* Boston: D. C. Heath.

1934. *Art as Experience.* New York: Minton Balch.

1938. *Experience and Education.* New York: Touchstone/Simon and Schuster, 1997.

1938. *Logic: The Theory of Inquiry.* New York: Henry Holt.

1948. *Reconstruction in Philosophy.* Boston: Beacon, 1957.

1949. *Knowing and the Known* (with A. P. Bentley). Boston: Beacon.

1967–1991. *The Collected Works of John Dewey,* edited by J. A. Boydston. 37 vols. Carbondale: Southern Illinois University Press.

About Dewey

Alexander, T. M. *The Horizons of Feeling: John Dewey's Theory of Art, Experience, and Nature.* Albany: SUNY Press, 1987.

Boisvert, R. D. *Dewey's Metaphysics.* New York: Fordham University Press, 1988.

*Boisvert, R. D. *John Dewey: Rethinking Our Time.* Albany: SUNY Press, 1998.

Bullert, G. *The Politics of John Dewey.* Buffalo, NY: Prometheus, 1983.

*Campbell, J. *Understanding John Dewey: Nature and Cooperative Intelligence.* Chicago and La Salle: Open Court, 1995.

Casparay, W. R. *Dewey on Democracy*. Ithaca, NY: Cornell University Press, 2000.

Damico, A. J. *Individuality and Community: The Social and Political Thought of John Dewey*. Gainesville: University of Florida Press, 1978.

Dykhuizen, G. *The Life and Mind of John Dewey*. Carbondale: Southern Illinois University Press, 1973.

Gouinlock, J. *John Dewey's Philosophy of Value*. New York: Humanities Press, 1990.

Hickman, L. *John Dewey's Pragmatic Technology*. Bloomington: Indiana University Press, 1990.

Sleeper, R. *The Necessity of Pragmatism: John Dewey's Conception of Philosophy*. New Haven: Yale University Press, 1987.

*Tanner, L. N. *Dewey's Laboratory School: Lessons for Today*. New York: Teachers College Press, 1997.

*Tiles, J. E. *Dewey*. London: Routledge, 1988.

Relevance for Education

Althouse, R., M. H. Johnson, and S. T. Mitchell. *Colors of Learning: Integrating the Visual Arts into the Early Childhood Education Curriculum*. New York: Teachers College Press, 2003.

Arcilla, R. V. "Why Aren't Philosophers and Educators Speaking to Each Other?" *Educational Theory* 52 (2002): 1–11.

Dwight, J., and J. A. Garrison. "A Manifesto for Instructional Technology: Hyperpedagogy." *Teachers College Record* 105 (2002): 699–728.

Fendler, L. "Teacher Reflection in a Hall of Mirrors: Historical Influences of Political Reverberations." *Educational Researcher* 32 (2003): 16–25.

Fishman, S. "Deweyan Hopefulness in a Time of Despair." *JAC: A Journal of Composition Theory* 22 (2002): 765–804.

Gallagher, C. W. *Radical Departures: Composition and Progressive Pedagogy*. (Refiguring English Studies.) Urbana, IL: National Council of Teachers of English, 2002.

Garrison, W. "Democracy, Experience, and Education: Promoting a Continued Capacity for Growth." *Phi Delta Kappan* 84 (2003): 525–529.

Girod, M., and D. Wong. "An Aesthetic (Deweyan) Perspective on Science Learning: Case Studies of Three Fourth Graders." *Elementary School Journal* 102 (2002): 199–224.

Girod, M., C. Rau, and A. Schepige. "Appreciating the Beauty of Science Ideas: Teaching for Aesthetic Understanding." *Science Education* 87 (2003): 574–587.

Gosselin, C. "'In a Different Voice' and the Transformative Experience: A Deweyan Perspective." *Educational Theory* 53 (2003): 91–105.

Halliday, J., and P. Hager. "Context, Judgment, and Learning." *Educational Theory* 52 (2002): 429–443.

Johnston, J. S. "John Dewey and the Role of the Scientific Method in Aesthetic Experience." *Studies in the Philosophy of Education* 21 (2003): 1–15.

Mullen, C., and A. R. Kohan. "Beyond Dualism, Splits, and Schisms: Social Justice for a Renewal of Vocational-Academic Education." *Journal of School Leadership* 12.6 (2002): 40–62.

O'Brien, L. "Teacher Education for a Democratic Society: Issues in Education." *Childhood Education* 79 (2003): 376–378.

Roberts, G. T. "An Interpretation of Dewey's Experiential Learning Theory." Washington, DC: ERIC Document Reproduction Service No. ED481922, 2003.

Rodgers, C. "Defining Reflection: Another Look at Dewey and Reflective Thinking." *Teachers College Record* 104 (2002): 842–866.

Schecter, C. "Deliberation: The Communal Negotiation of Meaning in Schools." *Planning and Changing* 33 (2002): 155–170.

Smith, J. P., and M. Girod. "John Dewey and Psychologizing the Subject Matter: Big Ideas, Ambitious Teaching, and Teacher Education." *Teaching and Teacher Education* 19 (2003): 295–307.

SIGMUND FREUD

Key Concepts

- psychosexual stage theory
- Oedipus Complex
- id, ego, and superego
- unconscious
- defense mechanisms
- dreams
- psychoanalysis
- talking cure

Sigmund Freud (1856–1939) was born to a Jewish family in Freiburg, Germany. His father, a wool merchant, was extremely intelligent and had a good sense of humor. His mother was an energetic woman, Freud's father's second wife and twenty years younger than her husband. Freud had two older half-brothers and six younger siblings. When Sigmund was four, he moved with his family to Vienna, where he lived for most of his life.

Throughout his school years, Freud was an outstanding student. He graduated with distinction from gymnasium (secondary school) in 1878 and took his medical degree at the University of Vienna in 1881. Freud was an exceptional research scientist whose early work was primarily in neurophysiology; he invented a special cell-staining technique. In 1885 he won a modest medical scholarship that allowed him to travel to Paris to work under the great Jean-Martin Charcot (1825–1893) at the Salpêtrière hospital. Freud was fascinated with Charcot's work on hysteria, which he treated as a disease, and with his use of hypnotism to reproduce symptoms of hysteria in his patients. In 1886 Freud began his practice as a physician in Vienna, focusing likewise on nervous disorders. Vienna remained his home until 1938, when he was forced to flee Austria for England following the Nazi takeover. Freud was a founder of psychoanalysis. In a 1922 essay for a general audience ("Two Encyclopedia Articles"), he provided three interrelated definitions of psychoanalysis: (a) a discipline focused on investigating the unconscious, (b) a therapeutic method for treating nervous disorders, and (c) a growing body of research data. Together these three definitions provide a helpful introduction to Freud's work.

Freud's books and lectures brought him both fame and ostracism from the mainstream medical community. He attracted a number of bright sympathizers who became the core of the psychoanalytic movement. Unfortunately, Freud had a tendency to alienate people who did not agree completely with him. Some separated from him on friendly terms; others did not, and went on to found competing schools of thought.

Freud believed that sexual energy (libido) was the primary motivating force of development, not only for adults but for children and infants as well. His conception of sexuality was quite broad and included all pleasurable bodily sensations. During infancy, according to Freud, the greatest pleasure seems to come from sucking, especially sucking the breast. In fact, babies have a tendency to bring nearly everything they encounter into contact with their mouths. Later in a child's life, the greatest pleasure seems to be located in the anal regions and to involve holding in and letting go. By three or four years of age, pleasure is often derived by touching or rubbing against the genitalia. Only much later in life is the greatest bodily pleasure associated with sexual activity, including intercourse.

Freud translated these observations and insights into a **psychosexual stage theory** of personality development. According to it, the first stage is the oral, which lasts from birth to about eighteen months. The focus of pleasure is the mouth: sucking, biting, chewing, licking. The next is the anal stage, which lasts from about eighteen months to three or four years old; the focus of pleasure is the anus. The next, the phallic stage, lasts from about three or four to six or seven years. The focus of pleasure is the genitalia, and masturbation typically begins during this stage. The next stage of psychosexual development is the latent stage, which lasts roughly from six or seven years of age until puberty. During this stage, Freud believed, the sexual impulse is suppressed in the service of learning, though masturbation is not uncommon. The genital stage begins at puberty and represents the resurgence of the sex drive in adolescence. For Freud, who regarded masturbation, oral sex, homosexuality, and many other things we find normal today as immature, sexual intercourse was the hallmark of this stage.

Freud's theory of psychosexual development is a true stage theory. Freudians believe that all human beings go through these stages in the same order and at roughly the same ages. Freud developed explanations or rationales, which nowadays can seem rather bizarre, for each of the stages, their focal objects, and the psychic mechanisms involved in moving from one stage to the next. Each stage involves certain problems or issues that must be worked through. In the oral stage, this is weaning. In the anal stage, it is toilet training. In the phallic stage, it is the **Oedipus Complex**. The Oedipus Complex is particularly important for understanding both human consciousness and the origins of most neuroses. The name comes from the Greek legend of Oedipus, who unwittingly killed his father, married his mother, and then blinded himself when he realized what he has done.

Freud explained the Oedipus Complex as follows. The child's first love-object is the mother. The child wants her attention, affection, milks, caresses—wants her in a broadly sexual way. Young boys, however, are in competition with their fathers for the mother's offerings, but their fathers are bigger, stronger, and smarter than they are, and the fathers get to sleep with the mothers. At around the time boys recognize this archetypal situation, they have become aware of some of the secondary sexual characteristics of boys and girls. From their naive perspective, the primary difference is that boys have penises and girls do not. At this point in life, it seems to the child that having something is better than not having something, and he is pleased to be a boy. He is also haunted, however, by wondering what might have happened to girls' penises. This is the beginning of what Freud called "castration anxiety," a slight misnomer for the fear of losing one's penis. Returning to Oedipus, in the face of the father's superiority and fear for his penis, the boy engages some ego defenses. He displaces his sexual impulses from his mother to girls and later to women, and he identifies with his rival (that is, his father) and tries to become just like him. After a few years of latency, boys become adolescents and enter the world of mature heterosexuality.

Girls, too, begin life in love with their mothers. Their problem is the need to switch their affection to their fathers before the Oedipal process can take place. Freud solved this problem with his concept of penis envy: Like boys, girls notice the advent of secondary sexual characteristics and feel that they do not measure up somehow. They would like to have penises and the power that seems to go along with them. Minimally, they desire penis substitutes, such as babies. Because girls know that a father as well as a mother is needed to have a baby, they transfer their love for their mothers onto their fathers. Unfortunately, those fathers are already spoken for, so young girls displace their desires from their fathers to boys and men. They also begin to identify with their mothers, the women who got the men they really wanted. Note that there is no parallel among girls for castration anxiety, and Freud believed that the absence of castration anxiety explains why women are both less firmly heterosexual than men and somewhat less morally inclined. Not surprisingly, this claim has been strongly critiqued, and not only by feminist scholars.

In sum, the Oedipus Complex concerns the young child's attraction to the parent of the opposite sex and jealousy of the parent of the same sex. Although girls and boys experience this attraction and negotiate this complex differently, in both cases the goal is to move from jealousy of the same-sex parent to identification with her or him. Freud believed that the Oedipus Complex is a universal human experience, and that the failure to negotiate it successfully is the primary cause of neuroses.

Freudian psychological theory involves the constant interaction of three forces or dimensions of human mental activity: the id, the ego, and the superego. Human psychic reality, for Freud, begins with the human as an organism designed to survive and reproduce, and guided toward those ends by its basic needs—hunger, thirst, the avoidance of pain, and sex. Central to the satisfaction is the working of the **id**. The human mind, as id, translates the organism's needs into motivational forces called "instincts" or "drives." The id works in keeping with the pleasure principle, or the propensity to take care of needs immediately. The infant, in Freud's view, is pure or nearly pure id, and the id is thus little more than a psychic interpretation of biology. The id, Freud thought, represents eternal desire and is thus a primordial or primary process.

Besides unconscious drives, the human mind also has consciousness and self-consciousness, which mediate the individual's experience of reality through the senses. Freud referred to this conscious mediational activity as the **ego**. The ego relates the individual to others and the world by what Freud called the "reality principle." It searches for objects to satisfy the wishes that the id creates but it does so with long-term consequences in mind. This problem-solving activity is referred to as a "secondary process" and is governed by reason. According to Freud, the ideal adult state is characterized by a strong ego and the ability to delay need gratification.

However, as the ego struggles to keep the id happy, it encounters both enablements and constraints, which it records and remembers. During childhood, memories of rewards and punishments meted out by the child's mother and father are particularly important because they predispose the child to avoid certain activities and embrace others. This set of predispositions is called the **superego** and comes to represent society and the ways in which society wants the individual to act. The superego is well developed when the child is about seven years of age. In some people, however, it never becomes well developed; in others, it becomes overdeveloped.

There are two key dimensions to the superego: (a) the conscience, which is an internalization of warnings and punishments, and (b) the ego ideal, or the internalization of rewards and positive experiences. The conscience and ego ideal modulate the workings of the ego with feelings such as pride, shame, and guilt.

In sum, the ego serves both the desires of the id and the policing control of the superego, both of which are forces of desire that have been internalized and made part of the personality. The ego is the site of the compromise between unfulfilled desires on one hand (id) and acceptable social relations and action on the other (superego).

The concept of the **unconscious** did not originate with Freud, but he redefined the concept and used it to explain a range of philosophical, cultural, and clinical issues and problems. The unconscious is the non-conscious part of the mind, which affects conscious thought and behavior but is not directly accessible for interpretation. For Freud, the primary value of the unconscious lies not in exactly what it is or where it may be found but in the ways it helps explain the mental work inherent in all psychic life. This work is largely a matter of mediating between conscious activity and unconscious forces such as desire. None of the key dimensions of psychic life (id, ego, superego) or the relations between and among them can be understood without the concept of the unconscious.

Freud's most innovative work on the unconscious addresses how to access and interpret it. He did this through analyses of slips of the tongue, jokes, free associations, and especially dreams, which he called the "royal road" to the unconscious. According to Freud, dreams represent fulfillments of unconscious wishes and desires that the conscious mind has censored because they are socially taboo or threaten the integrity of the self. For Freud, the content of the unconscious is essentially those drives that are inadmissible to the conscious self and are therefore forced out of consciousness through various mechanisms of repression. These include, for example, drives and memories related to the "primal scene" (childhood recollection of seeing one's parents having sex) and taboos on desires related to the Oedipus Complex. Although repressed, these drives invariably resurface in dreams, "Freudian slips," free associations, and other expressive modalities.

The ego deals with the demands of reality, the id, and the superego as well as it can. But when the anxiety becomes overwhelming, the ego must defend itself. It does so by unconsciously blocking the impulses or distorting them into more acceptable, less threatening forms. The strategies by which the ego does this are called the ego **defense mechanisms**, of which Freud posited quite a few, such as denial, repression, asceticism, isolation, displacement, turning against the self, projection, altruistic surrender, reaction formation, undoing, introjection, identification with the aggressor, regression, rationalization, and sublimation. To illustrate the basic functions of defense mechanisms, we discuss just a few of them here.

Denial involves blocking external events out of conscious awareness. If a situation is too traumatic, a person simply denies having experienced it. For example, a student who has failed an exam miserably may claim he or she thought it was a breeze and aced it. Denial is a primitive and dangerous defense. One cannot disregard reality and get away with it forever.

Displacement involves redirecting a desire or impulse onto a substitute target. The desire or impulse is acceptable to the person who has it, but that person is threatened by the object of his or her impulse, so the impulse is redirected toward a symbolic substitute. For example, a person may hate his father for having been a tyrant and redirect this hatred toward authority figures in general (teachers, police, employers). Similarly, a person who wants a romantic relationship but does not have one may turn this desire into a love for pets.

Projection is the tendency of a person to see his or her unacceptable desires in other people. A husband, for example, who lusts after a co-worker may become increasingly jealous of his wife and even accuse her of lust or infidelity rather than owning up to his own desires.

Reaction formation transforms an unacceptable desire into its opposite. Reaction formation is quite typical for children entering the phallic stage of development. Both boys and girls often turn their emerging interest in and desire for the opposite sex into claims of disgust. ("Girls are yucky!") Similarly, a person who feels homosexual desires may become adamant about how wrong, evil, and disgusting homosexuality is.

Sublimation is a matter of transforming an unacceptable desire into a socially acceptable, even productive activity. A person with pent-up hostility, for example, may become a police officer, soldier, or demolition expert; a person who always feels like the world is falling down around him may become an accountant, a businessperson, or a scientist.

Probably the best-known of all defense mechanisms, repression is a matter of pushing an unacceptable impulse or desire out of conscious awareness, burying it in the unconscious. A person who feels sexually attracted to her best friend's lover, for example, might repress this desire. Repression, however, is seldom completely successful, and the repressed desire often returns in some alternative guise, such as hysterical or neurotic symptoms. Some of these symptoms are antisocial manifestations of the repressed desire, such as sticking out the tongue or making rude noises or gestures.

According to the sciences of Freud's time, **dreams** were not considered psychological but biological or somatic. Popular accounts of dreams, however, rendered them as symbolic or coded, and the images and experiences represented in dreams were believed to have specific and interpretable meanings. Two methods of interpreting dreams were common. Dreams were either regarded as global representations of some hidden meaning that required understanding, or each image or experience in a dream was seen to have a specific meaning that required decoding according to a "dream dictionary." Each method had its problems. The more global method of dream interpretation could not handle the unintelligible and contradictory content with which dreams are packed. The more specific method had no checks on the validity of preestablished correspondences between image and meaning. To solve this problem, Freud combined the two methods. Specifically, he argued that the analysis of outlier images or symbols complemented global analysis, and that global analysis helped contextualize (and thus validate) the interpretation of specific images and symbols.

Dreams were important to Freud because he viewed them as symptomatic of repressed desires and thus as windows into neuroses and other psychological disorders. Interpreting dreams was therefore indispensable to understanding both psychological problems and the nature and functions of the mind. Interpreting dreams involves three steps or phases. First, the dream is broken up into its basic elements, and any associations the dreamer makes in relation to each element are used to contextualize interpretations. Second, based on the assumption that the meaning of the dream has a composite character, relations between and among dream elements (and their contextualization) are constructed.

Finally, symbolic details are interpreted to reveal the dream as a distorted version of a coherent psychic formation of unconscious thoughts.

Through this interpretive process, Freud claimed that dreams are secret fulfillments of repressed desires, and he suggested that two fundamental psychic forces operate in dreams. One force constructs the desire or wish represented in the dream. The other censors this desire or wish, which distorts the expression of the desire. The simultaneous working of these opposing forces is what accounts for the often unintelligible and contradictory nature of dreamscapes and the corresponding need to discover their hidden meanings.

Freud's account of psychosexual development and certain psychic disorders (neuroses) that arise from developmental blockages led him to develop a clinical treatment for these disorders that came to be known as **psychoanalysis**. When people speak of psychoanalysis they often mean clinical treatment exclusively, but the term equally designates both the clinical treatment and the theory that underlies it. The goal of psychoanalysis is to reestablish a harmonious relationship between the three elements that constitute the mind (id, ego, and superego) by excavating and resolving unconscious repressed conflicts. The actual method of treatment pioneered by Freud grew out of Josef Breuer's work on hysteria. Breuer had shown that when a hysterical patient was encouraged to talk freely about the earliest occurrences of her symptoms and fantasies, the symptoms began to go away. And if the patient was induced to remember the trauma that originally created the problem, these symptoms went away entirely. Based on the assumption that repressed conflicts are buried in the deepest recesses of the unconscious, Freud extended Breuer's techniques in what is now commonly known as the **talking cure**. He got his patients to relax and encouraged them to talk freely and uninhibitedly about whatever came to their minds (free association). He believed that in such a relaxed state, these free associations would eventually lead them to access material that would allow him to discern the unconscious forces lying behind this material. More specifically, Freud believed that free association disarmed the superego, allowing repressed material to cross the threshold from the unconscious to the conscious mind. Because this process is necessarily difficult and protracted, the primary task of the analyst is to help the patient recognize and overcome the natural resistances and defense mechanisms, which often manifest themselves as hostility toward the analyst. Thus, resistance is seen as a sign of progress in tapping the underlying unconscious causes of a patient's disorder. The patient's dreams are particularly important in psychoanalysis because, as in free association, the superego is partially disarmed in sleep. In this regard, Freud distinguished between the *manifest* content of dreams (what they seem to be about) and their *latent* content (the repressed desires or wishes that they are really about). Interpreting dreams correctly allows the analyst to locate ideas and events repressed in the unconscious that produce neurotic symptoms. Because Freud's theory is a psychosexual theory, these ideas and events are inevitably about conflicts during psychosexual development and the libidinal content of the patient's relationships with his or her mother and father. Becoming "cured" is a matter of becoming conscious of unresolved conflicts, confronting them directly, and doing something productive with them. In other words, psychoanalysis is supposed to lead to self-understanding. Exactly what a patient does with this self-understanding is also negotiated in therapy. One strategy is sublimation, or redirecting the unconscious sexual energy toward social, artistic, or scientific pursuits. Freud saw sublimation as the motivating force behind most significant social, cultural, and scientific achievements. Another strategy is suppression, or the conscious, rational control of formerly repressed drives. A third strategy is to blame the superego and the social constraints it embodies and to go ahead and satisfy repressed desires or drives. Whatever strategies are enacted, the talking cure involves a release of the pent-up psychic energy, the constriction of which was the original cause of the neurotic illness.

Despite obvious problems with respect to its biological determinism, the exclusivity of its practice, and its gender blindness, psychoanalysis provides one of the best available theoretical models of the psychic processes that contribute to our resistance to change—why we often repeat courses of action that are not desirable and even constrain us. Conversely, psychoanalysis is implicated in any attempt to understand the forms and possibilities for change—for resistance against these habitual behavioral patterns. These spaces are cleared by an appeal to a theory of the unconscious, a theory that is necessary to any discussion of the dialectic between social and ideological formations and agents. In connection with this point, the notions of a unitary subject, a totally determined subject, and an impossible subject are rendered untenable from the start by psychoanalysis with its emphasis on unconscious processes. Additionally and equally important, psychoanalysis sees cognition and affect not as separate entities but as dialectically related in complex ways. Finally, psychoanalysis accounts both for the continuity of the self and for a locus of motivation and desire, in that it views the past as implicated in the present. In short, psychoanalysis profoundly challenges any attempt to separate the individual from the social, to think of the individual solely in terms of his or her consciousness of self, to conceive subjectivity as a unitary capacity for rational action, or to deny individuals any grounds for resisting social and ideological forces.

Freud's greatest reach into education is probably the extent to which his basic structural model of ontogenesis has been used to theorize intellectual, social, and moral development. His theories have also been foundational within the fields of counseling psychology and school psychology. Freudian ideas helped to create an entire school of literary interpretation—psychoanalytic criticism. They provided the foundation for a diverse range of pedagogical theories, including various forms of feminist pedagogy. And they have been instrumental in the development and refinement of theories of motivation and engagement.

Further Reading

By Freud

1953–1974. *The Standard Edition of the Complete Psychological Works of Sigmund Freud*, edited by J. Strachey with A. Freud. 24 vols. London: Hogarth.

*The Interpretation of Dreams, First Part. In *The Standard Edition*, vol. 4.

Totem and Taboo: Some Points of Agreement between the Mental Lives of Savages and Neurotics. In *The Standard Edition*, vol. 13.

*Introductory Lectures on Psycho-Analysis. In *The Standard Edition*, vols. 15–16.

"The Uncanny." In *The Standard Edition*, vol. 17.

*1922. "Two Encyclopedia Articles." In *The Standard Edition*, vol. 18.

"The Future of an Illusion." In *The Standard Edition*, vol. 21.

Moses and Monotheism: Three Essays. In *The Standard Edition*, vol. 23.

About Freud

Bettelheim, Bruno. *Freud and Man's Soul*. New York: Knopf, 1982.

Cavell, M. *The Psychoanalytic Mind: From Freud to Philosophy*. Cambridge, MA: Harvard University Press, 1993.

Chessick, R. D. *Freud Teaches Psychotherapy*. Indianapolis: Hackett, 1980.

Dilman, I. *Freud and the Mind*. Oxford: Blackwell, 1984.

Edelson, M. *Hypothesis and Evidence in Psychoanalysis*. Chicago: University of Chicago Press, 1984.

Fancher, R. *Psychoanalytic Psychology: The Development of Freud's Thought*. New York: W. W. Norton, 1973.

Farrell, B. A. *The Standing of Psychoanalysis*. Oxford: Oxford University Press, 1981.

Frosh, S. *The Politics of Psychoanalysis: An Introduction to Freudian and Post-Freudian Theory*. New Haven: Yale University Press, 1987.

*Gay, Peter. *Freud: A Life for Our Times*. New York: W. W. Norton, 1988.

Grünbaum, A. *The Foundations of Psychoanalysis: A Philosophical Critique*. Berkeley: University of California Press, 1984.

*Hook, S., ed. *Psychoanalysis, Scientific Method, and Philosophy*. New York: New York University Press, 1959.

Jones, E. *Sigmund Freud: Life and Work*. 3 vols. New York: Basic Books, 1953–1957.

MacIntyre, A. C. *The Unconscious: A Conceptual Analysis*. London: Routledge & Kegan Paul, 1958.

Mackay, N. *Motivation and Explanation: An Essay on Freud's Philosophy of Science*. Guilford, CT: International Universities Press, 1989.

Pendergast, M. *Victims of Memory*. New York: Harper Collins, 1997.

*Ricoeur, P. *Freud and Philosophy: An Essay in Interpretation*, translated by D. Savage. New Haven: Yale University Press, 1970.

Schafer, R. *A New Language for Psychoanalysis*. New Haven: Yale University Press, 1976.

Wallace, E. R. *Freud and Anthropology: A History and Reappraisal*. Guilford, CT: International Universities Press, 1983.

Relevance for Education

Bowlby, J. *Attachment and Loss*. 2nd ed. New York: Basic Books, 1983.

Britzman, D. P., and A. J. Pitt. "Pedagogy and Transference: Casting the Past of Learning into the Presence of Teaching." *Theory into Practice* 35 (1996): 117–123.

Diaz-de-Chumaceiro, C. L. "Hamlet in Freud's Thoughts: Reinterpretations in the Psychoanalytic Literature." *Journal of Poetry Therapy* 11 (1998): 139–153.

Elkind, D. *Reinventing childhood: Raising and Educating Children in a Changing World*. Rosemont, NJ: Modern Learning, 1998.

Erikson, E. H. *Identity and the Life Cycle*. New York: W. W. Norton, 1994.

Ginter, E., and W. Bonney. "Freud, ESP, and Interpersonal Relationships: Projective Identification and the Mobius Interaction." *Journal of Mental Health and Counseling* 15 (1993): 150–169.

Gallop, J. *Feminist Accused of Sexual Harassment*. Chapel Hill, NC: Duke University Press, 1997.

Garcia, J. L. "Freud's Psychosexual Stage Conception: A Developmental Metaphor for Counselors." *Journal of Counseling and Development* 73 (1995): 498–502.

Gartner, S. L. *A Freudian Approach to Education*. Washington, DC: ERIC Document Reproduction Service No. ED339994, 1991.

Kohlberg. L. *The Philosophy of Moral Development: Moral Stages and the Idea of Justice*. New York: Harper Collins, 1981.

Maslow, A. *Toward a Psychology of Being*. 3rd ed. New York: Wiley, 1998.

Moddelmog, D. A. *Readers and Mythic Signs: The Oedipus Myth in Twentieth-Century Fiction*. Carbondale, IL: Southern Illinois University Press, 1993.

Mowery, D. "The Phrase of the Phallic Pheminine: Beyond the 'Nurturing Mother' in Feminist Composition Pedagogy." Paper presented at the Annual Meeting of College, Composition, and Communication, San Diego, CA, 1993.

Munteanu, M. A. "Psychodynamic Interpretations of the Immigrant's Dream: Comments on Adler's (1993) Refugee Dreams and Attachment Theory." *Guidance and Counseling* 10 (1994): 21–24.

Murphy, A. "Transference and Resistance in the Basic Writing Classroom: Problematics and Praxis." *College Composition and Communication* 40 (1989): 175–187.

Quandahl, E. "More than Lessons in How To Read: Burke, Freud, and the Resources of Symbolic Transformation." *College English* 63 (2001): 633–654.

Weiland, S. "Erikson after Dewey: Education, Psychology, and Rhetoric." *Educational Theory* 44 (1994): 341–369.

Wheeler, R. P. "Psychoanalytic Criticism and Teaching Shakespeare." *ADE Bulletin* 87 (1987): 19–23.

KARL MARX

Key Concepts

- historical materialism
- dialectic
- mode, relations, and forces of production
- proletariat, capitalist, and bourgeoisie
- means of production
- base and superstructure
- alienation
- ideology

Karl Marx (1818–1883) was a German political philosopher. He was born in Trier, Germany, to liberal Jewish parents who had converted to the Protestant Evangelical Established Church in order to advance the law career of his father. In 1836, after a year at the University of Bonn, Marx entered the University of Berlin, where he concentrated on philosophy. Deeply influenced by Hegelian thought, he was a member of a student group known as the Young Hegelians who espoused a radical, atheistic version of Hegel's dialectic.

Marx's doctoral thesis on Greek philosophy was accepted in 1841. Unable to find a university position, he became a journalist for a liberal newspaper, the *Rhenish Gazette*. He wrote articles on a wide range of topics, especially on political and social concerns, and served briefly as the paper's editor before it was censored by the Prussian government for, among other things, articles about workers' conditions.

In 1843, Marx, newly married, moved to Paris to take a position as co-editor of a new publication, the *German-French Annals*. This journal expressed communist ideas and failed to draw the interest of French. Deemed subversive by the Prussian government, the publication was confiscated and its editors sought for arrest. Once again unemployed and now unable to return to Germany, Marx devoted his energy to writing a work of political philosophy that would express his socialist views. At this time (1844), Marx befriended Friedrich Engels (1820–1895), the socialist son of a German industrialist, who became Marx's lifelong collaborator and benefactor.

At the insistence of the Prussian government, the French expelled Marx and other German communists from Paris. Marx moved to Brussels, supported financially by Engels. In 1847, Marx and Engels attended the Congress of the Communist League in London, where Marx asserted his views on how to bring about a communist revolution. As a result, he and Engels were commissioned to articulate the League's working doctrines. This commission led to the publication of *The Communist Manifesto* (published in German in 1848).

After the 1848 French revolution, Marx moved first to Paris, then to Cologne, then back to Paris as conservative factions regained control of Germany, and then, late in the summer of 1849, to London, where he remained throughout the rest of his life. Marx lived in poverty for a time, but with Engels's support and his own family inheritances, he eventually enjoyed a comfortable lifestyle in London with his family. He continued to organize social movements and to write. In 1852 he became a regular contributor to the *New York Tribune*, continuing for ten years. Marx published the first volume of *Capital*, a critique of capitalist economics, in German in 1867. *Capital* brought attention to Marx's ideas, and a second edition appeared in 1871. Translations into other languages soon followed, though an English translation did not appear until after Marx's death. Two subsequent volumes of *Capital* remained unfinished at Marx's death and were completed later by Engels.

Marxism, or Marxist theory, is based on ideas formulated by Marx and Engels as a critique of industrial capitalism. It focuses attention on social history in relation to political economy, especially class struggle. From a Marxist perspective, history is not driven by ideas, values, or some overarching spirit. Rather, it is a record of struggle, rooted in material existence, for food, shelter, products of labor, and control over the means of production. Marx's ideas—disseminated in part through various interpretations of and elaborations on Marxism—have had a tremendous impact on twentieth-century politics as well as on critical theory, literary theory, cultural studies, history, sociology, economics, the arts, philosophy, religion, and education.

We can conceive of Marxist theory in at least two ways. First, it is a revolutionary critique of capitalist society. Marx was personally concerned with the need for social change in light of what he saw as the injustice and oppression caused by nineteenth-century industrial capitalism and the economic relations it engendered. His analysis of how industrial capitalism operated and how it caused oppression was directed at changing this system and thereby ending the human suffering it produced. Second, and more important for our purposes, Marxist theory is a way to analyze not only economic relations but also those values and viewpoints created by industrial capitalism that affect ostensibly nonpolitical endeavors such as education, religion, literature, and other cultural products and practices. Marxist theory underscores the ideological nature of all human enterprises.

Central to Marxist thought is Marx's philosophy of history. Known as **historical materialism**, it views historical change as the result of the actions of human beings within the material world, and not as caused by God or some other extra-human or spiritual force. In this materialist view of history, Marx was influenced by Ludwig Feuerbach (1804–1872), who emphasized the material conditions of the world and was critical of the idealism of Hegelian thinking, which stressed ideas and the spiritual nature of the universe and historical change. For Marx, what propels history is a **dialectic** expressing economic and other conflicts between social classes. Hegel, too, had understood history as dialectical, with change taking place as a series of successive movements from thesis to antithesis to synthesis. But whereas Hegel saw this as a history of the human spirit, Marx saw it as a history of human struggle over material goods and their production. This is why Marx is said to have "stood Hegel on his head." Material circumstances shape ideas, not vice versa.

Marxism describes the historical development of different **modes of production**, a concept referring to the ways societies organize economic relations in order to allow for the production of goods. The Marxist characterization of capitalism as an oppressive and unjust system of labor and production centers on social relations and the tools used in the production of goods. Labor is not performed in isolation but within larger human networks. Human patterns of economic organization, or **relations of production**, interact with human labor and technologies, or **forces of production**, to create the mode of production.

Modes of production differ across historical periods. Marxist cultural analysis is especially focused on industrial capitalism, viewing it as an economic system that promotes an unequal and therefore unjust mode of production. Marx's discussion of class struggle in capitalist society predicates that economic development progresses from primitive to feudal to capitalist, and that class struggle corresponds to the dominant mode of production in each society. It is only with the development of a socialist mode of production that class distinctions and conflicts end. Historical change can occur only within the context of dialectical conflicts between classes. Contradictions between those in control and those controlled inevitably lead to class conflict. It is the dialectic of class confrontation that engenders a new society. The ultimate goal is a socialist, classless state.

In a capitalist mode of production, the relations of production are such that workers labor to turn raw materials into finished goods, and owners control the sale and distribution of these products, collecting their surplus value. Such a system, says Marx, inevitably results in the creation of class distinctions in which the **proletariat**—workers who sell their labor power for a wage in order to make a living—enables the **capitalists** who own and control the **means of production** (that is, the natural resources, factories, machines, and other material resources) to recover profits at the expense of the workers. A third class, the **bourgeoisie**, are neither owners nor workers but service providers such as teachers and doctors. Although they provide services to both the other classes, they are usually identified as having the same class characteristics as capitalists.

For Marx, economic organization—that is, modes of production—shape other aspects of society. The concepts of **base** and **superstructure** explain this relationship. "Base" refers to a society's economic mode of production, which determines its superstructure—that is, its political, social, religious, artistic, moral, scientific, and other cultural productions. From this perspective, education is not an independent or autonomous mode of human activity but is conditioned and determined by a society's mode of production and the relations of production it engenders. This is a materialist theory of education, viewing it as part of a society's superstructure.

The economic base is supported by a superstructure that justifies the base and seeks to naturalize class differences as an overarching reality that people have no possibility of changing. Such a system is understood by Marxism as fundamentally exploitative and changeable only through the dialectical struggle between classes. Struggle occurs because the inequities and contradictions of an unequal system become evident over time. Marxism forecasts that the dialectical struggle will eventually destroy capitalism and establish a class-free socialism in its place. This event will mark the end of history, in the sense that further economic change will no longer occur because the unequal class relations that fueled the dialectical struggle will have ceased to exist.

Marxism draws attention to processes of **alienation**, especially through the stratification of society into different social classes, where the upper classes have privileged access to the goods produced by the lower classes. Alienation—a result of unequal class relations caused by a capitalist mode of production—occurs in two ways. First, a capitalist mode of production is a system in which workers produce goods from which only capitalist owners profit. Thus, labor is alienated from its own efforts. Second, workers are alienated from themselves in a capitalist system. According to Marx, this occurs because workers become commodities when they must sell their alienated labor in the marketplace, just as other goods are sold. Thus, workers are alienated from their own humanity.

Marxist theory conceives of **ideology** as a false consciousness that distorts social and material reality, functioning to keep people in their place within the capitalist system. This distortion prevents people from viewing relations of production as they really are. Therefore, ideology is an aspect of superstructure: it is produced by the economic base and functions to legitimate that base. Ideologies determine what can be thought and believed about politics, education, literature, and other aspects of culture. But ideologies are not autonomous; they depend, said Marx, on the prevailing economic mode of production and serve as a justification for its continued existence. For example, Marxist scholars of education argue that schools provide key support for the popular ideology of "meritocracy," the notion that one has earned one's place in a capitalist society through individual effort (Bowles and Gintis, 1976). Even though family income at birth is the single best predictor of life chances, schools claim to sort young people fairly by ability and effort. In doing so, they reinforce the notion that one has earned his or her place in society. Schooling in capitalist America is, ultimately, about reproducing the capitalist class system, making it seem fair and "natural."

Schools reproduce and naturalize class divisions in several different ways. Jean Anyon (1980), for example, traced how schools serving young people at different ends of the class spectrum used the same basic curricula in radically different ways. The school that served working-class youth, she showed, stressed mechanical approaches to problem solving. Following clear rules in a step-by-step, rote fashion was emphasized. Teachers did not make real connections to underlying thought processes nor to authentic problem solving. Work was fragmented across different subjects. It is perhaps not surprising that students saw the teacher's authority as capricious and arbitrary. In contrast, the executive elite school stressed reasoning through problem solving, as well as organic connections between subject areas. Students were not encouraged simply to follow rules—quite the opposite: they were expected to figure out the rules themselves. The correct answer was less important than the thought processes behind it. Teachers were partners in this process. Anyon concluded that working-class youth were being prepared for arbitrary and demeaning work, as well as for a conflictual relationship with authority. In contrast, the students of the executive elite were learning to make the rules and to control the lives and labor of others. In both cases, capitalist ideology was reproduced through the education process.

Marxism has thus been employed in exploring how school systems broadly support the capitalist economic structure. Other thinkers, however, have looked more closely at how capitalist ideology is negotiated as well as at the cultural dimensions of economic reproduction and resistance. Often called "Neo-Marxism," much of this school of thought has been influenced by Antonio GRAMSCI. This work has been picked up and extended by educational theorists and researchers including Paul Willis and Michael Apple. Yet for Marxism, the most important fight remains the fight against capitalism. Other struggles—including those around gender and race—can be explained and contested largely through a focus on economic class.

Further Reading

By Marx

1978. *The Marx-Engels Reader*, edited by R. Tucker. 2nd ed. New York: W. W. Norton.

1986. *Karl Marx: A Reader*, edited by J. Elster. Cambridge: Cambridge University Press.

2000. **Karl Marx: Selected Writings*, edited by D. McClellan. 2nd ed. Oxford: Oxford University Press.

About Marx / Relevance for Education

Anyon, J. "Social Class and the Hidden Curriculum of Work." *Journal of Education* 162 (1980): 67–92.

*Apple, M. *Ideology and Curriculum*. New York: Routledge, 1979.

*Bowles, S., and H. Gintis. *Schooling in Capitalist America*. New York: Basic Books, 1976.

Carver, T., ed. *The Cambridge Companion to Marx*. Cambridge, UK: Cambridge University Press, 1992.

Dolby, N., and G. Dimitriadis, with P. Willis, eds. *Learning To Labor in New Times*. New York: Routledge, 2004.

Elster, J. *Making Sense of Marx*. Cambridge: Cambridge University Press, 1985.

Hill, D., P. McLaren, M. Cole, and G. Rikowski, eds. *Marxism against Postmodernism in Educational Theory*. Lanham, MD: Lexington, 2002.

Kenway, J., and A. Kraak. "Reordering Work and Destabilizing Masculinity." In Dolby and Dimitriadis, eds.

*McLellan, D. *Karl Marx: His Life and Thought*. New York: Harper and Row, 1973.

Singer, P. *Marx: A Very Short Introduction*. Oxford: Oxford University Press, 2000.

Weis, L. *Class Reunion*. New York: Routledge, 2004.

*Willis, P. *Learning To Labor*. New York: Columbia University Press, 1979.

Wolff, J. *Why Read Marx Today?* Oxford and New York: Oxford University Press, 2002.

FERDINAND DE SAUSSURE

Key Concepts

- structuralism
- structural linguistics
- semiology and semiotics
- *langue* and *parole*
- synchronic and diachronic
- sign, signifier, and signified
- arbitrary nature of the sign
- binary opposition (meaning as difference)

Ferdinand de Saussure (1857–1913) was a Swiss linguist whose posthumously published *Course in General Linguistics* (1916) became a catalyst for the development of **structuralism**. Saussure was born in Geneva into a family with a lineage of noted academics going back to the eighteenth century. He displayed a gift for languages from an early age. At the University of Geneva, he studied not only linguistics but also theology, law, and chemistry. In 1878, at age twenty-one, he published *Memoir on the Original System of Vowels in the Indo-European Languages*, a reconstruction based on historical-comparative study of phonological patterns in Indo-European languages.

Saussure received his doctorate from the University of Leipzig in 1880. From 1881 through 1891 he taught linguistics at the École des Hautes Études in Paris. In 1891 he returned to the University of Geneva, where he taught courses on Sanskrit and general linguistics for the remainder of his career. Although he published very little, his students at Geneva compiled and transcribed their notes from his general linguistics course lectures and had them published in 1916 as *Course in General Linguistics*.

That statement of Saussure's perspective on language has affected many fields of academic inquiry, including religion, literature, philosophy, anthropology, and psychology. In the work of influential twentieth-century critical theorists such as Michel FOUCAULT, Louis Althusser, Roland Barthes, Claude Lévi-Strauss, Jacques LACAN, Julia Kristeva, and Jacques DERRIDA, Saussure's assertion that linguistic meaning resides in the relationships among words constitutes a critical point of departure. Saussure's philosophy of language is commonly referred to as **structural linguistics** because its strategy for examining language and meaning centers on investigating structures within a system. In concert with the work of Martin Heidegger and other philosophers of being, structuralism brought about a major shift in twentieth-century thought often referred to as the "linguistic turn," which has become shorthand for the conviction that meaning does not exist outside language.

In *Course in General Linguistics*, Saussure advocated the scientific study of language, which, for him, concerned "the life of signs within society." This method contrasts with historical linguistics as then practiced by European philologists, who sought to trace Indo-European languages back to a common origin. Saussure called his new linguistic science **semiology**, a term derived from the Greek word for "**sign**" (*semeîon*). Semiology, also called **semiotics**, is the science of signs—that is, the study of the structure of language as a system of signification rather than of the history of languages.

To study language as a system of signs, Saussure made a distinction between *langue* and *parole*. *Langue* ("language") refers to language as a structured system operating at a particular time and place, and to the linguistic rules that determine how a language can be used in practice. In contrast, *parole* ("speech") refers to particular occurrences of speech within the system. Without *langue*, argued Saussure, *parole*—actual language use—would be impossible. For Saussure, the primary object of inquiry, then, is *langue*, which constitutes overarching linguistic systems that make specific utterances possible.

As the terms *langue* and *parole* suggest, the study of language as a system requires a **synchronic** ("at the same time") approach rather than a **diachronic** ("across time") one. "Synchrony" refers to the study of language, especially spoken language, as it is used at a particular moment in time. "Diachrony" refers to the study of language change over time. Nineteenth-century philology employed a diachronic methodology that derived from a central assumption that language could be comprehended only through a study of its historical changes.

Thus, if a word could be traced back to its origin, then the path to its present meaning could be followed.

Saussure advocated a synchronic approach to language as a system, asserting that language can be understood only in terms of relationships. Instead of regarding etymology as the conveyor of a word's meaning, Saussure argued that meaning is produced by a word's relationship to other words occurring at a particular time, within a particular system of relationships. For instance, the contemporary word "dog" means something not because of its historical derivation from the Middle English *dogge*, which is in turn derived from the Old English *docga*, but rather because of the current relationship of "dog" to other words like "puppy" and "cat." In Saussure's analysis, all of these terms are part of a system, and their meanings and significances derive from relationships with other signs within that system.

As illustrated by the previous example, a central claim made by Saussure's synchronic linguistic analysis is that words do not have inherent meaning. Instead, meaning resides in relationships of difference and similarity within a larger linguistic system; words are not units of self-contained meaning. A related concern—whether language is natural or conventional—also plays an important role in Saussure's linguistic analysis. A natural view of language proposes that language names things in the world because there is some intrinsic relationship between a word and the thing named. By contrast, if language is conventional, both concrete things and abstract concepts are named on the basis of an arbitrary decision to use a certain sound to represent a certain idea: the **arbitrary nature of the sign**. Saussure developed a theory of language that clearly sides with the idea of language as a matter of historically constituted arbitrary convention.

How did Saussure arrive at the conclusion that language is primarily conventional? He began with the idea of the linguistic sign. A sign may be a word or some other semiotic form. Regardless of its particular form, however, every sign consists of a **signifier** and a **signified**. A linguistic sign comprises a sound-image, such as the sounds represented by the letters "d-o-g" (the signifier), and the object or concept associated with the sound-image (the signified). What determines the signification (that is, the meaning) of a sign is not its sound-image or linguistic origin but its place within the larger network of interrelationships—that is, within the larger linguistic structural system. Thus, a structuralist approach focuses on the relationship of individual parts to the larger whole—the structure—within which significance is determined.

One of Saussure's key insights, then, is that the sign is fundamentally relational. He argued further that the relation between the signifier and the signified is arbitrary. That is, any signifier can potentially stand for any signified. The fact that "dog" signifies a four-legged domestic animal in English, while *chien* and *inu* point to this same animal in French and Japanese respectively, is evidence that there is no necessary relationship between the sounds "d-o-g" and a common pet. The word "dog" is an arbitrary designation. We could call dogs by some other term as long as we agreed culturally on that usage. There is no particular dog designated by the word, nor is there some inherent quality ("dogness") contained in or conveyed by the sound-image "dog."

Because signs are arbitrary, the meaning of any particular sign is determined in terms of similarity and difference in relation to other signs. Thus, meaning is founded on **binary oppositions**, such as light/dark, good/bad, inside/outside, margin/center, male/female, positive/negative, immanent/transcendent, life/death, or sacred/profane. Within these binary pairs, the meaning of one is basically the opposite of the other. Meaning, then, is predicated on difference. Sacred means "not profane," inside means "not outside," and so on. Saussure wrote:

> In language there are only differences. Even more important: a difference generally implies positive terms between which the difference is set up, but in language there are only differences without positive terms. Whether we take the signified or the signifier, language has neither ideas nor sounds that existed before the linguistic system, but only conceptual and phonic differences that have issued from the system. The idea or phonic substance that a sign contains is of less importance than the other signs that surround it. (1959, p. 150)

Although the direct appropriation and application of Saussure's work in education has not been extensive, he seems to be mentioned everywhere, usually as a central theorist on whose work other theorists (including Basil BERNSTEIN, Jean PIAGET, Sigmund FREUD, Derrida, Lacan, and Mikhail BAKHTIN) drew heavily to develop their own ideas. For example, critics of Bernstein's code theory claim that Saussurean structuralism lies at the heart of much of Bernstein's sociological work on elaborated and restricted codes, including the prescriptivist values that Bernstein explicitly rejected. The importance of binaries in the work of Derrida was clearly inspired by Saussure. Bakhtin's ideas about the utterance as a foundational unit of analysis in linguistics, the importance of "actual language" to linguistic study, dialogism, and heteroglossia were all reactions to problems inherent in Saussurean structuralism. These scholars, in turn, have exerted influence in more direct and directly traceable ways than has Saussure within education and educational research.

Saussure's work has, however, been appropriated in direct ways by some educational scholars. Tochon (2000) drew on Saussurean linguistics to develop a framework for semiotic research into disciplinary didactics as a prototype discipline. Gathering data on oral communication in classrooms from a large sample of small group learning circles in elementary schools, he showed how lived experience transcended subject-matter planning, concluding that the effects of planning for authentic educational experiences are indeed paradoxical.

Much important research has used Saussurean linguistics for thinking about literary analysis and English education more generally. Orr (1986), for example, criticized poststructural interpretations of Saussure's work that challenged its usefulness for literary studies. He went on to discuss intertextuality in the interpretive process, concluding that semiotics generally, and Saussure's work in particular, provide important tools for understanding the relations between specific cultural texts and historical epistemes, between microtexts and cultural macrocontexts. Drawing on Saussure's theories about the construction of texts, Garner and Newsome (1979) explored the use of derivation in literature classes, showing that sensitivity to students' lived experiences facilitates their ability to make text-to-life and life-to-text connections, and thus their understanding and appreciation of literary texts.

Somewhat surprisingly, Saussure's structural linguistics has been deployed extensively to conduct research on mathematics and science learning. Using Saussure's ideas about the structural organization of language as a system, McNamara (1995) explained how language (and understanding how language works) is fundamental to the process of learning mathematics. Based on his findings, he explored what Saussure's work can offer to enhancing and enriching the theoretical lenses through which mathematical activity in classrooms is typically viewed, described, interpreted, and explained. Focusing on science learning, Kawasaki (1996) used Saussurean structural linguistics to offer what he considered an "impartial" frame of reference to analyze science education in non-Western countries. Among other things, he outlined the associative relations between linguistic units proposed by Saussure and examined how they function in science teaching and learning. Kawasaki also identified specific problems with science education and its effectiveness in Japan and argued that science education curricula and practice should be reconstructed to resemble more closely foreign language education curricula and practice.

Finally, Saussure's linguistic model has been applied within the subfield of practitioner research. Drawing together ideas from Saussure and hermeneutic theory, Brown (1996), for example, studied how writing within school-based teacher research projects functioned in framing and guiding teachers' efforts to conduct research on their own practice and its effects. Based on this research, he drew a useful analogy between Saussure's descriptions of linguistic analysis (especially syntagmatic analysis) and the generation and analysis of ongoing writing and revising in the service of engaging in teaching as reflective practice.

To conclude, Saussure's structuralism provided the foundation for all future structuralisms, including those of scholars as diverse as Bernstein, Piaget, Freud, and Noam Chomsky. However, Saussure's work has probably been felt most heavily in education in the ways it has constituted a foil for poststructuralist theorizing on language, literacy, learning, and even educational research itself. Additionally, various dimensions of Saussure's structuralist linguistics have been used to frame educational inquiry and practice across many disciplinary domains—literary analysis, mathematics teaching and learning, science education, and inquiry-based pedagogy.

Further Reading

By Saussure

1959. *Course in General Linguistics*, translated by W. Baskin. New York: McGraw-Hill.

About Saussure

Belsey, C. *Poststructuralism: A Very Short Introduction*. Oxford: Oxford University Press, 2002.

Culler, J. *The Pursuit of Signs: Semiotics, Literature, Deconstruction*. Ithaca, NY: Cornell University Press, 1981.

*Culler, J. *Ferdinand de Saussure*. Rev. ed. Ithaca, NY: Cornell University Press, 1986.

Lévi-Strauss, Claude. "The Structural Study of Myth." In his *Structural Anthropology*. New York: Basic Books, 1963.

Relevance for Education

Brown, T. "Creating Data in Practitioner Research." *Teaching and Teacher Education* 12 (1996): 261–270.

Garner, M., and B. Newsome. "Hangman and Associations: The Final Analysis." *English in Australia* 48 (1979): 18–28.

Kawasaki, K. "The Concepts of Science in Japanese and Western Education." *Science and Education* 5 (1996): 1–20.

McNamara, O. "Saussurian Linguistics Revisited: Can It Inform Our Interpretation of Mathematical Activity?" *Science and Education* 4 (1995): 253–266.

Orr, L. "Intertextuality and the Cultural Test in Recent Semiotics." *College English* 48 (1986): 811–823.

Tochon, F. V. "When Authentic Experiences Are 'Enminded' into Disciplinary Genres: Crossing Biographic and Situated Knowledge." *Learning and Instruction* 10 (2000): 331–359.

THE THEORISTS

MIKHAIL BAKHTIN

Key Concepts

- actual language
- utterance
- unfinalizabilty
- dialogism
- heteroglossia
- addressivity
- voice
- genre
- social language
- carnival

Mikhail Bakhtin (1895–1975) was born in Orel, Russia, south of Moscow, and grew up in Vilnius and Odessa, cosmopolitan border towns that offered an unusually heterogeneous mix of languages and cultures. He studied classics and philology at St. Petersburg University (later Petrograd University) and then moved to the country, first to Nevel and then to Vitebsk, where he taught high school. While there, he married Elena Aleksandrovna and became part of an intellectual circle that also included Valentin Voloshinov and Pavel Medvedev. He moved to Leningrad in 1924 and five years later was arrested for alleged participation in the underground Russian Orthodox Church. Because of his ill health resulting from a degenerative bone disease, Bakhtin's initial sentence of ten years in a Siberian labor camp was reduced to six years of internal exile in Kazakhstan, where he worked as bookkeeper on a collective farm. For a full decade after his exile, he was unable to find stable employment; then, in 1945, he secured a position teaching Russian and world literature at Mordovia Pedagogical Institute in Saransk. After sixteen years of teaching, he retired from this position in 1961. In 1969 he moved to Moscow, where he remained until his death in 1975.

Bakhtin worked on many topics during more than a half-century of scholarship, notably epistemology, ethics, aesthetics, and education. In all his work, however, there are abiding concerns with ethical responsibility, creativity, and the relations between the two. He was particularly interested in the relations between structure and agency, and between convention and invention.

Bakhtin's experiences in Vilnius and Odessa exposed him to a rich and complex mix of different language groups, cultures, and classes. In fact, these experiences probably laid the foundation for his theories of dialogism and heteroglossia, discussed at length below. His reading in contemporary German philosophy and physics introduced him to the problem of unity amid difference that would persist throughout his work and influence its reception in both Russia and the West. Bakhtin resisted the Neo-Kantian emphasis on all-embracing unity: "The original Kantian concept of the heterogeneity of ends is much closer to Bakhtin's work than the later Neo-Kantian lust for unity" (Holquist, 1990, p. 6). He was more receptive to Einstein's revelation of a complex unity of differences, from which Bakhtin seems to have inferred that all meaning is relational, the result of a "dialogue" between and among bodies—physical, political, and conceptual (Holquist in Bakhtin, 1990, pp. 20–21). Finally, Bakhtin's religious activities as an intellectual from the Russian Orthodox tradition disposed him to value *sobornost*, a deep investment in togetherness and community responsibility.

From his earliest writings, Bakhtin attacked "theoretism," the reduction of human generativity to a priori theoretical systems (for example, Saussurean linguistics, Freudianism, Marxism, or Russian Formalism). Theoretism, he argued, impoverishes the truth of human life by reducing all of life's phenomenological complexity and messiness to static universal laws and structures. Indeed, much of his work is devoted to demonstrating the fallacy of theoretism, either as an adequate philosophical anthropology or as an approach to human activity in a variety of settings.

Actively resisting theoretism as it had been applied to philosophical anthropologies, Bakhtin attended to the particularities (not the generalities) of **everyday life**. He claimed that such a stance mitigates the academic impulse toward universalizing experience within theories.

Instead of being drawn to the grand or catastrophic events of human history—wars, disasters, revolutions, inaugurations—he was fascinated by the "prosaic" details of the lives of ordinary people, details that are in many ways most revealing of how self re-creation and social transformation take place on the ground rather than in history books. In this regard, his work is very much like that of Michel FOUCAULT.

Bakhtin resisted over-theorizing language, as linguistic structuralism (for example) seemed to do. Thus, a thorough understanding of Bakhtin's take on language presupposes an understanding of the fundamental linguistic innovations developed by Ferdinand de SAUSSURE. In particular, we need to understand Saussure's distinction between *langue* (language as a structured system that operates according to discernible rules) and *parole* (the specific utterances of individual speakers at particular historical moments). Saussure's linguistics concentrates on *langue* and involves (a) distilling lexicons and fundamental grammatical rules, (b) comparing the structures of different languages, and (c) examining the implications of structural differences across languages. In contrast, Saussure considered *parole*, or the instantiations of language in the utterances of particular speakers at particular moments, to be too unpredictable, heterogeneous, and context-contingent to be relevant to understanding language as a system.

For Bakhtin, though, what is most interesting about language is the individual, temporally specific, highly context-dependent phenomenon of language-in-use. He viewed the fundamental Saussurean dichotomy between *langue* and *parole* as overly simplistic and incapable of describing the complex reality of **actual language** in use. Although languages often do undergo a centralizing pull toward unification, singularity, and systemic integrity, they are simultaneously drifting and being pulled toward multiple peripheries. Canons and codes are developed (most commonly by an elite group holding power), while elsewhere a wide variety of individual speakers are innovating and modifying the canons and codes through their improvisational acts of language use. These two sets of competing forces—centripetal (centralizing and unifying) and centrifugal (decentralizing and disunifying)—always operate simultaneously. For Bakhtin, then, studying only sanitized, unified languages systems severely limits and distorts the attempt truly to understand the nature and functions of language, and it misconstrues how language actually functions in human society and human life.

For Bakhtin, the **utterance** is the most important linguistic unit of analysis. Utterances are discernible chunks of language-in-use. They may be as short as a single word (for example, "Damn!") or as long as a novel. Utterances may also be multiply embedded within other utterances, which is indeed the case with much social discourse and many written texts. This is true partly because utterances involve both the physical artifacts produced—either spoken or written language—and a host of extralinguistic forces that helped to shape them. Those extralinguistic forces derive both from the social world and from the thinking processes of individuals. As such, utterances are both social and individual.

The framing context of utterances includes both the author of the utterance (as speaker or writer) and the persons to whom the author responds and from whom the author expects a response. Utterances also come with histories of meaning potential. In most forms of actual language practice, utterances have been used before and are appropriated and redeployed for new purposes in new contexts. In other words, speakers/writers always use chunks of language they have heard in the past and reconfigure and reaccent them for their own purposes.

Utterances are also saturated with the ideologically charged valuations of the social worlds in which they occur. Whether implicitly or explicitly, speakers/writers always express evaluative attitudes toward the subjects or themes of their utterances, "subjective emotional evaluation(s) of the referentially semantic content" (Bakhtin, 1986, p. 84). The referentially semantic content of the utterance captures its *meaning* and is accessible to traditional studies of language as system, such as linguistics (1986, pp. 84–86). The evaluative attitude captures the *specific sense* of the utterance and is discernible only in the context of "a particular actual reality and particular real conditions," which are extralinguistic or metalinguistic (1986, pp. 85–86).

Throughout his life Bakhtin emphasized the concept of **unfinalizability**, or the impossibility of arriving at final conclusions for anything. In *Problems of Dostoevsky's Poetics*, for example, he wrote: "Nothing conclusive has yet taken place in the world, the ultimate word of the world and about the world has not yet been spoken, the world is open and free, everything is still in the future and will always be in the future" (1981, p. 166). Life is riddled with surpluses, remainders, loopholes, and anomalies that keep things unfinalizable and therefore always hold open the possibility of surprise, change, and transformation.

Dialogism is a kind of a formalization of Bakhtin's insistence on unfinalizability, and it is his most central and most important theoretical construct. The central focus of Bakhtin's theory of dialogism is language. A secondary focus is the human subject as an unfinalizable complex of identities, desires, and voices. With respect to language, Bakhtin claimed that all discourses—literature, everyday talk, military commands, and so on—are dialogic, a complex amalgam of multiple voices. When someone speaks or writes, her words are not simply streaming forth from within herself as sole author and source. Rather, her discourse, like her identity, is essentially a coalescence of the many voices and languages that constitute her as a subject. Every subject is made up of multiple voices, past and present. The subject is thus a space of dialogue. One's speech and writing issue forth from that dialogical space.

Polyphony is a key characteristic of Bakhtin's theory of dialogism. In this regard, he identified two kinds of discourse: monologic and dialogic discourse. As the word implies, monologic discourse embodies a single voice. It is one with itself and allows for no contradiction, no counter-voice, like a declaration from a pope or president. It is presented as though it is the final word, impossible as that may be. Dialogic discourse, in contrast, emerges in the midst of several unmerged voices. It is an undirected intersection of voices manifesting a "plurality of consciousnesses" that do not all join together in one monologic voice. It cannot be systemized or finalized. Dialogic discourse manifests the particularity and uniqueness of speech event itself. It is not the unity of a system but the unity of a dynamic event, a dialogue that involves struggle and contradiction. Dialogic discourse is discourse that contains a deliberate reference to someone else's words but also inserts "a new semantic intention into a discourse which already has, and which retains, an intention of its own" (Bakhtin, 1981, p. 189).

Another key characteristic of dialogism is **heteroglossia**. This is a broader concept than polyphony. It is a complex mixture of languages and world views that is always (except in some abstracted ideal conditions) dialogized, as each language is viewed from the perspective of the others. This dialogization of languages, or dialogized heteroglossia, creates a complex unity, for whatever meaning language has resides neither in the intention of the author nor in the text but in a space where the semantic histories of both collide or intersect. "For any individual consciousness living in it, language is not an abstract system of normative forms but rather a concrete heteroglot conception of the world. All words have the 'taste' of a profession, a genre, a tendency, a party, a particular work, a particular person, a generation, an age group, the day and hour" (Bakhtin, 1986, p. 293). This complex content of any utterance is not merely a mixture, however, but a dialogized heteroglossia, a viewing of the utterance from the perspectives of others (1986, pp. 295–296).

In this matrix of dialogicality, the specific contexts in which utterances are produced, distributed, and consumed are influenced by at least four levels of intentionality: (a) the intentionality of the historical moment, (b) the intentionality of the social and cultural frames at work, (c) the intentionality of the culture in which the utterance is produced, and (d) the intentionality of the individual speaker(s) and audience(s) involved. Thus, concrete heteroglossic speech events propel language toward multiplicity—not in the poststructural sense that they disconnect the signifier from the signified, but in the sense that they constantly proliferate different ways of speaking, different rhetorical strategies, different vocabularies, and different meaning potentials.

Bakhtin refined his notion of an utterance by developing the concept of **addressivity**, which he defined as "the quality of turning to someone" (1986, p. 99). Addressivity is this act of turning (and of being turned to) that defines the dialogic utterance. It requires addressees who participate together in the creation of the meaning of any utterance. Bakhtin also noted that the addressor takes "into account possible responsive reactions" of the addressee (1986, p. 94) when constructing an utterance. This means that the addressor anticipates the responses of the audience. Addressivity, then, marks a highly charged recursive relationship between interlocutors. The author/speaker is never free from the audience in this model of understanding because "anticipation" is an essential mechanism by which the social situation establishes the basic structure of the utterance.

Because heteroglossia involves the interanimation of voices, social languages, and genres, each of these constructs merits discussion. Bakhtin (1981, 1984) developed an interesting model of voice that simultaneously involves multiple dimensions. For Bakhtin, **voice** is a packet of discourse replete with an ideology. It is the verbal-ideological perspective expressed within a particular utterance. Voice "is the speaking personality, the speaking consciousness. A voice always has a will or desire behind it, its own timbre and overtones" (1981, p. 434). The speaking consciousness referred to here is quite different from the notion of an individual author in that it always belongs simultaneously to a speech community and to an individual speaker. Importantly, the semantic intention of any voice is always transformed in some way each time it is used by a new speaker or writer. It is thus always "double-voiced" or, perhaps more accurately, "multiple-voiced." Finally, because texts are usually composed of multiple utterances, they usually embody multiple voices or ideological perspectives, which enter into various relationships of support, indifference, or competition.

Bakhtin argued that even the expert novelist's voice is never unitary, except in the historical sense of its control and exploration of voices that are borrowed from a variety of discursive communities and allowed (or encouraged) to intermingle in the novel. Thus, Bakhtin viewed the individual author not as an inherent subjectivity but as a complex dialogic construction that involves knowledge of a variety of discourse communities, the appropriation of a variety of discursive practices, and the active orchestration and transformation of a symphony of voices.

Bakhtin (1973, 1986) emphasized that among the concrete forces that shape individual language users, no force is stronger than the talk that they experience over time in the primary socialization settings of the family, the community, and the school. Thus, the utterances of individual people always contain traces of the utterances experienced by those people in the past, as they have interacted with others. These traces breathe life into each new utterance, indexing past experiential histories, social interactions, and ideological perspectives. As individuals experience the language of others through social interaction, they collect words, phrases, styles, and structures and integrate them, forming a new synthetic object that we might call their individuality as language users and social beings. Individuals become laminates (or mosaics) of discourse practices who are only partially responsible for their own uniqueness.

Genres are discursive frames that organize discourse into typified or durable text structures and social practices that accomplish specific purposes within typical communicative activities. Examples of speech genres include conversations, academic lectures, service encounters, stories, proverbs, military commands, and Initiation–Response–Evaluation/Initiation–Follow-up–Evaluation (IRE/IRF) (Bakhtin, 1986). In addition, speech genres are historically and ideologically saturated "aggregate[s] of the means for seeing and conceptualizing reality" (Bakhtin and Medvedev, 1985, p. 137). They are also indexical, signaling the ideologies, norms, values, and social ontologies of the social contexts in which they typically function. When people appropriate and use genres, they also inherit these ideologies as obvious and familiar horizons against which their actions and the actions of others make sense.

Whereas genres are cultural frames that organize discourse practice at the level of whole texts or communicative events, **social languages** organize discourse practice at the more local levels of lexicon, syntax, semantics, and pragmatics. Analyzing the social languages that occur with discourse activities helps us understand where people got the language forms they use, as well as the concrete histories and nuanced local meanings of these forms. Such understandings are possible because social languages are typically associated with local social contexts or domains of practice (for example, profession, age group, social set, cult) at particular times and places in history (Bakhtin, 1986). An attorney, for example, would probably use what we might call "legalese" when in court, but almost never when playing with her children or relaxing with friends. Among other things, she would adjust her lexicon, grammar, forms of address, substantive content, and tone— often considerably—for these various audiences and contexts. Just as there are tacit conventions for the appropriate use of social languages, there are consequences for importing certain social languages into social contexts where these languages are unwelcome.

Carnival is another Bakhtinian concept that has gained much attention from scholars in a wide range of disciplines. Carnival may be imagined as heteroglossia gone wild. Bakhtin's fullest treatment of carnival appears in *Rabelais and His World* (1973), in which he mapped the origins, nature, and function of this construct. More specifically, he showed how the extraordinary and grotesque representation of the human body, the lavish linguistic diversity, and the parodies and travesties that characterize Rabelais's writings can be seen as derived from the widespread practices of carnival in Renaissance Europe. Bakhtin went on to argue that carnivals are playful subversions of the established social and political orders, which might otherwise appear fixed. Through common practices of masquerade, the burning of effigies, the desecration of sacred objects and spaces, role reversals, and excessive indulgence of the body, carnivals loosen the hold of the dominant order, breaking free—though only temporarily—from law, tradition, and all that enforces normative social behavior. Carnival is thus an invitation to become a part of an embodied collective. "In this whole the individual body ceases to a certain extent to be itself; it is possible, so to say, to exchange bodies, to be renewed (through change of costume and mask). At the same time the people become aware of their sensual, material bodily unity and community" (Bakhtin, 1973, p. 255).

In the field of education, Bakhtin's theoretical constructs (especially dialogism and carnival) have become increasingly influential, especially within literacy studies. The interactive and responsive approach to teaching–learning processes that his work encourages provides educational researchers and practitioners alike with ways to integrate theory, method, and practice. Additionally, his notions of dialogism and heteroglossia provide the foundation for transforming education in the twenty-first century by blurring the boundaries between research and practice to develop *"the potential to generate innovative research and new kinds of knowledge as well as new tensions and professional dilemmas"* (Cochran-Smith and Donnell, in press). This boundary work holds promise for pushing beyond current monologic rhetorics and practices about what counts as research and whose research counts. It also moves us toward newer, more dynamic ideas about the power of research to transform both theory and practice.

Such new ideas are sorely needed in most teacher education programs, which typically focus on teaching methods or techniques without considering the underlying epistemological and ontological views guiding their practices. Bakhtin's ideas (especially voice, dialogism, and genre) suggest that epistemological and ontological perspectives are central in shaping teachers' and students' understandings. A more Bakhtinian approach to teacher education would underscore the importance of helping teachers reflect on and interrogate their understandings of language and learning and of how these understandings function in classrooms and beyond.

Bakhtin's insights could also contribute in significant ways toward shaping future research and academic discussions about the impact of opportunities for learning on access to academic knowledge. Such discussions could pave the way for the critical dialogues across multiple disciplines that are needed to disrupt current archaic and somnambulistic ideas about "best practices" in education and why they are deemed "best."

Further Reading

By Bakhtin

1973 [published under the name of V. N. Voloshinov]. *Marxism and the Philosophy of Language*, translated by L. Matejka and I. R. Titunik. Cambridge, MA: Harvard University Press.

1976 [published under the name of V. N. Voloshinov]. *Freudianism*, translated by I. R. Titunik. Bloomington: Indiana University Press.

1981. **The Dialogic Imagination*, translated by C. Emerson and M. Holquist. Austin: University of Texas Press.

1984a. *Problems of Dostoevsky's Poetics*, translated by C. Emerson. Minneapolis: University of Minnesota Press.

1984b. *Rabelais and His World*, translated by H. Iswolsky. Cambridge, MA: MIT Press.

1985 [with P. N. Medvedev]. *The Formal Method in Literary Scholarship: A Critical Introduction to Sociological Poetics*, translated by A. J. Werhle. Cambridge, MA: Harvard University Press.

1986. *Speech Genres and Other Late Essays*, translated by V. W. McGee. Austin: University of Texas Press.

1990. *Art and Answerability: Early Philosophical Essays*, translated by V. Liapunov, edited by M. Holquist amd V. Liapunov. Austin: University of Texas Press.

1993. *Toward a Philosophy of the Act*, translated by V. Liapunov, edited by V. Liapunov and M. Holquist. Austin: University of Texas Press.

About Bakhtin

*Clark, K., and M. Holquist. *Mikhail Bakhtin*. Cambridge, MA: Harvard University Press, 1984.

Emerson, C. *The First Hundred Years of Mikhail Bakhtin*. Princeton: Princeton University Press, 1997.

Kristeva, Julia. *Desire in Language: A Semiotic Approach to Literature and Art*, translated by T. Gora, A. Jardine, and L. S. Roudiez. New York: Columbia University Press, 1980.

Morson, G. S., and C. Emerson, eds. *Rethinking Bakhtin: Extensions and Challenges*. Evanston, IL: Northwestern University Press, 1989.

*Morson, G. S., and C. Emerson. *Mikhail Bakhtin: Creation of a Prosaics*. Stanford: Stanford University Press, 1990.

Wertsch, J. V. *Voices of the Mind: A Sociocultural Approach to Mediated Action*. Cambridge, MA: Harvard University Press, 1990.

Relevance for Education

Bazerman, C. *Shaping Written Knowledge: The Genre and Activity of the Experimental Article in Science*. Madison: University of Wisconsin Press, 1988.

Beach, R., and C. M. Anson. "Stance and Intertextuality in Written Discourse." *Linguistics and Education* 4 (1992): 335–358.

Bennett, T. *Outside Literature*. London: Routledge, 1990.

Berkenkotter, C., and T. N. Huckin. "Rethinking Genre from a Sociocognitive Perspective." *Written Communication* 10 (1993): 475–509.

Bloome, D., and A. Egan-Robertson. "The Social Construction of Intertextuality in Classroom Reading and Writing Lessons." *Reading Research Quarterly* 28 (1993): 304–333.

Chapman, M. L. "The Emergence of Genres: Some Findings from an Examination of First-grade Writing." *Written Communication* 11 (1994): 348–380.

Chapman, M. L. "The Sociocognitive Construction of Written Genres in First Grade." *Research in the Teaching of English* 29 (1995): 164–192.

Chapman, M. L. "Situated Social Active: Rewriting Genre in the Elementary Classroom." *Written Communication* 16 (1999): 469–490.

Cochran-Smith, M., and K. Donnel. "Practitioner Inquiry: Blurring the Boundaries of Research and Practice." In J. Green, G. Camilli, and P. Elmore, eds., *Complementary Methods for Research in Education*. 3rd ed. Washington, DC: American Educational Research Association (in press).

Cope, B., and M. Kalantzis. *The Powers of Literacy: A Genre Approach to Teaching Writing*. Pittsburgh: University of Pittsburgh Press, 1993.

Coulter, D. "The Epic and the Novel: Dialogism and Teacher Research." *Educational Researcher* 28 (1999): 4–13.

Devitt, A. J. "Generalizing about Genre: New Conceptions of an Old Concept." *College Composition and Communication* 44 (1992): 573–586.

Dyson, A. H. *Social Worlds of Children Learning To Write in an Urban Primary School*. New York: Teachers College Press, 1993.

Dyson, A. H. *Writing Super Heroes: Contemporary Childhood, Popular Culture, and Classroom Literacy*. New York: Teachers College Press, 1997.

Freedman, A., and P. Medway, eds. *Genre and the New Rhetoric*. London: Taylor and Francis, 1994.

Gutierrez, K., E. Rymes, and J. Larson. "Script, Counterscript, and Underlife in the Classroom: James Brown versus *Brown v. Board of Education*." *Harvard Educational Review* 65 (1995): 447–471.

Hartman, D. "Intertextuality and Reading: The Text, the Author, and the Context." *Linguistics and Education* 4 (1992): 295–312.

Hengst, J. A., and P. J. Miller. "The Heterogeneity of Discourse Genres: Implications for Development." *World Englishes* 18 (1999): 325–341.

Hicks, D. "Narrative Skills and Genre Knowledge: Ways of Telling in the Primary School Grades." *Applied Psycholinguistics* 11 (1990): 83–104.

Hicks, D. "Discourse, Learning, and Teaching." In M. W. Apple, ed., *Review of Research in Education, Volume 21*. Washington, DC: American Educational Research Association, 1995–1996.

Hicks, D. "Narrative Discourses as Inner and Outer Word." *Language Arts* 75 (1998): 38–34.

Ivanic, R. "Intertextual Practices in the Construction of Multimodal Texts in Inquiry-based Learning." In N. Shuart-Faris and D. Bloome, eds., *Uses of Intertextuality in Classroom and Educational Research*. Greenwich, CT: Information Age, 2004.

Kamberelis, G. "Genre as Institutionally Informed Social Practice." *Journal of Contemporary Legal Issues* 6 (1995): 115–171.

Kamberelis, G. "Genre Development: Children Writing Stories, Science Reports and Poems." *Research in the Teaching of English* 33 (1999): 403–460.

Kamberelis, G. "Producing Heteroglossic Classroom (Micro)cultures through Hybrid Discourse Practice." *Linguistics and Education* 12 (2001): 85–125.

Kamberelis, G., and K. Scott. "Other People's Voices: The Coarticulation of Texts and Subjectivities." *Linguistics and Education* 4 (1992): 359–403.

Kumamoto, C. D. "Bakhtin's Others and Writing as Bearing Witness to the Eloquent 'I'." *College Composition and Communication* 54 (2002): 66–87.

Lemke, J. L. *Talking Science: Language, Learning, and Values*. Norwood, NJ: Ablex, 1990.

Lensmire, T. J. *When Children Write: Critical Re-visions of the Writing Workshop*. New York: Teachers College Press. 1994.

Lensmire, T. J. "The Teacher as Dostoevskian Novelist." *Research in the Teaching of English* 31 (1997): 367–392.

Lillis, T. "Student Writing as 'Academic Literacies': Drawing on Bakhtin To Move from 'Critique' to 'Design'." *Language and Education* 17 (2003): 192–207.

Marsh, M. *Social Fashioning of Teacher Identities: Rethinking Childhood*. New York: Peter Lang, 2003.

Maybin, J. "Reported Speech and Intertextual Referencing in 10- to 12-year-old Students' Informal Talk." In N. Shuart-Faris and D. Bloome, eds., *Uses of Intertextuality in Classroom and Educational Research*. Greenwich, CT: Information Age, 2004.

Miller, C. R. "Genre as Social Action." *Quarterly Journal of Speech* 70 (1984): 151–167.

Myers, G. *Writing Biology: Texts in the Social Construction of Scientific Knowledge*. Madison: University of Wisconsin Press, 1990.

Nystrand, M., and A. Gamoran. *Opening Dialogue: Understanding the Dynamics of Language and Learning in the English Classroom*. New York: Teachers College Press, 1996.

Prior, P. "Response, Revision, and Disciplinarity: A Microhistory of a Dissertation Prospectus in Sociology." *Written Communication* 11 (1994): 483–533.

Prior, P. *Writing/Disciplinarity: A Sociohistoric Account of Literate Activity in the Academy*. Mahwah, NJ: Erlbaum, 1998.

Rockwell, E. "Teaching Genres: A Bakhtinian Approach." *Anthropology and Education Quarterly* 31 (2000): 260–282.

Rosmarin, A. *The Power of Genre*. Minneapolis: University of Minnesota Press, 1985.

Scollon, R., W. K. Tsang, D. Li, L. Yung, and R. Jones. "Voice, Appropriation and Discourse Representation in a Student Writing Task." *Linguistics and Education* 9 (1998): 227–250.

Short, K. "Researching Intertextuality within Collaborative Classroom Learning Environments." *Linguistics and Education* 4 (1992): 313–334.

Sipe, L. "Talking Back and Taking Over: Young Children's Expressive Engagement during Storybook Read-alouds." *Reading Teacher* 55 (2002): 476–483.

Skidmore, D. "From Pedagogical Dialogue to Dialogical Pedagogy." *Language and Education* 14 (2000): 283–296.

Solsken, J., J. Willett, and J. Wilson-Keenan. "Cultivating Hybrid Texts in Multicultural Classrooms: Promise and Challenge." *Research in the Teaching of English* 35 (2000): 179–212.

Swaim, J. F. "Laughing Together in Carnival: A Tale of Two Writers." *Language Arts* 79 (2002): 337–346.

Swales, J. *Genre Analysis*. Cambridge, UK: Cambridge University Press, 1990.

Wells, G. "Reevaluating the I-R-F Sequence: A Proposal for the Articulation of Theories of Activity and Discourse for the Analysis of Teaching and Learning in the Classroom." *Linguistics and Education* 5 (1993): 1–37.

Zack, V., and B. Graves. "Making Mathematical Meaning through Dialogue: 'Once you think of it, the z minus three seems pretty weird.'" *Educational Studies in Mathematics* 46 (2001): 229–271.

BASIL BERNSTEIN

Key Concepts

- elaborated codes
- restricted codes
- collection codes
- integrated codes

Basil Bernstein (1924–2000) had a working-class childhood in London's East End. He worked his way through the London School of Economics, where he earned a degree in sociology, and Kingsway Day College, gaining a degree in teacher education. Bernstein later received a Ph.D. in linguistics from University College, London. He taught at the Institute of Education in London for his entire career, eventually being named to the Karl Mannheim Chair in the Sociology of Education. He retired in 2000, having continued to be a prolific writer and influential thinker until his death.

Bernstein's earliest work looks at class differences and language use. In his own words, he was interested in the "fundamental linkage of symbolic systems, social structure and the shaping of experience," as well as "*how* such shaping takes place" (1972, p. 159). Bernstein wanted to know how social orders reproduce themselves through micro-level speaking practices. Yet he sought not just to describe these practices but also to find out how language use could intervene critically in the reproduction of unfair social structures. Throughout this career, he looked for ways "to prevent the wastage of working-class educational potential" (quoted in Sadovnik, 2001, p. 8).

In his first book, *Class, Codes, and Control, Volume 1*, Bernstein developed an important and often misunderstood distinction between **elaborated** and **restricted codes** in speech. Elaborated codes are rooted in middle-class dispositions (or ways of interacting with the world). They indicate a context-independent way of speaking, a way of cueing the addressee into the background material necessary to make sense out of talk. This kind of speech is not tied to any kind of local social order. Speakers have the freedom to define and negotiate the context of their speech. Restricted codes, in contrast, are rooted in working-class dispositions. They indicate a very context-dependent way of speaking, a sparse use of language that largely assumes that the addressee shares the speaker's background. This kind of speech is closely tied to local social orders. Working-class youth are thus predisposed to deal with local, concrete sets of circumstances, while middle-class youth are predisposed to communicate with multiple and overlapping audiences in a variety of ways. As Bernstein wrote, "Elaborated codes orient their users towards universalistic meanings, whereas restricted codes orient, sensitize, their users to particularistic meanings" (1972a, p. 164). His second book, *Class, Codes, and Control, Volume 2*, gathers empirical examples (largely from his students) to work through some of these ideas.

Bernstein's notions of elaborated and restricted codes were quite controversial. In fact, he was accused of supporting what is sometimes called a "deficit" model of language use, and of making normative value judgments about language varieties and the people who use them. He was also accused of implying that marginalized youth—for Bernstein, working-class youth in Britain—were marginalized because their language was somehow deficient or "broken." The strongest such charge came from the linguist William Labov, who did early important work on African American narrative. He wrote, "Bernstein's views are filtered through a strong bias against all forms of working-class behavior, so that middle-class language is seen as superior in every respect" (1972, p. 204). Bernstein denied any such value judgment in his work, but the debate remains important for those in education. How can one work toward an equitable education system while respecting and valuing the home cultures of students?

Bernstein soon took up questions of education and the ways these codes prepare youth for school success in distinct ways. In early articles like "On the Classification and Framing of Educational Knowledge," Bernstein explored how curricular knowledge is "framed" in school settings. He was less interested in the particular content of curricula than in the formal dimensions of how knowledge is dispensed and controlled. He highlighted the idea that different kinds of knowledge (for example, different school subjects) can be rigidly separated from one another or can interpenetrate more loosely. He called the former the **collection code** type of curriculum, and the latter an **integrated code** type. He wrote:

> Classification, here, does not refer to *what* is classified, but to the *relationship* between contents. Classification refers to the nature of the differentiation between contexts. Where classification is strong, contents are well insulated from each other. Where classification is weak, there is reduced insulation between contexts for the boundaries between contents are weak or blurred. *Classification thus refers to the degree of boundary maintenance between contents.* (1977, p. 49; italics in original)

For Bernstein, the degree of "boundary maintenance" between different kinds of knowledge is a function of power. He was also interested in the ways teachers and students were able to "frame" curricular knowledge in pedagogical settings. Here, Bernstein asked whether or not students and teachers could freely rearticulate these boundaries. He wrote: "*The frame refers to the degree of control teacher and pupil possess over the selection, organization, and pacing of the knowledge transmitted and received in the pedagogical relationship*" (p. 50; italics in original). A key question here is to what degree students can introduce their own everyday knowledge into school settings.

Bernstein used this typology to explain different educational systems throughout the world. Some of these systems tightly control the relationships between school subjects as well as the ability of teachers and students to rearticulate them. Others allow for a more fluid relationship between subjects as well as for the possibility that students and teachers can rework them. Importantly, there are key relationships between these educational codes and the social structures of power that support them. Collection codes tend to exist along with very authoritarian and hierarchical systems that support rigid structures of power. Integrated codes tend to accompany more egalitarian and nonhierarchical systems that support less rigid structures of power. However, Bernstein wanted not merely to describe these systems, but also to change them. For him, changes in the ways knowledge is ordered, separated, and taught have the potential to change social structures. Speech and educational codes are micro-level instantiations of larger power structures. Like much work in the sociology of knowledge, this work held out the hope that educational practices could help reorder larger systems.

Bernstein was thus centrally concerned with questions of power and authority in school settings, with particular attention to how knowledge is organized and disseminated. His work is often associated with what is sometimes called the "new sociology of education," a movement that emerged in England in the 1970s and included the work of Geoff Whitty and Michael Young. These scholars attempted to map the ways in which broader social hierarchies are connected with and instantiated in the organization of school knowledge. Their work wrestles with the ways decisions about knowledge or curricula stratification could both support and disrupt broader social stratification. Like Bernstein's, their focus is primarily on questions of social class.

Bernstein continued in his interest in pedagogy and social control. He published two more volumes of *Class, Codes, and Control*, each developing the framework described above. Bernstein's language became increasingly dense and baroque in his treatment of these codes, but he also continually clarified his own investments in education—and the kinds of educative systems that would nurture true democracies. In his last book (2000), a revised version of an earlier text, he discussed the "rights" necessary for a democratic education system and the conditions that would enable them. These include the right to what he called "enhancement," "inclusion," and "participation," which play out (respectively) at the individual, social, and political levels. Throughout all this work, Bernstein explored the underlying codes that explain how knowledge is distributed and picked up.

Bernstein's work has been of continuing interest to scholars and researchers in education, although much of it is arcane and specialized. Two edited collections provide a good overview of the various ways his work has affected the field: *Knowledge and Pedagogy: The Sociology of Basil Bernstein* (1995) and *Towards a Sociology of Pedagogy: The Contribution of Basil Bernstein to Research* (2001). This work has picked up and attempted to extend the various pieces of the puzzle that Bernstein laid out—the complex interconnections among language codes, school knowledge, pedagogy, and social and economic reproduction.

Several theorists have put Bernstein's work into dialogue with that of social theorists such as Émile Durkheim, Karl **MARX**, and Michel **FOUCAULT**. As Atkinson (1995) argues, Bernstein is best seen as a structuralist, drawing on Durkheim's concerns with mechanical versus organic solidarity—respectively, social cohesion based on shared in-group ritual and routine, and social cohesion based on the complex differentiation of labor. Clearly, these different ways of approaching social cohesion informed Bernstein's notions of restricted and elaborated codes, yet he was also concerned with social control and regulation, particularly as they are linked to the organization of knowledge. In this respect, he shared much with the work of Foucault, according to Atkinson, and Foucault's interest in knowledge, power, and discipline. In addition, Bernstein's work is centrally concerned with the lived realities of economic inequality and can be seen as advancing a post-Marxist sociology of education (Apple, 1995).

Others have put Bernstein's work into dialogue with VYGOTSKY and activity theory more broadly (Daniels, 2001). This work has looked to the ways in which cognitive capacities are mediated by symbolic interaction in context. According to Hasan (1995), there is important overlap between these thinkers in this regard, although Vygotsky developed a more acute theory of the semiotic while Bernstein developed a more compelling vision of the social. Several recent empirical studies have picked up this important point of overlap between Vygotsky and Bernstein. These include studies of cognitive socialization and educational attainment (Nash, 2001), curriculum-specific talk around mathematics and art (Daniels, 1995), and second-language learning (Foley, 1991).

This does not exhaust the range of theoretical and empirical studies that have taken up Bernstein's work. His oeuvre has informed work on home literacy practices (Williams, 2001), classroom discourse (Neves and Morais, 2001), and the role of authority in pedagogy (Finn, 1999). Much of this work is narrowly specialized and dense; however, the continuing interest in Bernstein speaks to the potential of his work to link the broadest of social processes (for example, capitalism) with specific ways of talking about symbolic interaction practices.

Further Reading

By Bernstein

1972. "Social class, language and socialization." In P. Gigioli, ed., *Language and Social Context*. Middlesex, England: Penguin.

1973a. *Class, Codes and Control, Volume 1*. London: Routledge.

1973b. *Class, Codes and Control, Volume 2*. London: Routledge.

1977. *Class, Codes and Control, Volume 3*. London: Routledge.

1990. *Class, Codes and Control, Volume 4*. London: Routledge.

2000. *Pedagogy, Symbolic Control, and Identity*. Lanham, MD: Rowman and Littlefield.

About Bernstein / Relevance for Education

Apple, M. "Education, Culture, and Class Power: Basil Bernstein and the Neo-Marxist Sociology of Education." In A. Sandovnik, ed., *Knowledge and Pedagogy*. Norwood, NJ: Ablex, 1995.

Atkinson, P. "From Structuralism to Discourse: Bernstein's Structuralism." In A. Sandovnik, ed., *Knowledge and Pedagogy*. Norwood, NJ: Ablex, 1995.

Daniels, H. "Pedagogic Practices, Tacit Knowledge, and Discursive Discrimination: Bernstein and Post-Vygotskian Research." *British Journal of the Sociology of Education* 16 (1995): 517–532.

Daniels, H. "Bernstein and Activity Theory." In A. Morais, I. Neves, B. Davies, and H. Daniels, eds., *Knowledge and Pedagogy: The Sociology of Basil Bernstein*. New York: Peter Lang, 2001.

Finn, P. *Literacy with an Attitude*. Albany, NY: SUNY Press, 1999.

Foley, J. "Vygotsky, Bernstein and Halliday: Towards a Unified Theory of L1 and L2 Learning." *Language, Culture, and Curriculum* 4 (1991): 17–42.

Hasan, R. "On Social Conditions for Semiotic Mediation: The Genesis of Mind in Society." In A. Sandovnik, ed., *Knowledge and Pedagogy*. Norwood, NJ: Ablex, 1995.

Labov, William. *Language in the Inner City*. Philadelphia: University of Pennsylvania Press, 1972.

Morais, A., I. Neves, B. Davies, and H. Daniels, eds. *Knowledge and Pedagogy: The Sociology of Basil Bernstein*. New York: Peter Lang, 2001.

Nash, R. "Class, 'Ability' and Attainment: A Problem for the Sociology of Education." *British Journal of the Sociology of Education* 22 (2001): 189–202.

Neves, I., and A. Morais. "Texts and Contexts in Educational Systems." In A. Morais et al., eds., *Knowledge and Pedagogy*. New York: Peter Lang, 2001.

*Sandovnik, A. "Basil Bernstein (1924–2000)." *Prospects: The Quarterly Review of Comparative Education* 31 (2001): 687–703.

*Sandovnik, A. *Towards a Sociology of Pedagogy: The Contribution of Basil Bernstein to Research*. Norwood, NJ: Ablex, 1995.

Williams, G. "Literacy Pedagogy Prior to Schooling: Relations between Social Positioning and Semantic Variation." In A. Morais et al., eds., *Knowledge and Pedagogy*. New York: Peter Lang, 2001.

PIERRE BOURDIEU

Key Concepts

- practice
- field
- habitus
- taste
- doxa
- cultural capital

Pierre Bourdieu (1930–2002) was a French sociologist whose work has been widely influential in both the social sciences and the humanities. He was born in rural southwestern France, where his father was a postal worker. Bourdieu received a scholarship that enabled him to attend the prestigious Lycée Louis-le-Grand in Paris. He subsequently enrolled at the École Normale Supérieure, where he studied with Louis Althusser. After graduating with a degree in philosophy, Bourdieu taught first at the high school level. In 1959 he was appointed to a position in philosophy at the Sorbonne; after that he taught at the University of Paris from 1960 to 1964. In 1964 he was named Director of Studies at the École des Hautes Études en Sciences Sociales and founded the Centre de Sociologie de l'Education et de la Culture (Centre de Sociologie Européenne). In 1982 he was named to the Chair of Sociology at the Collège de France. He received the Medaille d'Or (Gold Medal) from the Centre Nationale de la Recherche Scientifique in 1993.

During his military service, Bourdieu spent time teaching in Algeria. This experience made him acutely aware of the social effects of French colonialism and the social inequality embedded in the colonialist Algerian social system. He later conducted ethnographic fieldwork in Algeria that was the foundation for many of his concepts and theories. Bourdieu also conducted research in France, where he studied the structures of social and class differences. Interested in how systems of social inequality are embedded in cultural practices, he paid particular attention to the study of the French education system and demonstrated how it reproduced class differences, despite its claims to the contrary. Bourdieu was a consummate public intellectual. In 2001, he became a celebrity with the appearance of a popular documentary film about him, *Sociology Is a Combat Sport*. His books were often best-sellers in France. He matched his status as a public intellectual with political activism, publicly criticizing the inequalities in the French social class structure and urging better conditions for, among others, the working classes and the homeless. He was also closely associated with antiglobalization movements.

Bourdieu's large body of work—he authored more than twenty-five volumes—covers many different areas, including the sociology of culture and taste, education, language, literature, and cultural aspects of museums. Among his best-known texts are *Outline of a Theory of Practice* (published in French in 1972), *Distinction* (published in French in 1979), and *The Logic of Practice* (published in French in 1980). Many of his key concepts (for example, field, practice, habitus, doxa, cultural capital, and taste) have exerted significant and ongoing influences on the humanities and social sciences, including education.

We begin with **practice** because it is the central construct, the engine, that drives Bourdieu's entire sociological theory about the relations between structure and agency. The construct of practice is developed most fully in *Outline of a Theory of Practice* and *The Logic of Practice* and is essential for explaining the processes by which social patterns of behavior reproduce (or transform) structures of domination. In an equation that is as illustrative as it is cryptic, Bourdieu posited that "(habitus)(capital) + field = practice." This equation is a bit misleading; in fact, reading it backwards more accurately represents the relations between and among practice, habitus, capital, and field in Bourdieu's theory. Both field and habitus are continually produced and reproduced in flows of practice. In other words, there is not a field (structure) separate from a habitus (agency), the two of which somehow get connected through practice. Instead, neither field nor habitus could exist in the absence of practice. Both are produced in and through social practice. This is one of Bourdieu's most brilliant insights, and one that resolved the dilemma of structure and agency in a unique and creative way.

People who occupy the same field share similar habituses (see below for definitions) and produce/reproduce that field through practice in fairly similar ways. Social practices that materially produce/reproduce culture are not, however, objectively determined, nor are they exclusively effects of intentional activity by individuals. Paradoxically, they are the conditions of possibility for both field and habitus, and they are constituted/reconstituted as agents act within the limits of action afforded by the field. They are neither entirely rule-governed nor entirely random. Practices are predictable within limits, but they also change over time as people engage in them in partially idiosyncratic ways.

From the perspective of the individual habitus, practices involve conscious, intentional action and unconscious, unintentional action. Social actors develop a certain "feel for the game" of any field, which enables them to act more or less automatically. This is what Bourdieu refers to as "embodied learning," through which trained actions are not the result of logical reasoning but occur through processes that take place outside conscious control. Bourdieu contended that it is not only a sense of the game that is embodied; through regulated management of the body within particular social and cultural contexts, the logic of the world within which the individual acts is also embedded in the habitus. Yet because practices are not solely rule-governed, all individuals take them up in partially unique ways. This social fact means that the organization or logic of the field itself is constantly being reconfigured by the specific ways in which the practices within it are enacted.

A **field** is perhaps best understood as a field of forces. It is a dynamic social arena where exchanges and struggles take place involving particular forms of capital. A field is thus defined primarily in terms of the kinds of practices that are common within it and the kinds of capital that may accrue to individuals who engage in those practices, and secondarily as the kinds of social relations that develop as people work to acquire and maintain the kinds of capital with the most purchase in the field. The boundaries of any specific field with respect to the stakes, and the kinds of individuals drawn into its domain of practice, are not fixed but fluid, because fields develop and are maintained by the practices that occur in them.

There are as many social fields as there are kinds of practices and forms of capital—the field of gender, for example with masculine and feminine practices and forms of capital, or the field of class with working-class, middle-class, and upper-class practices and forms of capital. Any social field can be located within or across a number of levels of a given social formation and may be largely inclusive or exclusive in terms of size or reach. Multiple fields overlap and are interrelated to make up the larger society, or social space. Over the timespan of an individual's life, he or she may pass through different fields and compete for capital with varying degrees of success within them. An individual habitus is always constructed at the intersection of many social fields, which may be related in mutually supportive or contradictory and conflicting ways. Similarly, depending on his or her habitus, an individual will feel more or less "at home" in any particular social field.

Habitus is the structuring mechanism that operates from within agents, though it is neither wholly individual nor itself wholly determinative of conduct. In Bourdieu's words, habitus is

> the strategy generating principle enabling agents to cope with unforeseen and ever-changing situations ... a system of lasting and transposable dispositions which, integrating past experiences, functions at every moment as a *matrix of perceptions, appreciations, and actions,* and makes possible the achievement of infinitely diversified tasks, thanks to analogical transfers of schemes permitting the solution of similarly shaped problems and, and thanks to the unceasing corrections of the results obtained. (1977, pp. 72, 82–83)

In other words, a habitus is a set of dispositions that generate and structure human actions and behaviors. Habitus develops through accumulated socialization experiences and represents the sedimentation, internalization, or embodiment of these experiences within the individual. Thus, particular dispositions and tastes come to mirror (more or less) those of particular social fields through engagement in social practice within those fields. These dispositions and inclinations can be usefully perceived as **taste**. Taste is inculcated through participation in social practices in particular social environments over time. Although each habitus is unique, people who have moved through similar social contexts develop similar habituses. Habitus is thus the embodied social history of the individual. It is a durable set of socially constructed predispositions that structure social action, largely in unconscious ways. In turn, habitus shapes the ways individuals deal with both familiar and novel social situations. However, habitus is also creative or inventive, even though it must work within the limits of its own structures:

> Habitus is not the fate that some people read into it. Being the product of history, it is an *open system of dispositions* that is constantly subjected

to experiences, and therefore constantly affected by them in a way that either reinforces or modifies its structures. It's durable but not eternal. (Bourdieu and Wacquant, 1992, p. 133)

Finally, field and habitus are both relational constructs, and they function fully only in relation to each other.

Knowing the habitus of a particular person does not provide the social scientist with predictive power to know what practices a person will engage in. To claim this would be to remove agency from individual actors and valorize structure over practice. Bourdieu criticized any method that attempted to remove agency and practice from our understanding of social structure. Similarly, habitus is not fixed or static. Indeed, Bourdieu argued that distinctions between one habitus and another are not rigidly set. They are different but have a shared and processual quality. Dispositions are also multiple and nonexclusive. We may, for example, apply one set of dispositions in our home life and another while at work. Our dispositions also change over time. How does one come to or learn a particular habitus? Bourdieu described this process as one of informal, unconscious learning rather than formal instruction. One learns to inhabit a habitus through practice, such as using a particular space for a specific purpose, listening to particular kinds of music, cooking, drinking, wearing clothes, driving cars, celebrating holidays, and giving gifts. Conversely, the habitus one occupies shapes the practices one engages in. The important point here is that much of the motivation for people's behavior is hidden, implicit knowledge learned informally and embodied in specific social practices. Once internalized, dispositions seem natural. They are taken for granted. Bourdieu used the term **doxa** to refer to the taken-for-granted, unquestioned, unexamined nature of dispositions.

Importantly, Bourdieu's notion of habitus is not simply about how socialization or enculturation experiences become dispositions; it is also about power relations, especially those that exist between social classes. Indeed, perhaps his most intense intellectual concern was to understand how social inequality is perpetrated and maintained. Habitus functions to distinguish social classes from each other. It is a sort of pragmatic version of ideology. Habitus contrasts the different sets of dispositions (social expectations, lifestyle choices, and so forth) that exist between different classes. Class distinctions appear clearly in the complex of practices embedded in a particular habitus. One reason why this is so socially powerful, according to Bourdieu, is that class inequalities and the dominance of one class over another occur covertly. Rather than the application of overt force, symbolic power is harnessed to maintain class distinctions and the appearance of their naturalness. Money may have economic exchange value for food and other commodities, but the possession and use of it also have symbolic exchange value that marks one as wealthy and upper-class or poor and lower-class. Domination occurs, in part, because the exchange value system is itself controlled by the dominant class.

In order to explain the relation between habitus and social stratification within fields more fully, Bourdieu used the term "capital" (typically considered an economic concept), but he employed it to refer not only to financial resources but also to other resources that confer and reveal social status of one kind or another. Financial capital matters for the establishment of class distinctions, of course, but so does **cultural capital**, including educational level, linguistic competence, and other forms of capital that mark social class. Cultural capital is used to distinguish and maintain class distinctions and, by extension, social inequality.

Bourdieu's insistence that cultural capital *is* capital crucially underpins his social analysis. The existence of different but convertible forms of capital—economic, cultural, and social capital—requires us to part company with Marx, "to abandon the economic/non-economic dichotomy [in favor of] ... a science capable of treating all practices" (1990, p. 122). The concept of cultural capital enables the general theory's articulation because "agents are distributed within [the social world], in the first dimension, according to the overall volume of the capital they possess and, in the second dimension, according to the composition of their capital—i.e., according to the relative weight of the different kinds of assets within their total assets" (1985, p. 724).

Bourdieu and Passeron's (1979) work on reproduction in education has had considerable impact on educational research, and particularly on the sociology of education. This has seen widespread use of Bourdieu's concept of cultural capital in research on education and schooling. His conception of capital is far broader than that of Marx. Capital can be something that is owned, such as real estate, a car, or money in the bank. It can also be something that is embodied. The amount of capital an individual may accumulate makes a significant contribution to determining the range of her or his available choices. Accumulated capital determines an individual's "distance from necessity," his or her distance from material want. This is why Bourdieu used the term "capital" to refer to both material and symbolic resources, the differential accumulation of which determines location in social space.

Importantly, as posited by Bourdieu, social, cultural, or economic forms of capital can be accumulated and converted from symbolic forms to more powerful, material, economic forms. The institutional cultural capital contained in a university degree, for example, can be converted into financial capital through the particular type of work to which it provides access. The social capital accumulated through the building of social connections made at an elite independent school or an exclusive golf club may also be converted into financial capital through the access that it provides to business exchanges and the possibility of more rewarding employment. Primarily concerned with the reproduction of culture in the broad anthropological sense, Bourdieu's analytical framework is focused on cultural capital, which he conceives as existing in three forms: institutional forms, objective forms, and embodied forms. Institutional forms of cultural capital exist as formal credentials, such as university degrees and school diplomas. Objectified forms of cultural capital may take the form of cultural goods such as books, musical instruments, or art works. Embodied forms of cultural capital exists in the form of long-lasting dispositions of the mind and body. These last forms are particularly relevant to the practices of education and educational research.

Further Reading

By Bourdieu

1977. *Outline of a Theory of Practice*, translated by R. Nice. Cambridge, UK: Cambridge University Press.

1979 [with J. C. Passeron]. *Reproduction in Education, Society and Culture*. London: Sage.

1984. *Distinction: A Social Critique of the Judgment of Taste*, translated by R. Nice. Cambridge, MA: Harvard University Press.

1987 [1979]. "The Forms of Capital." In J. G. Richardson, ed., *Handbook of Theory and Research for the Sociology of Education*. New York: Greenwood.

1988. *Homo Academicus*, translated by P. Collier. Stanford: Stanford University Press.

1990. *The Logic of Practice*, translated by R. Nice. Stanford: Stanford University Press.

1992 [with L. J. D. Wacquant]. *An Invitation to Reflexive Sociology*. Chicago: University of Chicago Press.

1993. *Sociology in Question*. Thousand Oaks, CA: Sage.

1994. *Language and Symbolic Power*. Cambridge, MA: Harvard University Press.

1998. *Practical Reason: On the Theory of Action*. Stanford: Stanford University Press.

About Bourdieu

Calhoun, C. C., E. LiPuma, and M. Postone, eds. *Bourdieu: Critical Perspectives*. Chicago: University of Chicago Press, 1993.

Connell, R. *Ruling Class, Ruling Culture*. Melbourne: Cambridge University Press, 1977.

Guillory, J. *Cultural Capital: The Problem of Literary Canon Formation*. Chicago: University of Chicago Press, 1993.

Hargreaves, J. *Sport, Power and Culture*. Cambridge, UK: Polity, 1986.

Jenkins, R. *Pierre Bourdieu*. Rev. ed. London: Routledge, 2002.

Lane, J. F. *Pierre Bourdieu: A Critical Introduction*. London: Pluto, 2000.

*Robbins, D. *The Work of Pierre Bourdieu*. Boulder, CO: Westview, 1991.

Shilling, C. *The Body and Social Theory*. London: Sage, 1993.

Shusterman, R., ed. *Bourdieu: A Critical Reader*. Oxford: Blackwell, 1999.

*Swartz, D. *Culture and Power: The Sociology of Pierre Bourdieu*. Chicago: University of Chicago Press, 1997.

Relevance for Education

Apple, M. *Ideology and Curriculum*. London: Routledge and Kegan Paul, 1979.

Armour, K. "The Case for a Body Focus in Education and Physical Education." *Sport, Education and Society* 4 (1999): 5–16.

DeFrance, J. "The Anthropological Sociology of Pierre Bourdieu: Genesis, Concepts, Relevance." *Sociology of Sport Journal* 12 (1995): 121–131.

Dressman, M. "Preference as Performance: Doing Social Class and Gender in Three School Libraries." *Journal of Literacy Research* 29 (1997): 319–361.

Driessen, G. "Ethnicity, Forms of Capital, and Educational Achievement." *International Review of Education* 47 (2001): 513–538.

Erickson, F. "Transformation and School Success: The Politics and Culture of Educational Achievement." *Anthropology and Education Quarterly* 18 (1987): 335–357.

Gallacher, J., B. Crossan, J. Field, and B. Merrill. "Learning Careers and the Social Space: Exploring Fragile Identities of Adult Returners in the New Further Education." *International Journal of Lifelong Education* 21 (2002): 493–509.

Horvat, E. M. "The Interactive Effects of Race and Class in Educational Research: Theoretical Insights from the Work of Pierre Bourdieu." *Penn GSE Perspectives on Urban Education* 2 (2003): 1–25.

Johannesson, I. A. "Principles of Legitimation in Educational Discourses in Iceland and the Production of Progress." *Journal of Education Policy* 8 (1993): 339–351.

Kirk, D. "Schooling Bodies in New Times: The Reform of Physical Education in High Modernity." In J. M. Fernandez-Balboa, ed., *Critical Postmodernism in Human Movement, Physical Education and Sport*. New York: SUNY Press, 1997.

Kirk. D. "Physical Education Discourse and Ideology: Bringing the Hidden Curriculum into View." *Quest* 44 (1992): 35–56.

Li, G. "Literacy, Culture, and Politics of Schooling: Counternarratives of a Chinese Canadian Family." *Anthropology and Education Quarterly* 34 (2003): 182–204.

Lofgren, K. "Habits among Students in Umea and Madison: A Contribution to the Understanding of Pierre Bourdieu's Scientific Methodology." Ph.D. dissertation, Umeå University, Sweden, 2000.

Luke, A. "The Body Literate: Discourse and Inscription in Early Literacy Training." *Linguistics and Education* 4 (1992): 107–129.

Mitchell, C. Preface. In C. Mitchell and K. Weiler, eds., *Rewriting Literacy: Culture and the Discourse of the Other*. New York: Bergin and Garvey, 1991.

Mutch, C. "The Long and Winding Road: The Development of the New Social Studies Curriculum in New Zealand." Paper presented at the New Zealand Educational Administration Society Biennial Conference, Wellington, 1998.

Paul, J. "Centuries of Change: Movement's Many Faces." *Quest* 48 (1996): 531–545.

Roth, W-M., D. Lawless, and K. Tobin. "Towards a Praxeology of Teaching." *Canadian Journal of Education* 25 (2000): 1–15.

Smrekar, C. *The Impact of School Choice and Community: In the Interest of Families and Schools*. Albany: SUNY Press, 1992.

Stone, L., and M. Gunzenhauser. "From Bourdieu and Wolin, Inside and Outside the Box: A Frame for the Special Issue." *Studies in Philosophy and Education* 20 (2001): 181–190.

Valadez, J. R. "Searching for a Path out of Poverty: Exploring the Achievement Ideology of a Rural Community College." *Adult Education Quarterly* 50 (2000): 212–230.

Walpole, M. B. "College and Class Status: The Effects of Social Class Background on College Impact and Outcomes." Paper presented at the Annual Meeting of the Educational Research Association, Chicago, IL, 1997.

JEROME BRUNER

Key Concepts

- cognitive revolution
- rhetorical turn
- culturalist approaches to education

Jerome Bruner (b. 1915) was born in New York City. He graduated with a B.A. degree from Duke University in 1937 and received a Ph.D. in psychology from Harvard in 1941. He was a professor at Harvard beginning in 1952, and at Oxford University from 1972 to 1980. He held concurrent appointments at the New School for Social Research in New York City and also at New York University. He later was named Research Professor of Psychology and Senior Research Fellow in Law at New York University.

Early in his career, Bruner was a central player in the so-called **cognitive revolution**. This movement looked beyond behaviorist models of mind to explore the mind in use. In his words, the cognitive revolution was "an all-out effort to establish meaning as the central concept of psychology—not stimuli and responses, not overtly observable behavior, not biological drives and their transformation, but meaning" (1990, p. 2). With time, however, this lofty goal was largely overtaken by other concerns that were more narrowly scientistic. Bruner noted for example, that the "emphasis began shifting from 'meaning' to 'information,' from the *construction* of meaning to the *processing* of information" (p. 4). With this move to "information processing," a narrower conception of mind took hold that largely elided the complexity of individuals and their relationships to the world—their agency. Parting ways with cognitive approaches to the mind, Bruner "return[ed] to the question of how to construct a mental science around the concept of meaning and the processes by which meanings are created and negotiated within a community" (p. 11).

Bruner's move away from behaviorist models had important implications for the field of education. His book *The Process of Education* was published in 1960 and quickly became a classic in the field. Here Bruner argued that meaning making is more important than training youth to perform tasks in narrow, behaviorist fashion. This necessitates an appreciation of the ways children learn, and a focus on how these processes happen in certain stages. The most famous claim in the book is that any subject can be taught to any young person of whatever age in some demonstrably "honest" form. This would be the book's central legacy—though the qualifying term "honest" and its importance would be debated for years to come. Bruner had a far-reaching approach to education and educational psychology, and his work would be picked up in several related disciplines.

Related important work has to do with language acquisition. *Child's Talk* (1983), Bruner's most comprehensive work on language acquisition per se, is based on two case studies of British toddlers. Bruner's model of language acquisition and developing communicative competence is quintessentially a contextual and pragmatic one. From the outset he gave priority to social and cultural factors involved in the process of learning language (the "Language Acquisition Support System"). He considered innate capacity (the "Language Acquisition Device") to be of secondary importance in the process—necessary but insufficient for actual language learning. Although innate capacity may be rule-governed, it is the regulatory aspects of social and cultural exchange that are formative.

Communication is the *modus operandi* for social and cultural processes. Indeed, one of the reasons that Bruner could argue for a sociocultural hypothesis is that language is not the only semiotic system used by the child, and it is, for the most part, the last mastered. However, even though language presupposes communication, it eventually becomes its "state-of-the-art" form. Being both the medium of and the primary instrument for these processes, language inhabits the peculiar position of being both necessary for them but secondary to them. Language both grows out of these processes and facilitates their accomplishments. Its key motive is the better regulation of individual as well as social and cultural processes. Learning how to communicate verbally, then, is part of the greater, more global, and more relevant processes of socialization and acculturation.

Among other things, the turn toward "meaning" signaled a **rhetorical turn** in psychology. This turn meant looking beyond a narrow focus on mental input and output toward the ways people construct meaning in context, including through language. For Bruner, this means opening up psychology to other kinds of influences, including literature, where ideas about the construction of meaning have always proliferated.

In his important *Actual Minds, Possible Worlds,* Bruner discussed the increasing interest in literature, linguistics, and the uses and functions of language beginning in the 1970s, and specifically the turn to narrative. This interest, he argued, all but took over several different fields across the social sciences and the humanities around this time. The first chapter of this book highlights two distinct ways of approaching narrative. In one camp are those who tend to focus on top-down models of narrative; they seek to develop models out of context, to discover deep structures that could be tested against particular "instances" of particular phenomena. Bruner offered structural linguistics as one domain of inquiry where such concerns are played out. In the other camp are those who favor bottom-up models. These models are not really models at all; rather, they tend to focus on particular texts and to build unique theories from the particularities of these texts. For example, these partisans might be "in search of the implicit theory in Conrad's construction of *Heart of Darkness* or the words that Flaubert constructs" (p. 10).

Bruner did not necessarily advocate either approach. He has been more intent on bringing the concerns of the literary, of narrative, to the social scientific study of psychology. Here as throughout his work, he remained interested in how individuals become meaning-making agents in cultural contexts. This necessarily implies an interest in the interplay between how we construct stories and how we are constructed by available cultural narratives. This tension is perhaps the most central undercurrent in Bruner's next book, *Acts of Meaning.* In this book he discussed the ways that cultural socialization necessitates making meaning in context. Narratives or stories make sense only against this backdrop. Culture renders these narratives understandable. Bruner focused on the durability of cultural values as well as their mutability:

Values inhere in commitment to "ways of life," and ways of life in their complex interaction constitute a culture. We neither shoot our values from the hip, choice situation by choice situation, nor are they the product of isolated individuals with strong drives and compelling neuroses. Rather, they are communal and consequential in terms of our relations to a cultural community. (1990, p. 29)

Here as elsewhere, Bruner explains how narratives provide people with a "basis for negotiation" in a culture.

Bruner has returned to questions of education again and again. *The Culture of Education* (1996) is key in this regard. It updates some of his earlier ideas about education, stressing throughout that all education happens in specific social contexts, as transactions between people. For Bruner, a **culturalist approach to education** means acknowledging the ways in which we live in a world saturated with cultural narratives: "Culturalism ... concentrates exclusively on how human beings in cultural communities create and transform meanings" (p. 4). Importantly, Bruner argues that much education assumes a narrow "computational" theory of the mind. Instead, he advocates emphasis on the situated, meaning-laden ways mind works in context. The goal of education, for Bruner, is to make individuals self-reflexive in this regard. The construction of valued selves is key.

Bruner's work has been critical for the field of education (Bakhurst and Shanker, 2001; Orlofsky, 2001). Bruner is one of several key thinkers, including Lev VYGOTSKY and John DEWEY, who brought a "constructivist" approach to learning and knowledge. For constructivists, knowledge is not simply handed down as whole cloth from teachers to students. Rather, students are co-participants in the construction of meaning. This means decentering the role and importance of the teacher, and focusing more on the child as knowledge-builder in context. For Bruner and others, knowing is "doing."

In addition, Bruner was very important for the turn toward narrative that resonated throughout the field of education since about 1980. According to Donald Polkinghorne:

Narrative is the cognitive process that gives meaning to temporal events by identifying them as parts of a plot. The narrative structure is used to organize events into various kinds of stories.... These are stories of the self. They are the basis of personal identity and self-understanding and they provide answers to the question "Who am I?" (1991, p. 136)

These "plots" mark stories within a temporal range, select relevant events to be included and excluded, and finally assign meaning to stories' events (Polkinghorne, 1995). The attention to narrative has led to a range of approaches in qualitative research in education, including narrative analysis, memoir, biography, autobiography, life history, and personal narrative (Alvermann, 2000).

Further Reading

By Bruner

1960. *The Process of Education*. Cambridge, MA: Harvard University Press.

1983. *Child's Talk*. New York: Norton.

1986. *Actual Minds, Possible Worlds*. Cambridge, MA: Harvard University Press.

1990. **Acts of Meaning*. Cambridge, MA: Harvard University Press.

1996. **The Culture of Education*. Cambridge, MA: Harvard University Press.

About Bruner / Relevance for Education

Alvermann, D. "Narrative Approaches." 2000. http://www.readingonline.org/articles/handbook/alvermann/. Accessed November 15, 2003.

Bakhurst, D., and S. Shanker. *Jerome Bruner: Language, Culture, Self*. Thousand Oaks, CA: Sage, 2001.

Orlofsky, D. *Redefining Teacher Education: The Theories of Jerome Bruner and the Practice of Training Teachers*. New York: Peter Lang, 2001.

Polkinghorne, D. E. "Narrative and Self-concept." *Journal of Narrative and Life History* 1 (1991): 135–153.

Polkinghorne, D. E. "Narrative Configuration in Qualitative Analysis." *International Journal of Qualitative Studies in Education* 8 (1995): 12–28. Reprinted in J. A. Hatch and R. Wisniewski, eds., *Life History and Narrative*. London: Falmer, 1995.

JUDITH BUTLER

Key Concepts

- gender/sex
- gender trouble
- performativity
- paradox of subjection
- face of the enemy

Judith Butler (b. 1956) received a Ph.D. in philosophy from Yale University in 1984. She is currently Maxine Elliott Professor in the departments of rhetoric and comparative literature at the University of California, Berkeley.

Butler is best known as a theorist of gender, identity, and power. Her most influential book to date, *Gender Trouble* (1990), makes the revolutionary argument that neither gender nor sex is a natural or given category of human identity. At the time of publication, this was a major challenge to the position then common among feminists that **gender** (masculinity and femininity) is culturally constructed whereas biological **sex** (male and female) is natural and innate. In *Gender Trouble* and the subsequent *Bodies That Matter* (1993), Butler countered that "gender must ... designate the very apparatus of production whereby the sexes themselves are established. As a result, gender is not to culture as sex is to nature; gender is also the discursive/cultural means by which 'sexed nature' or 'a natural sex' is produced and established as ... prior to culture, a politically neutral surface on which culture acts" (1990, p. 7). In other words, there is no male and female prior to cultural engenderings of those two categories of identity. We cannot think outside our culture, and "male" and "female" identities are as culturally determined as are "masculinity" and "femininity." That sexual identity is natural, that there are two sexes in nature, is a cultural idea.

Butler argued that these categories of identity take social and symbolic form in a culture through repeated action. Sexual identity is "performative": "There is no gender identity behind the expressions of gender ... identity is performatively constituted by the very 'expressions' that are said to be its results" (1990, p. 25). Gender is not being but doing; it is not who you *are* but what you *do*—that is, how you express your identity in word, action, dress, and manner.

Butler is critical of forms of feminism that assert "women" as a group with a distinct identity, set of political interests, form of social agency, and so on. In making such assertions, she contends, feminism risks reinforcing a binary conception of gender, thereby reducing the infinite possibilities of social identity for human beings to two categories, man and woman, defined in opposition to each other. Against this, Butler calls for performances that produce **"gender trouble"** within this social and symbolic order: drawing out the contradictions and excesses within oneself—the parts that do not "come together" into a simple, unified "whole" self—and acting out a multiplicity of gendered and sexual identities. Thus a multiplicity of gendered and sexual identities would be produced, troubling the binary oppositions that reduce woman to man's other and vice versa, and opening up new forms of social agency and ways of being in the world.

In developing her theory of the **performativity** of gender and sex, Butler drew from Michel FOUCAULT's understanding of power. Arguing against a reductionistic view of power as the dominant force of law, Foucault conceived of power as a "multiple and mobile field of force relations, wherein far-reaching, but never completely stable, effects of domination are produced" (*The History of Sexuality, Volume 1: An Introduction*, p. 102). Power takes form within society through ceaseless struggles and renegotiations. It does not simply come down from on high but circulates through society. In the process it materializes, takes a "terminal form," within a particular sociopolitical system of power/ knowledge. Yet the "terminal forms" power takes are never entirely stable because they can never contain or totalize all actual and potential forces within society. Although they appear to us as terminal and fixed, they are in fact quite temporary and precarious. There are always points of resistance that cut across the social order and its stratifications of power and privilege, opening possibilities for subversion.

In *Gender Trouble* and later works, Butler developed Foucault's critical insights into the formation and subversion of terminal forms of power in relation to gender and sexual identity politics. Butler conceives of every social-symbolic order as a regulatory consolidation of power in the Foucauldian sense. Such an order is established and maintained by prohibitions and repeated performances of identities within that order. Yet, as Butler puts it, to be *constituted* within such a social-symbolic order is not to be *determined* by it. There is always the possibility of agency, of acting out within the system in ways that are subversive and transformative of it, because there are always aspects of oneself that are "socially impossible," that cannot be reduced to the order of things, that exceed any particular identity (such as gender identity and sexual identity) within that order—hence her interest in drag, cross-dressing, and other "queer" forms of gender trouble. Butler calls for performances—that is, expressions of identity that exploit those subversive dimensions and thereby produce new possible ways of being in society.

In *The Psychic Life of Power* (1997), Butler engaged Foucault, FREUD, LACAN, Louis Althusser, and others to explore a related paradox of social-symbolic agency, which she described as the "**paradox of subjection**." The paradox lies in the fact that subjectivity is founded on subjection. That is, in order to become an acting subject in a society, one must be subjected to its order (its language, laws, values, and so forth). Note Luce Irigaray's description of the social-symbolic order of patriarchy as "a certain game" in which a woman finds herself "signed up without having begun to play" (*Speculum of the Other Woman*, p. 22). So it is, in fact, with all forms of subjectivity. One acts *within* a certain social-symbolic order, a certain "game" with certain rules to which and by which she is initially "subjected." Even if her actions are ultimately subversive of that order, her subjectivity is inaugurated through subjection to it. Thus Butler writes, "Subjection signifies the process of becoming subordinated by power as well as the process of becoming a subject" (1997, p. 2). "A power exerted on a subject, subjection is nevertheless a power assumed by the subject, an assumption that constitutes the instrument of that subject's becoming" (1997, p. 11). To have power is, paradoxically, to be subjected to power. "What does it mean" she asks, "that the subject, defended by some as the presupposition of agency, is also understood to be an *effect* of subjection?" (1997, p. 11). What it means, she argues, is that to be conditioned or formed by a certain terminal form of power is not to be determined by it. That is, a subject's agency, her own exercise of power, is not "tethered" to the conditions that formed her. The subject is, in one sense, an effect of power; through the same subject's own agency, power becomes the effect of the subject.

Recently Butler has applied her theoretical interests in identity politics, subjectivity, and power to issues of ethics and violence in the war-torn aftermath of September 11, 2001. In particular, she focuses on media representations of the **face of the enemy**. How is it that America's enemies have been "othered" in such a way as to render them inhuman and their lives "ungrievable," thereby turning us away from the reality of life as fragile and precarious? In exploring this problem in her essay "Precarious Life" (2003), Butler drew on Emmanuel Levinas's concept of the face-to-face encounter as an ultimate ethical situation, a moment of obligation to the other, who pleads "do not kill." Media images reduce the face of the other to enemy (both as target and as victim of war) and thereby rule out the possibility of a genuine face-to-face encounter in Levinas's sense. In these media representations, the "ultimate situation" of the face-to-face is foreclosed. How, Butler asks, has the face of the other been erased by these dehumanized faces, and how does one tell the stories of these lives in such a way as to recuperate the ethical possibility of opening oneself to them in obligation and grief?

Judith Butler has been a key theorist for advancing the concerns of poststructural feminism in education. As her collection *Working the Ruins: Feminist Poststructural Theory and Methods in Education* (2000) makes clear, both poststructuralism and feminism have powerfully destabilized the common-sense notions of "humanism" that have informed so much theory, practice, and research in education. This work has advanced feminist concerns without recourse to easy notions of "humanism" and "humanistic" education and their foundational claims. Echoing Butler, gender categories are assumed always to be already "produced," though in unstable ways and with real effects.

Butler's work is an excellent example of the poststructural concerns beginning to resonate in the field of education. This work takes seriously the ways schools "produce" gender while also "troubling" efforts to interrupt it, through either pedagogical practice or research.

Further Reading

By Butler

1990. *Gender Trouble: Feminism and the Subversion of Identity*. New York and London: Routledge.

1993. *Bodies That Matter: On the Discursive Limits of "Sex."* New York and London: Routledge.

1997. *The Psychic Life of Power: Theories of Subjection.* Stanford: Stanford University Press.

2002. "Judith Butler 1.22.02" [interview]. *Common Sense*, Winter, 9–12.

2003. "Precarious Life." Paper presented at Meeting of the Consortium of Humanities Centers and Institutes, Harvard University, 15 March.

About Butler / Relevance for Education

Davies, B. "Eclipsing the Constitutive Power of Discourse: The Writing of Janette Turner Hospital." In E. St. Pierre and W. Pillow, eds., *Working the Ruins: Feminist Poststructural Theory and Methods in Education.* New York: Routledge, 2000.

Lather, P., and C. Smithies. *Troubling the Angels: Women Living with HIV/AIDS.* Boulder, CO: Westview, 1997.

St. Pierre, E., and W. Pillow, eds. *Working the Ruins: Feminist Poststructural Theory and Methods in Education.* New York: Routledge, 2000.

GILLES DELEUZE AND FÉLIX GUATTARI

Key Concepts

- rhizome
- deterritorialization
- pack multiplicities
- schizoanalysis
- desiring-machines
- body without organs

Gilles Deleuze (1925–1995), a philosopher, was born in France. He studied at the Sorbonne under Georges Canguilhem and Jean Hyppolite. He later taught philosophy at the Sorbonne, the University of Lyon, and, at the invitation of Michel FOUCAULT, at the experimental University of Paris VIII. He retired in 1987. Deleuze was a prolific writer on both philosophy and literature, including studies of Hume, Bergson, Spinoza, Nietzsche, Proust, Artaud, and Lewis Carroll, critiques of Kantian and Platonic thought, and considerations of such issues as representation, linguistic meaning, subjectivity, and difference.

Félix Guattari (1930–1992), a noted psychoanalyst and political activist, was also born in France. He embraced both radical psychotherapy (which he called "anti-psychiatry") and Marxist politics, though he became disillusioned with the French Communist Party after the May 1968 Paris strikes. He was a psychoanalyst at the Clinique de la Borde from 1953 until his death and was known for his use of alternative psychoanalytic therapies. Guattari was closely associated with Lacanian psychoanalytic theory. He received training from Jacques LACAN and was in analysis with him from 1962 to 1969. He later came to critique at least some aspects of Lacanian analysis. Guattari individually published essays and two books on psychoanalytic theory. In addition to his work with Deleuze, he collaborated with other Marxist thinkers and psychoanalysts.

Deleuze and Guattari met in 1969 and started working together soon after. Their collaborations include four books that are especially noteworthy for their dual critiques of Marxist and Freudian thought. The writings we will deal with here are *Capitalism and Schizophrenia: Anti-Oedipus* (first published in French in 1972) and *A Thousand Plateaus* (first published in French in 1980). In these twin volumes, Deleuze and Guattari attempted to destabilize essentialism and grand theories, especially those of MARX, FREUD, and structuralism. Deleuze and Guattari left us a rich conceptual palette replete with neologisms, only a small part of which we can discuss here. Despite the tendency among many to associate Deleuze and Guattari with "postmodernism," they did not themselves see their intellectual project in this light. Guattari, for instance, repudiated postmodernism as "nothing but the last gasp of modernism; nothing, that is, but a reaction to and, in a certain way, a mirror of the formalist abuses and reductions of modernism from which, in the end, it is no different" (1996, p. 109). The postmodern label notwithstanding, Deleuze and Guattari crafted a view of the world critical of grand narratives, foundational thought, and essences. Resisting those tendencies of modern thought, their texts describe ways of seeing and understanding multiplicities both of individual subjects and of larger institutional entities. It was to the end of destabilizing what they refer to as "fascist ways of acting in the world" that they armed themselves with a battery of neologisms that force us to think and conceptualize outside established, hegemonic, and naturalized modes of modern common sense.

Because Deleuze and Guattari sought multiplicity in their writing style, it is difficult to derive a clear and linear outline of their ideas. Any attempt to do so runs counter to their own resistance to such modernist ways of thinking. Many of the neologisms they employed are more suggestive than definitive. But we can point out some of the recurring themes and concepts with which Deleuze and Guattari were concerned. In general, they engaged in insistent critiques of modern ideas concerning the primacy of hierarchy, truth, meaning, subjectivity, and representation. For instance, they attacked the notion that there exist individual subjects who can gain knowledge of the truth and then transmit (represent) that truth transparently to others.

One notion that underscores their attempt to derail modernist, linear thinking is their construct of the **rhizome**, an idea taken up at the beginning of *A Thousand Plateaus*. For Deleuze and Guattari, the rhizome is an oppositional alternative to what they call "arborescent" or "arboreal" ways of thinking, acting, and being, which have defined Western epistemologies at least since the Enlightenment and probably much earlier. As the name suggests, arborescent forms and structures may be imagined metaphorically as trees—linear, hierarchical, sedentary, striated, vertical, stiff, and with deep and permanent roots. They are structures with branches that continue to subdivide into smaller and lesser structures. In their various social and cultural instantiations, arborescent models of thinking, acting, and being amount to restrictive economies of dominance and oppression.

Deleuze and Guattari were clear that they opposed the arborescent model because of its inherent totalizing logic: "We're tired of trees. We should stop believing in trees, roots, and radicles. They've made us suffer too much. All of arborescent culture is founded on them, from biology to linguistics" (1987, p. 15). In the place of the tree, they offer the rhizome as an alternative theoretical model. In contrast to arborescent forms of thinking, acting, and being, rhizomatic forms are nonlinear, anarchic, and nomadic. The "rhizome is an acentered, nonhierarchical, nonsignifying system without a General and without an organizing memory or central automaton, defined solely by the circulation of states" (1987, p. 21). Rhizomes are networks. Rhizomes cut across borders. Rhizomes build links between preexisting gaps and between nodes that are separated by categories and orders of segmented thinking, acting, and being.

According to Deleuze and Guattari (1987), rhizomes develop and function according to six fundamental principles. The first two principles are *connection* and *heterogeneity*. "[A]ny point of a rhizome can be connected to anything other, and must be. This is very different from the tree or the root, which plots a point, fixes an order" (p. 7). Rhizomes are thus ever-growing horizontal networks of connections among heterogeneous nodes of discursive and material force. (Hall [1986] defines articulation as a non-necessary relation.)

The third principle of the rhizome is *multiplicity*. A rhizomatic system is comprised of a multiplicity of lines and connections. "There are no points or positions in a rhizome, such as those found in a structure, tree, or root. There are only lines" (Deleuze and Guattari, 1987, p. 8), and these lines are organized as ephemeral horizontal relations that are always proliferating. Multiplicity celebrates plurality and proliferative modes of thinking, acting, and being rather that unitary, binary, and totalizing modes. Rhizomatics "extirpate roots and foundations, to thwart unities and break dichotomies, and to spread out roots and branches, thereby pluralizing and disseminating, producing differences and multiplicities, making new connections. Rhizomatics affirms the principles excluded from classical Western thought and reinterprets reality as dynamic, heterogeneous, and non-dichotomous" (Best and Kellner, 1991, p. 99).

The fourth principle of the rhizome is the principle of *asignifying rupture*. This principle states: "A rhizome may be broken, shattered at a given spot, but it will start up again on one of its old lines, or on new lines" (Deleuze and Guattari, 1987, p. 9). Movements and flows are always rerouted around disruptions in a rhizomatic formation. Additionally, severed sections regenerate themselves and continue to grow, forming new lines, flows, and pathways.

The fifth and sixth principles of rhizomatics are *cartography* and *decalcomania*, which ensure that "a rhizome is not amenable to any structural or generative model. It is a stranger to any idea of genetic axis or deep structure" (1987, p. 12). Because Deleuze and Guattari viewed genetic axes and deep structures as reproductive rather than productive, they distinguished these from rhizomes by appealing to the metaphors of maps and tracings, and especially the differences between them. A tracing (or decalcomania) is a copy and operates according to "genetic" principles, evolving and reproducing from earlier forms. It is a reproduction of the world based on an a priori deep structure and a faith in the discovery and representation of that structure. A tracing is arborescent: "All tree logic is a logic of tracing and reproduction" (1987, p. 12). The tracing replicates existing striated structures. Deleuze and Guattari used Freudian psychoanalysis as an example of a historically powerful regime of truth within which tracings are always at work. No matter what an analysand utters, it is read against Oedipus, the phallus, lack, desire for the mother, rage against the father, and so on.

In contrast to tracings, maps (cartography) are open systems— contingent, unpredictable, and productive. Deleuze and Guattari invoked the sense of original cartographic work here and insisted that we think of maps as producing effective spatial articulations rather than simply (re)presenting space. From this perspective, a map produces an organization of reality rather than reproducing some prior representation of reality. Like the rhizome itself, the map is contingent and tentative. "The map is open and connectable in all of its dimensions; it is detachable, reversible, susceptible to constant modification. It can be torn, reversed, adapted, to any kind of mounting, reworked by an individual, group, or social formation" (1987, p. 12). The map is oriented to experimentation and adoption. Maps have multiple entryways. Unlike tracings, maps are based on rhizomatic or essentially unpredictable articulations of material reality. In drawing maps, the theorist (like an original cartographer) works at the surface, creating possible realities by producing new articulations of disparate phenomena and connecting the exteriority of objects to whatever forces or directions seem potentially related to them.

Although Deleuze and Guattari saw rhizomatics as necessary to any radical political work, they rejected utopianism and insisted, following Antonio GRAMSCI, that rhizomatic formations are always constructed in the struggle between stabilizing and destabilizing forces. To further explain the nature and functions of rhizomatic formations, Deleuze and Guattari suggested using the linear algebraic metaphors of lines or vectors to think about rhizomes. They posited two basic kinds of lines or vectors: lines of articulation (or consistency) and lines of flight, both of which project their effects across the rhizomatic field. Lines of articulation connect and unify different practices and effects. They establish hierarchies. They define center–periphery relations. They create rules of organization. They encourage stasis. In contrast, lines of flight disarticulate non-necessary relations between and among practices and effects. They open up contexts to their outsides and the possibilities that dwell there. They disassemble unity and coherence. They decenter centers and disrupt hierarchies.

Finally, every line or vector (of either kind) has its own quality, quantity, and directionality. Thus the effects of any line or vector will vary as a function of these characteristics, as well as of the particular densities built up at the intersection of various lines or vectors. From this perspective, rhizomes—as fields or contexts—are produced in the constant struggle between lines of articulation and lines of flight. The coherence and organization of a rhizome are effects or lines of articulation, and the instability and dissolution of a rhizome are effects of lines of flight. Lines of articulation make received models of reality eminently visible. Lines of flight expose these models as historically produced and power-laden (rather than natural and power-neutral). Lines of flight also open up new possibilities for seeing, living, and organizing political resistance. Effects are lines or vectors of force. Reality itself is constituted as configurations of these two kinds of lines or vectors. So, deploying or taking up lines of articulation or lines of flight has serious consequences for the production of reality. Taking up lines of articulation ("good student" or "heterosexual parent") helps to keep stable the current organization of a territorialized space and its relations to other territorialized spaces. Taking up lines of flight ("resistant but creative student" or "gay parent") helps open up new configurations of space (that is, reality) so that new possibilities for thinking, acting, and being may be opened up.

The goal of rhizomatics, then, is not the obliteration of existing strata (or organized, territorialized space) but the discovery of the available lines of flight within that space. Since the strata are inevitable and unavoidable, Deleuze and Guattari (1987) recommended "diving into the strata," becoming intensely familiar with them, and thus discovering the available lines of flight within them. Following this advice, working within the strata at the level of the lines of flight that continuously **deterritorialize** the strata, can, in some cases, lead to the complete abolition of the strata. At the very least, it can transform the strata into something new with new potentialities. Their project thus involves a radical opening up (more than an obliteration) of closed and repressive structures.

Deleuze and Guattari insisted that we not trace assumed reality, the taken-for-granted. Instead, we should map the real—not intentionally and structurally, but strategically and politically. Doing rhizomatics involves reconfiguring an understanding of reality according to strategic political interests. These reconfigurations, if not predictable, are readily understandable *ex post facto*.

Rhizomatics thus constitutes a critique of totalizing logics, of systems that attempt to explain all things within one interpretive framework or hierarchical master code. To this critical end, they mounted a blistering critique of the Freudian and Marxist master narratives that ultimately limit the complexity of reality with their transcendent interpretations of human subjectivity and history. They opposed to these dominant, transcendent modes of interpretation an immanent mode of interpretation that acknowledges and prizes complexities.

Deleuze and Guattari (1987) argued that "packs" (or **"pack multi-plicities"**) are particularly powerful deterritorializing/reterritorializing machines. The construct of the pack holds considerable promise for producing new and effective conceptions of collective affiliation/ action and political motivation. In this regard, Canetti (cited in Deleuze and Guattari, 1987, p. 33) distinguished between two kinds of multiplicities: mass multiplicities and pack multiplicities. Even though this is an analytic distinction, even though most multiplicities are probably mass–pack hybrids, and even though mass and pack multiplicities require each other for their existence, comparing Canetti's descriptions of these two kinds of formations is instructive here. Mass multiplicities (for example, government agencies, labor unions, professional organizations) are arborescent formations. They are composed of relatively large numbers of members. There is both divisibility and equality among the members. Mass multiplicities are focused around the concentration of form. The aggregate as a whole acts as a unit. There is a one-way hierarchy. Mass multiplicities are predisposed to territorialize, and they work to establish recognizable signs of power and stability.

In contrast, pack multiplicities are rhizomatic formations. They are small or have restricted numbers. They are not centralized but dispersed. They have no fixed territory and are motivated by an impetus to deterritorialize. Pack multiplicities experience qualitative metamorphoses in formation over time and space. They are thus neither totalizing nor finalizable. There are inequalities of membership in pack multiplicities, but these inequalities are impossible to hierarchize because they are often temporary and they shift continuously. Individual and collective action are blurred in the pack. Each member "takes care of himself at the same time as participating in the band" (1987, p. 33). Packs exhibit "a Brownian [random or apparently random] variability in directions" (p. 33) because they are constituted largely by articulated lines of flight or deterritorializations. Unlike mass multiplicities, pack multiplicities matter more in terms of their political motivations and effectivity than in terms of their forms of affiliation.

With pack multiplicities, there is no stable coherent whole to speak of, only assemblages of multiplicity. There is no politics of sublimation in the pack, no notion of transcendent similarity, only a constant becoming of multiply driven ethical and pragmatic singularities.

Although packs are not top-down structures or organized systems, they have specific sets of tactics. They are dynamic and complex webs of localized mobilizations. There are few, if any, hierarchical chains of command. No network has a single, specific leader, though at any given time someone may assume a leadership role. "In the changing constellation of the pack, in its dances and expeditions, he will again and again find himself at its edge; at the edge and then back in the center. He may be in the center, and then, immediately afterwards, at the edge again" (Canetti, cited in Deleuze and Guattari, 1987, p. 33). Pack leadership, then, is a continuous mobilization of positions. This mobility through constant repositioning in space means that each pack member is always both responsible for "guarding" a sector and also dependent on the whole pack for its survival.

A key question relevant to understanding and explaining mass multiplicities is what brings the mass together. This question is usually answered by some appeal to biological or social essentialism (for example, the identity politics of the civil rights movement or streams of second-wave feminism). Secondary questions thus include the following: Where is the center? Who is the leader? What does the multiplicity represent or stand for? What are its politics? What are its strategies? These questions, however, are all but irrelevant when one considers the forms and functions of pack multiplicities. Moreover, answering these questions for themselves would probably lead to co-optation and a weakening (or negation) of the pack's counter-hegemonic potential. Instead, the key questions to ask about pack multiplicities include the following: How do packs develop and flourish? How are packs and pack members mobilized? What do they deterritorialize and reterritorialize? What forces do they exert in the world, and what real effects does their work accomplish? How do new members learn about and join the pack?

Schizoanalysis is Deleuze and Guattari's name for doing anti-theory and anti-method, for resisting totalizing logics. The "schizo" does not care how others have organized the world. The schizo is immune to extant systems of meaning and structure. The schizo creates his or her own meanings and structures *ad infinitum*. The schizo is thus anti-theoretical and untheorizable.

Rather than defining schizoanalysis per se, Deleuze and Guattari used it as a tool. In the first volume of *Capitalism and Schizophrenia*, *Anti-Oedipus*, they took up the political nature of desire. Deleuze and Guattari's criticism of psychoanalysis is made under the banner of schizoanalysis, a rhizomatic alternative to the arborescent thinking of psychoanalysis. In their schizoanalytic critique of Freud, they refuted Freud's negative notion of desire as lack, which is explained through the Oedipus Complex. For Freud, the Oedipus Complex transcends time and place and is a natural human disposition that is inescapable. For Deleuze and Guattari, this perspective is repressive because it subjects everyone to the same transcendent structure (mother–father–child). Rather than viewing the unconscious as characterized by desire and its lack, Deleuze and Guattari saw the unconscious as productive of desire and hence in need of repressive control by the capitalist state. During psychoanalysis, the immanent interpretation of individuals is recast into the transcendent interpretation of Freudian desire, the family triangle. The individual is thereby subjected to the repression and restraint of the psychoanalytic interpretative framework, and the patient is subjected to the interpretation of the powerful and authoritative analyst. Libidinal impulses are instead to be understood as desire-producing and therefore potentially disruptive to the capitalist state, which wants to control desire by casting it in negative terms. Similarly, culture, language, and other symbolic systems are repressive because they subject people to their rules and codes. Deleuze and Guattari contrasted the symbolic with the imaginary. They referred to schizophrenia as enacting imaginative modes of thinking. The Oedipal is symbolic; the presymbolic is pre-Oedipal and therefore prior to the hierarchy and repression of families (an idea also pursued by Lacan).

Psychoanalysis is an arborescent system. Schizoanalysis is a critique of psychoanalysis, especially its conceptions of unconscious desire and the Oedipus Complex. In traditional psychoanalysis, negative Oedipal desire precedes any particular patient's narrative. That is, the interpretation of the reported narrative is known in advance by the analyst. The outcome of analysis is likewise predetermined and thus overdetermining. The only thing the analyst will find is Oedipal conflict. Desire is directed toward Oedipal prohibitions through this transcendent interpretation and as a means of internalized control: "The law tells us: You will not marry your mother and you will not kill your father. And we docile subjects say to ourselves: so that's what I wanted!" (Deleuze and Guattari, 1983, p. 114).

Deleuze and Guattari conceived of human beings (or human potential) with the term **"desiring-machines"** because desire stems from a moment prior to structure and representation. Bodies are desiring-machines in which such things as ideas, feelings, and desires flow in and out. Desire is like a machine. Both are productive. An engine produces torque, which produces speed and movement. A desiring-machine produces libidinal energy. The idea of machine subverts traditional views of subjectivity. Subjectivity is now an effect of production. A desiring-machine is connected to a **body without organs** (often abbreviated BwO). Deleuze and Guattari borrowed this term from the avant-garde playwright Antonin Artaud, who they claimed made himself a body without organs when he committed suicide. In *Anti-Oedipus*, the body without organs is posited to be a nonproductive entity that interrupts energy flows, arrests desire, and promotes stasis. In *A Thousand Plateaus*, though, the body without organs is recast as a productive force, a desiring-machine. By alluding to Artaud's suicide in describing the body without organs, Deleuze and Guattari were claiming that the person is not to be found inside the body, composed of autonomous, self-sustaining, and organized internal forms. Instead, the person/body is interconnected, exterior, open, multiple, fragmented, provisional, and interpenetrated by other entities. In their words:

> There is no such thing as either man or nature now, only a process that produces the one within the other and couples the machines together. Producing-machines, desiring-machines everywhere, schizophrenic machines, all of species life: the self and the non-self, outside and inside, no longer have any meaning whatsoever. (Deleuze and Guattari, 1977, p. 2)

Additionally, Deleuze and Guattari seem to use the term figuratively not so much to oppose organs as to oppose organization and the organism, much as they used the rhizome to combat arborescent thought. It is a body of affective energies, not an organization of parts:

> A body without organs is not an empty body stripped of organs, but a body upon that which serves as organs ... is distributed according to crowd phenomena ... in the form of molecular multiplicities.... Thus the body without organs is opposed less to organs as such than to the organization of the organs insofar as it composes an organism. (Deleuze and Guattari, 1987, p. 30)

The body without organs is also unlimited human potential on the move, perpetual creation: "It is not at all a notion of a concept, but an experimental practice, a set of practices. You never reach the Body without Organs, you can't reach it, you are forever attaining it, it is a limit" (1987, pp. 149–150). It is a space of deterritorialization, a space where desire is liberated from the constraints of all overdetermined and overdetermining system: psychoanalysis, Marxism, capitalism, and so on. This contrasts with the territorialization and reterritorialization dynamic—the attempts to totalize, to structure hierarchically, to contain, through institutions such as religion, family, and school. To (re)territorialize is to try to recontain and to replace boundaries around desire, to repress it. Deterritorialized space is fragmented, multiple, uncontained. It is space where boundaries are fluid, selves transform, desire flows in multiple directions. Deterritorialized space is space where everything flows and everything is made up of flows. What allows us to distinguish these flows from each other is a threshold or a plane that separates one from another. Every flow is made by cutting off or restricting another flow. But flows do not want to be cut off or restricted. The desire that drives a flow to flow unconstrained is the body without organs. It is real because the desire is real. In fact, the body without organs might just as well be called desire. But it is abstract desire, because it always gets limited by other flows of desire. Flows are never totally free, but always interrupted. Without the interruption and the desire, the flow and its break, there would be no world at all. Freedom, then, is paradoxical with respect to the body without organs. On the one hand, freedom is the freedom to flow without constraint, the freedom of autonomy. On the other hand, freedom is death. How else might a limited freedom be conceived?

The very complex spatial theories of Deleuze and Guattari have been appropriated and deployed in mostly sporadic, selective, and often tentative ways within education. Most of the attention to their trenchant social theories has been a matter simply of trying to figure out what they mean. There seem to be several key reasons for this. Although some of their work is relatively accessible, much of it is extraordinarily difficult to decipher because it is so dense and abstract. Additionally, because educational researchers have been so selective in taking up the ideas of Deleuze and Guattari, a more comprehensive understanding of the powerful ways in which this theoretical framework might be deployed for educational research and practice has been obstructed to a large extent. Unprincipled selectivity has also led to distortion of the few constructs that have been used (especially the rhizome). These tendencies are unfortunate. However, the same kinds of problems affected the application of Foucault's theories to educational issues for many years, but more recent Foucauldian work has been considerably better. It is to be hoped that the same pattern will obtain with respect to the ongoing uptake of Deleuze and Guattari's work. Indeed, more numerous, more principled, and more interesting uses of their theories could galvanize a rather patchy and dull history of theoretically informed empirical research in the field. It would also be good to see Deleuze and Guattari's work mobilized to reimagine how we "do" learning, teaching, and assessment, and to deterritorialize/reterritorialize the institutional space called school.

Further Reading

By Deleuze and Guattari

1983. G. Deleuze. *Nietzsche and Philosophy*, translated by H. Tomlinson. New York: Columbia University Press.

1988. G. Deleuze. *Foucault*, translated by S. Hand. Minneapolis: University of Minnesota Press.

1988. G. Deleuze. *Spinoza, Practical Philosophy*. San Francisco: City Lights.

1983. G. Deleuze and F. Guattari. **Anti-Oedipus: Capitalism and Schizophrenia*, translated by R. Hurley, M. Seem, and H. R. Lane. Minneapolis: University of Minnesota Press.

1986. G. Deleuze and F. Guattari. *Nomadology: The War Machine*. Paris: Semiotexte.

1987. G. Deleuze and F. Guattari. **A Thousand Plateaus: Capitalism and Schizophrenia*, translated by B. Massumi. Minneapolis: University of Minnesota Press.

1996. G. Deleuze and F. Guattari. *What Is Philosophy?*, translated by H. Tomlinson and G. Burchell III. New York: Columbia University Press.

1996. F. Guattari. "The Postmodern Impasse." In G. Genosko, ed., *The Guattari Reader*. Oxford: Blackwell.

About Deleuze and Guattari

Best, S., and D. Kellner. *Postmodern Theory: Critical Interrogations*. New York: Guilford, 1991.

Bogue, R. *Deleuze and Guattari*. London: Routledge, 1989.

Buchanan, I., and C. Colebrook, eds. *Deleuze and Feminist Theory*. Edinburgh: Edinburgh University Press, 2000.

Kaufman, E., and K. J. Heller, eds. *Deleuze and Guattari: New Mappings in Politics, Philosophy, and Culture*. Minneapolis: University of Minnesota Press, 1998.

*Massumi, B. *User's Guide to Capitalism and Schizophrenia: Deviations from Deleuze and Guattari*. Cambridge, MA: MIT Press, 1992.

Olkowski, D. *Gilles Deleuze and the Ruin of Representation*. Berkeley: University of California Press, 1999.

Rajchman, J. *The Deleuze Connections*. Cambridge, MA: MIT Press, 2000.

*Stivale, C. *The Two-fold Thought of Deleuze and Guattari: Intersections and Animations*. New York: Guilford, 1998.

Relevance for Education

Alvermann, D. "Researching Libraries, Literacies, and Lives: A Rhizoanalysis." In E. St. Pierre and W. Pillow, eds., *Working the Ruins: Feminist Poststructural Methods in Education*. New York: Routledge, 2000.

Clarke, J., R. Harrison, F. Reeve, and R. Edwards. "Assembling Spaces: The Question of 'Place' in Further Education." *Discourse* 23 (2002): 285–297.

Edwards, R., and J. Clarke. "Flexible Learning, Spatiality, and Identity." *Studies in Continuing Education* 24 (2002): 153–165.

Kamberelis, G. "The Rhizome and the Pack: Liminal Literacy Formations with Political Teeth." In K. Leander and M. Sheehy, eds., *Spatializing Literacy Research and Practice*. New York: Peter Lang, 2004.

Morgan, W. "Electronic Tools for Dismantling the Master's House: Poststructural Feminist Research and Hypertext Poetics." In E. St. Pierre and W. Pillow, eds., *Working the Ruins*. New York: Routledge, 2000.

St. Pierre, E. "Nomadic Inquiry in the Smooth Space of the Field: A Preface." *International Journal of Qualitative Studies in Education* 10 (1997): 365–383.

St. Pierre, E. "Poststructural Feminism in Education: An Overview." *International Journal of Qualitative Studies in Education* 13 (2000): 477–515.

Other Readings

Hall, S. "On Postmodernism and Articulation: An Interview." *Journal of Communication Inquiry* 10 (1986): 56–59.

Miller, T. *The Well-tempered Self: Citizenship, Culture, and the Postmodern Subject.* Baltimore: Johns Hopkins University Press, 1998.

JACQUES DERRIDA

Key Concepts

- dynamism of language
- *sous rature* (under erasure)
- deconstruction
- alterity
- logocentrism
- grammatology
- interiority and exteriority
- arche-writing
- undecidability
- *différance*
- *tout autre* (wholly other)

Jacques Derrida (1930–2004) was born into a middle-class Jewish family in the Algerian suburb of El-Biar. At ten years old, when World War II came to Algeria, he and the other Jews were expelled from the public school system and then later (with the arrival of the Allied forces) enrolled in a Jewish school. Derrida was twice refused a position in the prestigious École Normale Supérieure, where Jean-Paul Sartre, Simone de Beauvoir and most other French intellectuals and academics of the time began their careers, but he was eventually accepted to the institution and moved to France at age nineteen.

Derrida's initial work in philosophy was largely phenomenological, and his early training as a philosopher was done largely through the lens of Edmund Husserl. Other important inspirations of his early thought included Friedrich Nietzsche, Martin Heidegger, Ferdinand de SAUSSURE, Emmanuel Levinas, and Sigmund FREUD. Derrida acknowledged his indebtedness to all of these thinkers in the development of his approach to texts, which has come to be known as "deconstruction."

Derrida taught at the École Normale Supérieure and the École des Hautes Études in Paris, and he also held teaching posts at several American universities, including Johns Hopkins, New York University, and the University of California, Irvine. Throughout his career he demonstrated a strong commitment to public education, especially through his work with the Research Group on the Teaching of Philosophy, which advocates making philosophy a fundamental discipline in secondary school curricula. It would be impossible to summarize Derrida's work briefly, even if we were to limit ourselves to his most influential contributions to philosophy, religion, linguistics, literary theory, and cultural studies. Yet there is a certain orientation that is consistent throughout his many texts. We might describe it as a kind of close reading that raises questions about what is implicit in the accumulated reserve of intellectual history. Through relentlessly vigilant attention to the texts and discourses in which the fundamentals of Western thought are articulated, he worked to reveal the uncertainties, instabilities, and impasses implicit in those intellectual traditions, moving readers to the edges of knowing, where what once seemed certain begins to feel fragile, tentative, and precarious. This was not, as his critics allege, out of nihilistic contempt for all things Western or a fascination with groundless intellectual free play. Instead, it was an effort to destabilize assumptions enough to open up spaces for continued reflection and the possibility of innovation and creative thinking. He treated the Western intellectual tradition as a living discourse and worked to keep its intellectual disciplines and educational institutions from ossifying.

Throughout his career, Derrida was criticized for writing texts that are too difficult for many readers to understand. He defended his writing against these criticisms by pointing out that it is so difficult because it is fundamentally concerned with questioning precisely those things readers think they understand, and by arguing that new ways of thinking demand new ways of speaking and writing: "No one gets angry with a mathematician or with a doctor he doesn't understand at all, or with someone who speaks a foreign language, but when somebody touches your own language ..." (David, 1985, p. 107).

Derrida's theories on the nature and functions of language, characterized under the heading of the **dynamism of language**, were developed in large measure as a critique of structuralist theories of language, especially that of Ferdinand de Saussure. According to

Saussure, the sign is made up of the connection between a signifier and a signified, and there is a one-to-one correspondence between these two basic components. For Derrida, such a correspondence is analytic but not real. In the actual development and use of language, the sign is always a structure constituted by difference. Half of the sign is always "there" and half of it is always "not there." Because signifiers and signifieds are always coming apart and coming together in new ways, Saussure's idealist, structuralist theory of language cannot be wholly right.

Derrida's concept of *sous rature* (usually translated as "**under erasure**") is instructive here. *Rature* (or erasure) is the act of writing a word and then crossing it out (for example, ~~language existence truth~~). Based on earlier work by one of his mentors, Heidegger, Derrida developed this concept to indicate both the necessity and importance of the word and the necessity and importance of its erasure. Any word is both necessary (and thus its inscription is preserved) and inadequate (and thus its inscription is crossed out) for conveying the meaning it means to convey, for capturing the complexity, richness, and multiplicity of its referent. In other words, all signifiers are polysemic and always transcend their signifieds. In defining a word, for example, we use other words that lead to other words that lead to other words indefinitely, in a process of unlimited semiosis. Signifiers keep referring to new signifieds, and vice versa. We never end up at one stable relation between a single signifier and a single signified. Meaning is always elusive, always deferred, always multiple, always somewhat paradoxical.

Another reason why Derrida posited language as dynamic rather than stable is that meaning is never immediate or "present" (see the discussion of logocentrism below). Signs always refer to concepts (or things) that are absent. That is the basic definition of a sign: something that refers to something else. So meanings are, in a sense, absent (or something else), too. Meaning continually moves (changes) as signs refer to other signs that refer to other signs in an endless chain of deferral. Because no word/sign can ever function to connect once and for all any particular referent (concept or thing) with any particular meaning, all words/signs must be considered *sous rature*, as always already inhabited by the traces of other words/signs and as moving toward yet others. Additionally, meaning is never identical with itself. At another time or in another context, a meaning becomes a different meaning because of new interactions between relevant signifieds and signifiers.

Another reason for the dynamism of language is that language use is a temporal activity. When we listen to others speak or read what others have written, the meanings of these utterances unfold over time; we do not always comprehend these meanings until the utterances are over, and even then, the meanings can change as we continue to think about them in and through language (that is, other signifiers). Again, all words/signs always contain traces of other words/signs in an indefinite backward arc of connections, and all words/signs index future words/signs in an indefinite forward arc of connections. Together, these forward and backward arcs constitute an inexhaustible complexity, an infinite semantic potential.

Derrida first used the term "**deconstruction**" in *Of Grammatology* (published in French in 1967) while trying to translate Heidegger's term *Destruktion*; French *destruction* translates to both "annihilation, demolition" and "destructuration." At the time, the word *deconstruction* was used very little in French; its primary sense was mechanical, referring to the process of disassembly in order to understand parts in relation to the whole. For Derrida, deconstruction is conceived not as a negative operation aimed only at tearing down, but rather as a kind of close analysis that seeks "to understand how an 'ensemble' was constituted and to reconstruct it to this end" (Wood and Bernasconi, 1985, p. 4). It is in the process of reading closely, with an eye for how an idea is constructed, that one also comes to see the points of potential rupture, the cracks and other points of instability within the structure. It is in the process of close reading that one sees deconstruction happening.

Deconstruction contends that in any text, there are inevitably points of equivocation and **undecidability** that betray any stable meaning that an author might seek to impose upon his or her text. The process of writing always reveals that which has been suppressed, covers over that which has been disclosed, and more generally breaches the very oppositions that are thought to sustain it. This is why Derrida's philosophy is so textually based, and it is also why his key terms are always changing, because depending on who or what he is seeking to deconstruct, that point of equivocation will always be located in a different place. This also ensures that any attempt to describe what deconstruction is must proceed cautiously. Nothing would be more antithetical to deconstruction's stated intent than to define it once and for all. There is a paradox involved in trying to restrict deconstruction to one particular and overarching meaning or purpose when it is predicated on the desire to expose that which is wholly other (*tout autre*, discussed below) and to open us up to alternative possibilities. Although we will doubtless violate its fullness and dynamism as we try to write about it, deconstruction is never the closing down of one meaning or purpose to set up another in its place. Rather, it is the persistent opening up of meanings and purposes to their own **alterity**, that which is other and toward which they are changing.

Derrida introduced the construct of **logocentrism** in *Of Grammatology* (published in French in 1976), a book on the relations between speech and writing in which he contested the assumption that writing is derivative of speech, and the companion assumption that speech is closer than writing to the truth or *logos* of meaning and representation. He argued that the development of language actually occurs through the interplay of speech and writing, and because of this interplay, neither speech nor writing is more foundational to the development of language. Somewhat paradoxically, he argued further for the primacy of written language because of its unique and powerful semiotic quality of leaving a permanent trace, which defies the constraints of time and space and realizes discourse as material practice.

According to Derrida, logocentrism is the attitude that *logos* (the Greek term for "speech, thought, law, reason") is the foundational principle of language and philosophy. Logocentrism privileges speech over writing. **Grammatology** (a term that Derrida coined to mean the science of writing) was introduced as a way to begin to deconstruct this privileging of speech over writing. Grammatology is a method of destroying/constructing the origins of language in a way that enables writing to be equivalent to speech—logically and historically. Derrida's main target here was Saussure's structuralist linguistics. According to Saussure (and other logocentric theorists), speech is the original signifier of meaning, and the written word is derived from the spoken word. The written word is thus a representation of the spoken word.

Working against this binary in deconstructive fashion, Derrida argued that the play of difference between speech and writing is the play of difference between **interiority and exteriority**. This means that writing is both exterior to and interior to speech, and that speech is both interior to and exterior to writing. This play of difference also means that interiority and exteriority are erased. The outside is, and is not, the inside. Outside and inside become inadequate concepts to describe either speech or writing. As a theory of language development, then, logocentrism is inadequate. Derrida went on to show that, according to logocentrist theory, speech is a kind of presence, because the speaker is simultaneously present for the listener. If this were so, then writing would be a kind of absence because the writer is not simultaneously present for the reader. Writing may be regarded by logocentrist theory as a substitute for the simultaneous presence of writer and reader. If the reader and the writer were simultaneously present, then the writer would communicate with the reader by speaking instead of by writing. Logocentrism thus asserts that writing is a substitute for speech, and that writing is an attempt to restore the presence of speech.

Derrida claimed that logocentrism operates according to a "metaphysics of presence" logic motivated by a desire for a "transcendental signified." A transcendental signified is a signified that transcends all signifiers, a meaning that transcends all meanings. A transcendental signified is also a signified concept or thought that transcends any single signifier but that is implied by all determinations of meaning. Derrida went on to argue that the transcendental signified may be deconstructed by an examination of the assumptions that underlie the metaphysics of presence. If presence, for example, is assumed to be the essence of the signified, then the proximity of a signifier to a signified may imply that the signifier is able to reflect the presence of the signified. Operating with the same assumption, then the remoteness of a signifier from a signified may imply that the signifier is unable, or only barely able to reflect the presence of the signified. This interplay between proximity and remoteness is also an interplay between presence and absence, and between interiority and exteriority.

Derrida used the term "**arche-writing**" to describe a form of language that cannot be conceptualized within the metaphysics of presence. Arche-writing (or writing in general) is an original form of language, distinct from any historical system of writing, including speech. Arche-writing is a form of language that is unhindered by the difference between speech and writing. Arche-writing is also a condition for the play of difference between written and nonwritten forms of language. Derrida contrasted the concept of arche-writing with the vulgar concept of writing. The vulgar concept of writing, which is proposed by the metaphysics of presence, is deconstructed by the concept of arche-writing.

Derrida went even further and criticized structural anthropologists like Claude Lévi-Strauss for not realizing that logocentrism promotes ethnocentrism, especially because of structural anthropology's tendency to compare different cultures according to their writing systems. An unbiased approach to anthropology, he argued, would have to acknowledge the social fact that writing may function as a form of social or cultural domination and oppression, by which those who use writing subjugate those who do not.

Derrida developed two key constructs to demonstrate the internal inconsistencies of logocentrism, especially its rooting in binarisms. The first is undecidability; the second is *différance*. Developing the notion of undecidability was one of Derrida's most important attempts to trouble dualisms, or more accurately, to reveal how they are always already troubled. In his early work, an undecidable phenomenon (for example, ghost, pharmakon, hymen) was defined as something that cannot conform to either polarity of a dichotomy (for example, present/absent, cure/poison, and inside/outside). The figure of a ghost, for instance, is neither present nor absent but both present and absent at the same time. In later iterations of deconstruction, undecidability took on additional valences.

The term *différance* figures most prominently in *Dissemination*, where Derrida used the term to describe the origin of presence and absence. It is the basis on which Derrida explained his entire theory of meaning production. At the same time, the construct contributes to the explanation of that theory. *Différance* is indefinable and cannot be explained by the metaphysics of presence. In French, the verb *différer* means both "to defer" and "to differ." Thus, in relation to any signifier, *différance* may refer not only to the semantic state or quality of being deferred (in the sense of postponed or deflected toward other words and other meanings), but also to the semantic state or quality of being different from (or not quite the same as). *Différance* may be the condition for that which is deferred, and may be the condition for that which is different. *Différance* is the word that Derrida coined to describe and perform the way in which any single meaning of a concept or text arises only by the effacement of other possible meanings, which are themselves only deferred and may be activated at another time or in other contexts. *Différance* thus both describes and performs the conditions under which all identities and meanings can occur. Any text can be repeated in an infinite number of possible contexts with an infinite number of meanings for an infinite number of potential but undetermined audiences. It is a powerful modification of the ordinary notions of identity and difference.

Probably the most remarkable aspect of Derrida's later philosophy is his attention to *le **tout autre***, the "wholly other." This aspect of his work flowed from his later thinking about undecidability as "possible-impossible" aporias (logical contradictions) and figures, most prominently in *The Gift of Death* (1995). Our explanation of the wholly other derives primarily from this book, which is extremely difficult because of the ways it demands recognizing a certain incommensurability between the particular and the universal, as well as the dual demands placed upon anybody who wants to act responsibly. Responsible action always involves both being responsible to/before a singular other (for example, a friend, a child, God) and also being responsible toward others generally and to what we share with them. Derrida insisted that this type of aporia is too often ignored by the "knights of responsibility" who presume that accountability and responsibility in all aspects of life is readily established (1995, p. 85). These are the same people who insist that concrete ethical guidelines should be provided by any philosopher worthy of that title (p. 67). To their fault, these people ignore the difficulties involved in a notion like responsibility, which demands something importantly different from merely behaving dutifully (p. 63). Clearly, Derrida's targets here are reactionary philosophical and religious movements afoot at the time.

In *The Gift of Death*, Derrida seems to had wanted to free us from the common-sense assumption that ethical responsibility is action that flows seamlessly from general principles and is capable of justification in the public realm through reason (as assumed in, e.g., humanism and liberalism). In place of such an assumption, he insisted that the demands placed on Abraham by God, as well as those that might be placed on us by our own loved ones, constitute a "radical singularity." Ethics, with its dependence on generality, must be continually sacrificed as an inevitable aspect of the human condition and its aporetic demand to decide (p. 70). Choice and singularity take a front seat in this perspective. When we work for one particular cause instead of another, when we pursue one passion over another, when we choose to spend time with our spouse or children, we inevitably ignore "generalized others" (p. 69). This is a fundamental condition of existence: "I cannot respond to the call, the request, the obligation, or even the love of another, without sacrificing the other other, the other others" (p. 68). A universal community that excludes no one is a contradiction in terms because

> I am responsible to anyone (that is to say, to any other) only by failing in my responsibility to all the others, to the ethical or political general-ity. And I can never justify this sacrifice; I must always hold my peace about it ... What binds me to this one or that one, remains finally unjustifiable. (p. 70)

Derrida thus implied that responsibility to any particular individual is possible only if one is irresponsible to the "other others," that is, to the other people and possibilities toward others that haunt any and every existence.

Derrida's influence on education seems much like Gertrude Stein's description of Oakland, California: "there is no there there." Or perhaps more aptly, his influence is everywhere and nowhere. The name "Derrida" and the term "deconstruction" pervade educational discourse, whether in universities or public schools and whether in relation to theoretical or practical matters, but direct applications of Derrida's work (except in literary studies) are few and far between. Nevertheless, the man and his work have been taken up in significant enough ways in several specific domains: English education, writing and writing pedagogy, multicultural education, critical pedagogy, and the nature and functions of educational inquiry.

Derrida's work has indeed found its way into the field of education. Deconstruction, in particular, has helped education scholars investigate social-cultural-historical-political forces behind educational theories, practices, and policies, especially the extent to which these forces have privileged certain theories, practices, and policies while marginalizing others. Deconstruction has also been taken up to create new pedagogical theories and practices. Yet educators and education scholars have failed adequately to tap the scope and richness of Derrida's work for reimagining educational possibilities and making these possibilities realities. This is particularly true with respect to Derrida's later work on the wholly other, which cries out to be used to explore educational issues as diverse as the writing process, dialogic pedagogy, historical understanding, moral development, and character education.

Further Reading

By Derrida

1973. *Speech and Phenomena, and Other Essays on Husserl's Theory of Signs*, translated by D. B. Allison. Evanston, IL: Northwestern University Press.

1978. *Writing and Difference*, translated by A. Bass. Chicago: University of Chicago Press.

1981. *Positions*, translated by A. Bass. Chicago: University of Chicago Press.

1981. *Dissemination*, translated by B. Johnson. Chicago: University of Chicago Press.

1982. *Margins of Philosophy*, translated by A. Bass. Chicago: University of Chicago Press.

1985. "Letter to a Japanese Friend." In *Derrida and Différance*, edited by D. Wood and R. Bernasconi. Warwick: Parousia.

1986. *Glas*, translated by J. P Leavy, Jr., and R. Rand. Lincoln: University of Nebraska Press.

1994. *Specters of Marx: The State of the Debt, Work of Mourning, and New International*, translated by P. Kamuf. New York: Routledge.

1995. *The Gift of Death*, translated by D. Willis. Chicago: University of Chicago Press.

1997. *Deconstruction in a Nutshell: A Conversation with Jacques Derrida*. New York: Fordham University Press.

1998 [1976]. *Of Grammatology*, translated by G. C. Spivak. Baltimore: Johns Hopkins University Press.

About Derrida

*David, C. "An Interview with Derrida." In D. Wood and R. Bernasconi, eds., *Derrida and Difference*. Warwick: Parousia, 1985.

Eagleton, T. *Literary Theory: An Introduction*. Oxford: Basil Blackwell, 1983.

*Nial, L. *A Derrida Dictionary*. Oxford: Blackwell, 2004.

*Norris, C. *Derrida*. London: Fontana, 1987.

Reynolds, J., and F. J. Roffe, eds. *Understanding Derrida*. New York: Continuum, 2004.

Royale, N. *Jacques Derrida*. London: Routledge, 2003.

Wood, D. *Derrida: A Critical Reader*. Oxford: Blackwell, 1992.

Wood, D., and R. Bernasconi, eds. *Derrida and Difference*, translated by D. Allison. Warwick: Parousia, 1985.

Relevance for Education

Biesta, G. J. J., and M. Stams. "Critical Thinking and the Question of Critique: Some Lessons from Deconstruction." *Studies in the Philosophy of Education* 20 (2001): 57–74.

Brooke, R. "Control in Writing: Flower, Derrida, and the Images of the Writer." *College English* 51 (1989): 405–417.

Crowley, S. *A Teacher's Introduction to Deconstruction*. Urbana, IL: National Council of Teachers of English, 1989.

Daesenbrock, R. W. "Taking It Personally: Reading Derrida's Responses." *College English* 56 (1994): 261–279.

Dumont, C. W. "Towards a Multicultural Society: Bringing Postmodernism into the Classroom." *Teaching Sociology* 23 (1995): 307–320.

Lather, P. "Critical Pedagogy and Its Complicities: A Praxis of Stuck Places." *Educational Theory* 48 (1998): 487–497.

Palermo, J. *Poststructuralist Readings of the Pedagogical Encounter*. New York: Peter Lang, 2002.

Peim, N. "The History of the Present: Towards a Contemporary Phenomenology of the School." *History of Education* 30 (2001): 177–190.

Rice, W. H. "Derrida Meets IBM: Using Deconstruction To Teach Business Communication Students." Paper presented at the Annual AGLS Conference, Daytona Beach, FL, 1996.

Stockton, S. " 'Blacks' vs. 'Browns': Questioning the White Ground." *College English* 57 (1995): 166–181.

Thaden, B. Z. "Derrida in the Composition Class: Deconstructing Arguments." *Writing Instructor* 7 (1988): 131–137.

MICHEL FOUCAULT

Key Concepts

- archaeology of knowledge
- discourse
- genealogy
- power
- ethics of self
- governmentality

Michel Foucault (1926–1984) was a French philosopher, social and intellectual historian, and cultural critic. He was born in Poitiers, the son of upper-middle-class parents. He went to Paris after World War II and was admitted to the esteemed École Normale Supérieure in 1946, where he received degrees in philosophy (1948) and psychology (1949), and his *agrégation* in philosophy (1952). Like many other French intellectuals in the 1940s and 1950s, Foucault became a member of the French Communist Party in 1950, but he left it in 1953 in response to his reading Nietzsche.

During the 1950s and early 1960s, Foucault held teaching positions at European universities while conducting research and writing his first widely influential books, including *Madness and Civilization* (published in French in 1961; submitted two years before for his doctorate), the *Birth of the Clinic* (published in French in 1963), and *The Order of Things* (published in French in 1966), which became a best-seller in France and made Foucault a celebrity.

In response to the May 1968 strikes and student demonstrations, the French government opened the University of Paris VIII at Vincennes. Foucault, who had been working in Tunisia in May 1968, was named chairman of its philosophy department. In 1970, he was elected to the Collège de France, the country's most prestigious academic institution. This permanent appointment—as professor of the history of systems of thought—provided Foucault with a position in which he could devote nearly all his time to research and writing. His only teaching-related responsibility was to give an annual sequence of a dozen or so public lectures on his work.

During this same period, Foucault became increasingly involved in social and political activism. His advocacy of prisoners' rights, for example, influenced his history of the prison system, *Discipline and Punish* (published in French in 1975). Around the same time he turned his attention to sexuality, publishing the first of three volumes of the *History of Sexuality* in 1976. He completed the other two volumes shortly before his death from AIDS-related complications in 1984.

Regardless of how one evaluates Foucault's scholarship, there is little doubt that the questions and issues he raised have permanently reshaped the humanities and social sciences. His scholarly output is impressive both for its quantity and for its breadth of interests and ideas. Among the topics he examined are madness, punishment, medicine, and sexuality.

Foucault's work relentlessly challenges what counts as common-sense knowledge about human nature, history, and the world, as well as the social and political implications of such knowledge. Along the way, it questions the assumptions of such modernist masters as Sigmund FREUD and Karl MARX, whose ideas often underpinned intellectual common sense in twentieth-century France. More specifically, Foucault explored the parameters of what he called the "human sciences," that academic field in which humanistic and social science discourses construct knowledge and subjectivity. He often wrote on how various institutions (psychiatric clinics, prisons, schools, and so forth) produce discourses that then constitute what can be known or practiced relative to that body of knowledge. People become disciplined subjects within these different discourses. In the process he showed how knowledge and power are intimately connected. Therefore, terms such as "discourse," "subjectivity," "knowledge," and "power" are key to understanding Foucault's theories. These concepts, in turn, can be positioned within three areas that are central to his cultural analysis: (1) archaeology of knowledge, (2) genealogy of power, and (3) ethics. Underlying all three areas is a concern with the notion of the "subject" and the process of "subjectivization"—that is, the process by which a human subject is constituted (see also Judith BUTLER on the paradox of subjection, which she developed in relation to Foucault).

The **archaeology of knowledge** is the name Foucault gave (in a book by that title first published in French in 1969) to his method of intellectual inquiry. For Foucault, "archaeology" refers to a historical analysis that seeks to uncover **discourses** operating within systems of meaning. His concern is not with uncovering historical "truth," but rather with understanding how discursive formations—for example, medical discourse or discourse on sexuality—come to be seen as natural and self-evident, accurately representing a world of knowledge. Influenced by structuralism, Foucault sought to uncover structures and rules embedded in discourse through which knowledge is constructed and implemented. Discursive knowledge regulates, among other things, what can be said and done, what constitutes right and wrong, and what counts for knowledge in the first place. In short, discourse establishes and controls knowledge. Medical discourse thus establishes medical knowledge and related practices, including the doctor–patient relationship, divisions between physical and mental illness, the value of medical services, status hierarchies within the medical profession, and who can produce medical discourse itself. Significantly, Foucault's archaeological method regards discourses as both fluid and mutable, and systematic and stable. Medical discourse during the Renaissance bears no necessary similarity to present-day medical discourse, yet each has a distinctive historical archive. It is these historical shifts that Foucault aimed to uncover through the archaeology of knowledge. He examined discourses of madness, reason, and mental asylums in *Madness and Civilization* and discourses of medical practices and the medical "gaze" in *The Birth of the Clinic*.

During the 1970s, Foucault devoted his research to what he described as the "genealogy of power"—that is, a history of the meanings and effects of power, and how discourse and "technologies of power" are employed to discipline human behavior. The term **"genealogy"** refers to a mode of historical analysis that Foucault developed in texts such as *Discipline and Punish* (1975) and *The History of Sexuality, Volume 1: An Introduction* (1976). The concept of genealogy, borrowed from Nietzsche, is explained in Foucault's 1971 article "Nietzsche, Genealogy, History."

Foucault's understanding of the nature of history is significant for the way in which it subverts the common-sense teleological view of history as a narrative of the causes and effects that produce human events and are thus traceable, in a linear and logically satisfying fashion, back to origins. Foucault also saw history as narrative, but as a narrative that is fragmented, nonlinear, discontinuous, and without the certitude of cause and effect. Foucault referred to this form of historical analysis as "genealogy" and described it thus: "Genealogy is gray, meticulous and patiently documentary. It operates on a field of tangled and confused parchments, on documents that have been scratched over and recopied many times" ("Nietzsche, Genealogy, History," p. 139). For Foucault, history is textual and conveys a narrative that is ambiguous and conflicting. History bears the marks of repeated emendations—additions, deletions, embellishments, and other textual tinkering that makes it impossible to follow a cause-and-effect lineage back to an origin. Any origin has long become obscured and unrecoverable. Historical truth suffers a similar fate, though truth claims are still made and are difficult to controvert. Foucault, following Nietzsche, saw truth as error: "Truth is undoubtedly the sort of error that cannot be refuted because it was hardened into an unalterable form in the long baking process of history" ("Nietzsche, Genealogy, History," p. 144).

Genealogy as a method underscores the interpretive nature of any narration of the past. Indeed, the historical past is always and inevitably read through contemporary interests and concerns. Objectivity is questioned in favor of acknowledging the historian's political and ideological investment in the narrative being told. Even if historical truth exists, historians have no particular or privileged access to it. Foucault was most interested, then, in understanding historical documents as discourses of knowledge that highlight some perspectives while suppressing others. Foucault wanted to reread the past and narrate that story from other perspectives. This genealogical approach runs counter to an idea of history as relating the "truth" of past events—of telling what "actually" happened. Rather than chasing after some ephemeral grand narrative that attempts to silence the discontinuities, Foucault sought to interpret the past in ways that highlight the ambiguity, fragmentation, and struggle that necessarily accompany any historical analysis. For Foucault, if the concept of historical origin must be invoked, then it also must be acknowledged that there are multiple origins for any historical trajectory. History as one unified story gives way to a multiplicity of narratives about the past. Thus, we begin to see history not in terms of a static and fixed past but as a continually changing narrative process.

Foucault applied his genealogical analysis to the history of **power**, exploring how power operates to produce particular kinds of subjects. For Foucault, power is not a monolithic force that appears in the same guises throughout all times and places. Instead, power has a genealogical history and is to be understood differently depending on place, location, and theoretical perspective. For instance, a Marxist view of power as that force wielded by governments, corporations, and others who control the economic means of production is very different from a feminist view of patriarchal power. Similarly, Foucault saw power as having a history that includes instances of both oppressive power and power as resistance to oppression. He argued in "The Subject and Power" (1982) that the concept of power must always include the possibility of resistance to power. Power, therefore, is always a relationship, one that creates subjects. But power relationships can be resisted, which means that we can oppose the subject positions that discourses and material practices attempt to impose on us. For Foucault, power is capillary, flowing throughout the social body and not simply emanating from on high.

Foucault used genealogical inquiry to explicate the ways in which power is implicated in how subjects and subjectivity are constructed. As he noted in a 1980 lecture at Dartmouth College, "I have tried to get out from the philosophy of the subject through a genealogy of this subject, by studying the constitution of the subject across history which has led us up to the modern concept of the self. This has not always been an easy task, since most historians prefer a history of social processes, and most philosophers prefer a subject without history" ("About the Beginning of the Hermeneutics of the Self," 1999, p. 160). A genealogical view of subjectivity is Foucault's way out of such essentializing views of the human subject as a singular, transcendent entity.

In his later work, Foucault took up the issue of the "**ethics of self.**" But "ethics of self" does not simply mean an individual's "morals." Rather, he was interested in identifying "techniques" or "technologies" of the self—that is, the regularized forms of behavior that constitute a particular human subject. Such technologies, which include sexual, political, legal, educational, and religious patterns of behavior, may be taken for granted or even go completely unnoticed by the subject who is constituted by them. Nonetheless they function to *discipline* the body and mind within a larger order of power/knowledge. Techniques are subjectivizing practices that create and shape one's sense of self. These subjectivizing practices are not universal, but variable over time and place. By focusing on these technologies of the self, he aimed to uncover how they are implicated in the construction of subjects.

For Foucault, technologies of the self are practices "which permit individuals to effect by their own means, or with the help of others, a certain number of operations on their own bodies and souls, thoughts, conduct, and way of being, so as to transform themselves in order to attain a certain state of happiness, purity, wisdom, perfection, or immortality" (2003, p. 46). Significant here is the ethical idea that individuals can resist power and transform their own subjectivity by applying techniques of the self. While techniques of the self are about discipline, they are not simply about discipline as domination of the self; they also entail positive transformations of the self.

Foucault argued that morality has three references: (1) to a moral code, (2) to behaviors in relation to that code, and (3) to ways that people conduct themselves. Foucault was primarily concerned with this last aspect. For him, self-conduct deals with how individuals view and create themselves as ethical subjects. This runs counter to notions of morality as measuring one's behavior against a transcendent moral code. In his three-volume study of sexuality, for instance, Foucault investigated how and why sexuality became an object of moral discourse as opposed to other areas—say, for example, food or exercise.

Foucault was interested, later in his career, in how these modes of self-governance were themselves governed across multiple sites. Foucault's (1979) notion of **governmentality**, in particular, attempted to bridge the micro level of personal conduct and the macro level of the state's ability to rule from a distance. Though Foucault died before he could more fully develop this idea, governmentality was his effort to come to terms with how the state was able to orchestrate and mobilize personal conduct in a variety of sites. It was a way to rethink the nature of state control, not as simply emanating from a series of top-down dictates, but as artfully managed across range of official and unofficial sites and spaces—from public policy to popular culture.

Foucault's notions of self-care and self-fashioning have also influenced some important work in teacher education. For example, recent work has looked at the role of "emotion" in teacher self-fashioning, particularly in the "care of the teacher self" (Zembylas, 2003). Other work has been done on the historical production of reflection itself in teacher education, situating it within a genealogical study of scientific practice (Fendler, 2003).

Further Reading

By Foucault

1970. *The Order of Things: An Archaeology of the Human Sciences*, translated by Alan Sheridan. New York: Vintage.

1973. "About the Beginning of the Hermeneutics of the Self." In J. R. Carrette, ed., *Religion and Culture*. London: Routledge.

1973. *Madness and Civilization: A History of Insanity in the Age of Reason*, translated by Richard Howard. New York: Vintage.

1973. *Discipline and Punish: The Birh of the Prison*, translated by A. Sheridan. New York: Vintage.

1973. *The Birth of the Clinic: An Archaeology of Medical Perception*, translated by A. M. Sheridan-Smith. New York: Pantheon.

1974. *The Archaeology of Knowledge*, translated by A. M. Sheridan-Smith. London: Tavistock.

1977. *"Nietzsche, Genealogy, History." In D. Bouchard, ed., *Language, Counter-memory, Practice: Selected Essays and Interviews*. Ithaca, NY: Cornell University Press.

1978. *The History of Sexuality, Volume I: An Introduction*, translated by Robert Hurley. New York: Vintage.

1983. *"The Subject and Power." In H. Dreyfus and P. Rabinow, eds., *Michel Foucault: Beyond Structuralism and Hermeneutics*. Chicago: University of Chicago Press, 1983.

2003. "Technologies of the Self." In P. Rabinow and N. Rose, eds., *The Essential Foucault*. New York: New Press.

About Foucault / Relevance for Education

Armstrong, F. "The Historical Development of Special Education." *History of Education* 31 (2002): 437–456.

Baker, B. "'Childhood' in the Emergence and Spread of US Public Schools." In T. Popkewitz and M. Brennan, eds., *Foucault's Challenge*. New York: Teachers College Press, 1998.

Baker, B. *In Perpetual Motion: Theories of Power, Educational History, and the Child*. New York: Peter Lang, 2001.

Baker, B., and K. Heyning, eds. *Dangerous Coagulations?: The Uses of Foucault in the Study of Education*. New York: Peter Lang, 2004.

Ball, S., ed. *Foucault and Education: Disciplines and Knowledge*. New York: Routledge, 1990.

Carroll, J. "Giving and Taking: A Note on Ownership." *Writing Instructor* 11 (1991): 17–22.

Danaher, G., T. Schirato, and J. Webb. *Understanding Foucault*. London: Sage, 2000.

Danforth, S. "What Can the Field of Developmental Disabilities Learn from Michel Foucault?" *Mental Retardation* 38 (2000): 364–369.

Dreyfus, H., and P. Rabinow. *Michel Foucault: Beyond Structuralism and Hermeneutics*. 2nd ed. Chicago: University of Chicago Press, 1983.

Fendler, L. "Teacher Reflection in a Hall of Mirrors: Historical Influences and Political Reverberations." *Educational Researcher* 32 (2003): 16–25.

Gelb, S. "'Be cruel'! Dare We Take Foucault Seriously?" *Mental Retardation* 38 (2000): 369–372.

Gore, J. "Disciplining Bodies: On the Continuity of Power Relations in Pedagogy." In T. Popkewitz and M. Brennan, eds., *Foucault's Challenge*. New York: Teachers College Press, 1998.

Himley, M., et al. "Answering the Word: Adult Literacy and Co-authoring." *Written Communication* 13 (1996): 163–189.

Keogh, J. "Governmentality in Parent-Teacher Communications." *Language and Education* 10 (1996): 119–131.

Kivinen, O., and R. Rinne. "State, Governmentality, and Education—the Nordic Experience." *British Journal of Sociology of Education* 19 (1998): 39–52.

Luke, A. "The Body Literate: Discourse and Inscription in Early Literacy Training." *Linguistics and Education* 4 (1992): 107–129.

McCarthy, C., and G. Dimitriadis. "Governmentality and the Sociology of Education: Media, Educational Policy, and the Politics of Resentment." *British Journal of Sociology of Education* 21 (2000): 169–186.

McNay, L. *Foucault and Feminism: Power, Gender and the Self.* Boston: Northeastern University Press, 1992.

*Mills, S. *Michel Foucault.* London and New York: Routledge, 2003.

Peter, D. "Dynamics of Discourse: A Case Study of Illuminating Power Relations in Mental Retardation." *Mental Retardation* 38 (2000): 354–362.

Popkewitz, T. *Struggling for the Soul: The Politics of Schooling and the Construction of the Teacher.* New York: Teachers College Press, 1998.

Popkewitz, T., and M. Brennan, eds. *Foucault's Challenge: Discourse, Knowledge, and Power in Education.* New York: Teachers College Press, 1998.

Stygall, G. "Resisting Privilege: Basic Writing and Foucault's Author Function." *College Composition and Communication* 45 (1994): 320–341.

Zemblyas, M. "Interrogating 'Teacher Identity': Emotion, Resistance, and Self-formation." *Educational Theory* 53 (2003): 107–127.

PAULO FREIRE

Key Concepts

- limit situations
- generative words
- conscientization
- dialogue

Paulo Freire (1921–1999) was born in Recife, Pernambuco, Brazil. He spent his early years in the Recife area, attending secondary school and teaching Portuguese, before graduating from Recife's School of Law in 1947. Soon after, he joined the Division of Education and Culture, holding several posts before completing his doctorate at the University of Recife in 1959. In 1959, Freire was invited by the mayor of Recife to develop a literacy program for the city. It was at this point—in the newly established post of director of the University's Extension Services—that he began to develop his novel approach to adult literacy. Freire began to use collective study circles as pedagogical sites and instruments throughout Brazil. These study circles, which addressed local politics and concerns for social justice, were astonishingly effective in helping rural farm workers become literate throughout the country.

In 1963, Freire was appointed coordinator of the National Program of Literacy of Adults in Brasilia (the capital of Brazil) by President João Goulart. However, a military coup ended Goulart's presidency and Freire's role in government. In 1964, Freire was arrested and imprisoned for seventy days. Soon after his release, he went into exile. He would remain abroad for the next several years, working on various literacy projects in countries such as Tanzania, Chile, Guinea-Bissau, Peru, and Nicaragua. He returned in 1979 to São Paulo, Brazil, where he taught in several university positions before being appointed secretary of education for the city. He served in this capacity from 1989 to 1991.

Freire published numerous books that have been translated and have sold well throughout the world. These include *Pedagogy of the Oppressed* (1973), *Pedagogy of Hope: Reliving Pedagogy of the Oppressed* (1995), and the posthumously released *Pedagogy of Freedom: Ethics, Democracy, and Civic Courage* (1998). Of these, *Pedagogy of the Oppressed* (1993 [1970]) is undoubtedly his masterwork. It can be read as equal parts social theory, philosophy, and pedagogical method. His claims about education are foundational, rooted in both his devout Christian beliefs and his Marxism. Throughout it, Freire argued that the goal of education is to begin to name the world, to recognize that we are all "subjects" of our own lives and narratives, not "objects" in the stories of others. We must acknowledge the ways in which we as human beings are fundamentally charged with producing and transforming reality together. Those who do not acknowledge this, those who want to control and oppress, are committing a kind of epistemic "violence":

> To surmount the situation of oppression, people must first critically recognize its causes, so that through transforming action they can create a new situation, one that makes possible the pursuit of a fuller humanity. But the struggle to be more fully human has already begun in the authentic struggle to transform the situation. (1993, p. 29)

Freire often referred to these situations as **"limit situations,"** situations beyond which people cannot imagine themselves. Limit situations naturalize people's sense of oppression, giving it a kind of obviousness and immutability.

To help people imagine lives beyond these limit situations, Freire spent much time in communities trying to understand community members' interests, investments, and concerns in order to elicit comprehensive sets of **"generative words."** He used these words as starting points for literacy learning, and literacy learning was deployed in the service of social and political activism. More specifically, generative words were paired with pictures that represented them and then were interrogated by people in the community for what they revealed and concealed with respect to the circulation of multiple forms of capital. Freire encouraged the people both to explore how the meanings and effects of these words functioned in their lives and also to conduct research on how their meanings and effects do (or could) function in different ways in different social and political contexts. The primary goal of these activities was to help people feel in control of their words and to be able to use them to exercise power over the material and ideological conditions of their own lives. Thus, Freire's literacy programs were designed not so much to teach functional literacy as to raise people's critical consciousness (a process he called "**conscientization**") and to encourage them to engage in "praxis," or critical reflection inextricably linked to political action in the real world. Freire clearly underscored the fact that praxis is never easy and always involves power struggles, often violent ones.

As this description of Freire's pedagogy for the oppressed suggests, he believed that human beings live both "in" the world and "with" the world, and thus can be active participants in making history. In fact, he argued that a fundamental possibility of the human condition is to be able to change the material, economic, and spiritual conditions of life itself through conscientization and praxis. He posited human agency, then, as situated or embodied freedom—a kind of limited but quite powerful agency that makes it possible to change oneself and one's situation for the better. To enact such agency, he argued, people need to emerge from their unconscious engagements with the world, reflect on them, and work to change them. Viewed in this way, the enactment of freedom is an unfinalizable process. In constantly transforming their engagements in and with the world, people are simultaneously shaping the conditions of their lives and constantly re-creating themselves.

Freire's insistence that the unending process of emancipation must be a collective effort is far from trivial. Central to this process is a faith in the power of **dialogue**. Importantly, dialogue, for Freire, is defined as collective reflection/action. He believed that dialogue, fellowship, and solidarity are essential to human liberation and transformation: "We can legitimately say that in the process of oppression someone oppresses someone else; we cannot legitimately say that in the process of revolution, someone liberates someone else, nor yet that that someone liberates himself, but rather that men in communion liberate each other" (1993, p. 103).

Within Freirean pedagogies, the development and use of "generative" words and phrases and the cultivation of conscientization are enacted in the context of locally situated study circles (or focus groups). The goal for the educator or facilitator within these study circles is to engage with people in their lived realities, producing and transforming them. Again, for Freire, pedagogical activity is always already grounded in larger philosophical and social projects that are concerned with how people might more effectively "narrate" their own lives:

The starting point for organizing the program content of education or political action must be the present, existential, concrete situation, reflecting the aspirations of the people. Utilizing certain basic contradictions, we must pose the existential, concrete, present situation to the people as a problem which challenges them and requires a response— not just at the intellectual level, but at the level of action.... The task of the dialogical teacher in an interdisciplinary team working on the thematic universe revealed by their investigation is to "re-present" that universe to the people from whom she or he first received it—and "re-present" it not as a lecture, but as a problem. (1993, pp. 76, 90)

To illustrate this kind of problem-posing education rooted in people's lived realities and contradictions, Freire discussed a research program designed around the question of alcoholism, a serious problem in the city. A researcher showed an assembled group a photograph of a drunken man walking past three other men talking on the corner. The group responded, in effect, by saying that the drunken man was a hard worker, the only hard worker in the group, and he was probably worried about his low wages and having to support his family. In their words, "He is a decent worker and a souse like us" (1993, p. 99). The men in the study circle seemed to recognize themselves in this man, noting both that he was a "souse" and situating his drinking in a politicized context. In this situation, alcoholism was "read" as a response to oppression and exploitation. The goal was to "decode" images and language in ways that eventually led to questioning and transforming the material and social conditions of existence. Freire offered other examples, including showing people different (and contradictory) news stories covering the same event. In each case, the goal was to help people understand the contradictions they lived with and to use these understandings to change their worlds.

Freire's pedagogical framework could not be readily contained within traditional educational contexts where the historical weight of the "banking model" imposed powerful and pervasive constraints. His work has inspired a wide range of important social movements within education, and the activities of these movements have provided yet more models for how intensive group activity can be imagined and enacted in innovative and politically charged ways. It is critical to note that Freire's posthumously released *Pedagogy of Freedom: Ethics, Democracy, and Courage* (1998) takes up more explicitly this notion that teacher training is not simply about acquiring "skills" but also about maintaining a critical, reflective, politically engaged consciousness.

Further Reading

By Freire

1973. *Pedagogy of the Oppressed*, translated by M. Bergman Ramos. New York: Continuum.

1992. *Pedagogy of the City*, translated by D. Macedo. New York: Continuum.

1995. *Pedagogy of Hope: Reliving Pedagogy of the Oppressed*, translated by R. Barr. New York: Continuum.

1998. *Pedagogy of Freedom: Ethics, Democracy and Civic Courage*, translated by P. Clarke. Lanham, MD: Rowman and Littlefield.

1998. *Pedagogy of the Heart*, translated by D. Macedo and A. Oliveria. New York: Continuum.

About Freire / Relevance for Education

Allman, P. "Paulo Freire's Contributions to Radical Adult Education." *Studies in the Education of Adults* 26 (1994): 144–161.

Holzman, M. "A Post-Freirian Model for Adult Literacy Education." *College English* 50 (1998): 177–189.

Ledwith, M. "Community Work as Critical Pedagogy: Re-envisioning Freire and Gramsci." *Community Development Journal* 36 (2001): 171–182.

*Mayo, P. *Gramsci, Freire, and Adult Education: Possibilities for Transformative Action*. London: Zed, 1999.

*McLaren, P. *Che Guevara, Paulo Freire, and the Pedagogy of Revolution*. Lanham, MD: Rowman and Littlefield, 2000.

Pietrykowski, B. "Knowledge and Power in Adult Education: Beyond Freire and Habermas." *Adult Education Quarterly* 46 (1996): 82–97.

Rossatto, C. "Social Transformation and 'Popular Schooling' in Brazil." *Childhood Education* 77 (2001): 367–374.

Schleppegrell, M. "Problem-posing in Teacher Education." *TESOL Journal* 6 (1997): 8–12.

Shor, I. *Critical Teaching in Everyday Life*. Chicago: University of Chicago Press, 1980.

Torres, C. *Education, Power, and Personal Biography*. New York: Routledge, 1998.

CLIFFORD GEERTZ

Key Concepts

- interpretive turn
- thick description
- symbolic anthropology

Clifford Geertz (b. 1926) was born in San Francisco, California. After what he has described as a "rural" childhood, he served in the U.S. Navy during World War II, then attended Antioch College on the G.I. Bill. With the ambition to become a journalist, Geertz first majored in English before graduating with a B.A. in philosophy in 1950. Geertz went on to study anthropology at Harvard University, where he worked with an experimental interdisciplinary program run by Clyde Kluckhohn. With the assistance of a Ford Foundation grant, Geertz studied religion in Indonesia. He received his Ph.D. in 1956. He taught at the University of Chicago from 1960 to 1970, then was professor of social science at the Institute for Advanced Study at Princeton University from 1970 to 2000.

Geertz is the author of many important anthropological texts, including *The Religion of Java* (1960), *Agricultural Involution: The Process of Ecological Change in Indonesia* (1963), *The Social History of an Indonesian Town* (1965), *Person, Time and Conduct in Bali: An Essay in Cultural Analysis* (1966), and *Islam Observed: Religious Development in Morocco and Indonesia* (1968). These texts reflect his important fieldwork in Java, Bali, and Morocco (among other places) throughout the 1950s, 1960s, and 1970s. Perhaps Geertz's most lasting contributions have to do with the nature and practice of interpretive inquiry. His landmark book *The Interpretation of Cultures* (1973) represented a turning point for anthropology. Here, Geertz argued that culture is "semiotic," that "man is an animal suspended in webs of significance he himself has spun." The study of culture is, in essence, the study of those webs. For Geertz, reading cultures is like reading texts: the analysis of culture is "therefore not an experimental science in search of law but an interpretive one in search of meaning" (1973, p. 5). From this perspective, anthropology is the construction of other people's constructions of their realities.

Geertz signaled an **interpretive turn** in anthropology. He argued that cultures were not "out there" to be objectively captured through neutral forms of representation. Rather, cultures are always already the product of interpretive work. Individuals are meaning-making agents in context; this includes research subjects and participants as well as the ethnographers who study them. This was a fundamentally innovative understanding of reality as well as of the methods for understanding it. In stressing the interpretive nature of reality, however, Geertz did not imply that we simply conjure up arbitrary realities at will. Reality is neither wholly objective or wholly subjective.

Instead, Geertz was interested in understanding the complexity of concrete, local events. In a fascinating discussion that begins *The Interpretation of Culture*, for example, he outlined the various ways a wink of the eye might be interpreted and understood and with what effects, underscoring the fact that the most plausible explanations require a thorough understanding of the cultural context in which the wink is enacted. It might be, he suggested, an involuntary twitch or a conspiratorial gesture: "The winker is communicating, and indeed communicating in a quite precise and special way: (1) deliberately, (2) to someone in particular, (3) to impart a particular message, (4) according to a socially established code, and (5) without cognizance of the rest of the company" (1973, p. 6). The goal is to understand the social life and meaning and relevance of these habits and gestures in context through a process Geertz calls "**thick description**," within which the researcher comes to understand culture by "isolating its elements, specifying the internal relationships among those elements, and then characterizing the whole system in some general way" (1973, p. 17).

Geertz's famous treatment of the Balinese cockfight is a key exemplar of this "thick description," in which Geertz describes this ritual event in detail and nuance and shows how its meaning and relevance can be understood only against the backdrop of a storehouse of cultural knowledge. In his analysis, he deeply contextualizes this particular event, describing where it was held, the audience, the preparation of the birds, the size of the ring, the rules of the game, the structure of gambling practices, and so on. The cockfight is shown to be a complex ritual that the Balinese enact to help them understand their own culture and its hierarchies. The cockfight competition provides a "metasocial commentary upon the whole matter of assorting human beings into fixed hierarchical ranks and then organizing the major part of the collective existence around that assortment.... Its function, if you want to call it that, is interpretive: it is a Balinese reading of Balinese experience, a story that they tell themselves about themselves" (1973, p. 448). It is a story, to evoke Geertz, that the anthropologist "strains to read over the shoulders of those to whom they properly belong" (1973, p. 452). In sum, Geertz both renders this event coherent and understandable for the outsider and also privileges its ritual significance for the Balinese.

Among other things, Geertz called for a different kind of anthropology—a **symbolic anthropology**—which implied different conceptual understandings of the field's goals and practices. Much of the work in the past had been built on what might be called a "foundational" model in which studies built on and supplanted one another in clear, linear fashion. Geertz instead asked both anthropologists and his readers to avoid scientism, to understand that our understandings of the world are not linear but come in "spurts," and that we should not be "predictive" in our writings. In this regard, he was post-foundational. Still, Geertz held firmly to the idea that one could do solid empirical work and argue for its validity. He did not question the possibility that we can understand others and their cultures (as did some in the next generation of anthropologists). Geertz is not a relativist, as the following statement attests:

> A good interpretation of anything—a poem, a person, a history, a ritual, an institution, a society—takes us into the heart of that of which it is the interpretation. When it does not do that, but leads us instead somewhere else—into an admiration of its own elegance, of its author's cleverness, or of the beauties of Euclidean order—it may have its intrinsic charms; but it is something else than what the task at hand ... calls for. (1973, p. 18)

Geertz's contributions have been many, including new and complex ways to think about the nature of culture. According to Sherry Ortner, Geertz offers a notion of culture that bridges the social scientific and the humanistic. He makes us think of culture "as the clash of meanings in the borderlands; as public culture that has its own textual coherence but is always locally interpreted; as fragile webs of meaning woven by vulnerable actors in nightmarish situations; as the grounds of agency and intentionality in ongoing practice" (Ortner, 1999, p. 11). For Geertz, culture is a text with identifiable internal structures. Drawing heavily from literary studies, semiotics, and hermeneutics, he celebrates the belief that new experiences (in new cultures, for example) can extend one's interpretive horizon and bring these structures into view, and that these extensions constitute more complex and adequate forms of understanding.

Geertz's notion of culture was critical to the so-called crisis of representation, which became pronounced in anthropology in the mid-1980s, particularly with the work of James Clifford and George Marcus and the volume *Writing Culture* (1986). In opening up a discussion about the textual nature of culture and the interpretive nature of inquiry, Geertz underscored a key insight of this move: that writing is not epiphenomenal to but constitutive of the research process itself. In the introduction to *Writing Culture*, James Clifford wrote, "We begin, not with participant-observation or with cultural texts ... but with writing, the making of texts. No longer a marginal, or occulted, dimension, writing has emerged as central to what we do both in the field and thereafter." He went on, "The fact that it has not until recently been portrayed or seriously discussed reflects the persistence of an ideology claiming transparency of representation and immediacy of experience" (Clifford, 1986, p. 2). Different genres of writing and different semiotic media (writing, photography, video) afford different kinds of access to experience and the world. Challenges to viewing writing and other semiotic forms uncritically as representational (and not performative and productive) led to critiques of work conducted by anthropologists in earlier times.

Although scholars like Geertz have reimagined fieldwork as text-making and thus world-making, however, their critiques of traditional ethnography are not deconstructive. Many anthropologists associated with this "crisis" gave up on the notion of fieldwork itself, but Geertz held to the idea that "accurate" representations are possible. The ethnographer's primary task is still to expand her "horizon of vision" through experience with exotic others and to inscribe their worlds from "their point of view" as accurately as possible. In this respect, Geertz was critical to much of the interpretive work that would take hold in education beginning in the 1980s. Knowledge, reason, and truth are not conceived as the representational mirroring (through language and other semiotic media) of an already existing world. Instead, knowledge, reason, and truth are believed to be constructed through the symbolic acts of human beings in relation to the world and to others. Inquiry is no longer about verification within a correspondence theory of truth but about human interaction, communication, dialogue, and reasoned argument.

Further Reading

By Geertz

1960. *The Religion of Java*. Glencoe, IL: Free Press.

1963. *Agricultural Involution: The Process of Ecological Change in Indonesia*. Berkeley: University of California Press.

1965. *The Social History of an Indonesian Town*. Cambridge, MA: MIT Press.

1966. *Person, Time and Conduct in Bali: An Essay in Cultural Analysis*. Southeast Asia Program Cultural Report Series, No. 14.

1968. *Islam Observed: Religious Development in Morocco and Indonesia*. New Haven: Yale University Press.

1973. **The Interpretation of Cultures*. New York: Basic Books.

1995. *After the Fact: Two Countries, Four Decades, One Anthropologist*. Cambridge, MA: Harvard University Press.

2000. *Available Light: Anthropological Reflections on Philosophical Topics*. Princeton: Princeton University Press.

About Geertz / Relevance for Education

Clifford, J., and G. Marcus, eds. *Writing Culture: The Poetics and Politics of Ethnography*. Berkeley: University of California Press, 1986.

Heath, S. B. *Ways with Words: Language, Life, and Work in Communities and Classrooms*. Cambridge, UK: Cambridge University Press, 1983.

Lofty, J. *Time to Write*. Albany, NY: SUNY Press, 1987.

*Ortner, S., ed. *The Fate of "Culture": Geertz and Beyond*. Berkeley: University of California Press, 1999.

Schaafsma, D. *Eating on the Street: Teaching Literacy in a Multicultural Society*. Pittsburgh: University of Pittsburgh Press, 1993.

ANTONIO GRAMSCI

Key Concepts

- *Prison Notebooks*
- civil society
- hegemony
- organic intellectuals
- war of position and war of maneuver

Antonio Gramsci (1891–1937) was born in Sardinia, Italy, and grew up in a largely middle-class setting, though this relative comfort ended when his father was arrested and imprisoned for financial wrongdoing. With the help of a scholarship, Gramsci attended the University of Turin, where he studied philology and linguistics.

Gramsci, however, never finished his degree. His studies were overwhelmed by his political activities. He became involved in the Italian Socialist Party (ISP), working tirelessly on several fronts, including several adult education initiatives as well as ongoing writing about culture. He helped establish a factory council movement that implemented factory-based educational programs promoting socialism and socialist relations between workers. Gramsci also did extensive writing and editorial work for the newspapers *Il Grido del Popolo* and *Avanti!* In addition to his more explicitly political writing, he wrote on Shakespeare, Chekhov, Ibsen, and other authors.

Gramsci was arrested and imprisoned in 1926. Fascists had come to power in Italy, and he was convicted of various political offenses. His difficult years in prison, lasting until his untimely death, were nonetheless productive. In addition to attempting to set up schools for prisoners, Gramsci used the solitude to write his *Prison Notebooks*. Here he developed many of the themes that have become important to critical theorists in education as well as in other disciplines of the humanities and social sciences. These evolving notebooks, smuggled out of Italy by Gramsci's sister for publication, have not all been translated into English at this writing.

Unlike many so-called scientific Marxists of the time, Gramsci was interested in questions of culture. This distinguished him from some more orthodox Marxists, who tended to see culture as a mere dependent variable to the economic base. Clearly Gramsci took culture more seriously than this, seeing it as the site of very important work. Individuals struggled over culture in the realm of **civil society**. For Gramsci, civil society was comprised of all the noncoercive public sites where social allegiances were forged and broken over time: church, school, and family, among other sites. The effectivity of these sites cannot be reduced to—or explained through—the economy alone, nor do they depend on the force or physical coercion of state police apparatus. They do their own work, independent of those sites. They have their own relative autonomy.

Perhaps Gramsci's best-known theoretical work has to do with the idea of **hegemony**. According to Gramsci, hegemony "is a social condition in which all aspects of social reality are dominated by or supportive of a single class" (quoted in Mayo, 1999, p. 35). Gramsci's notion of hegemony relies on particular notions of state and social reproduction. For him, the state does not rule only by force. Although the state does employ coercive means, such as the military and the police, it also rules by consent. And this consent is won on a complex and uneven terrain by invested actors. Indeed, according to Gramsci, the state necessarily maintains its power by striking accords between dominant interests and the interests of resistant groups. The state reproduces itself by incorporating and rearticulating the resistant impulses of subordinate groups, thus producing seemingly common sense ideas about how the world works. Gramsci wrote, "The life of the state is conceived as a continuous process of formation and superseding of unstable equilibria ... between the interests of the fundamental group and those of the subordinate groups—equilibria in which the interests of the dominant group prevail, but only up to a certain point" (quoted in Storey, 2000, pp. 211–212). This kind of power was envisioned, for Gramsci, largely in terms of economic class.

An example might help illustrate this idea of hegemony. Republican President George W. Bush has served largely to advance the interests of elites in the United States, particularly the very wealthy, yet he surrounded himself with a Cabinet that is remarkably diverse, including black male (Colin Powell) and black female (Condoleezza

Rice) secretaries of state. A Gramscian analysis would argue that Bush is simply "striking a bargain" with historically subordinate groups to appear fair, as if he is really working in the interests of all groups. This allows him to appear even-handed even as he advances the interests of elites. It allows him to work toward broad common sense consensuses across disparate groups in pursuing his agenda.

Hegemony is maintained by what Gramsci called "**organic intellectuals**." Such intellectuals are able to mediate the goals, needs, and interests of different classes, to win their consent. In this regard, they do much of the intellectual work of making civil society make sense. Such intellectuals can either help support or resist dominant hegemony. Gramsci wrote, "Every social group ... creates together with itself, organically, one or more strata of intellectuals which give it homogeneity and an awareness of its own function, not only in the economic but also in the social and political fields" (quoted in Storey, 2000, p. 212). In this sense, both the progressive filmmaker Michael Moore and conservative talk-show host Rush Limbaugh are organic intellectuals. They both appeal to current events in mobilizing popular common sense to their causes. Organic intellectuals cannot simply impose a set of beliefs or practices from above. Rather, they must engage in a "**war of position**." For Gramsci, a war of position was a long, ongoing struggle taking place in the realm of civil society. The fights here are over the production of particular notions of political common sense. A war of position, for Gramsci, is different from a "**war of maneuver**." The latter is a more violent and singular confrontation with state authority.

For Gramsci, the role of state is an educative one, as is the role of hegemony: "Every relationship of 'hegemony' is necessarily an educational relationship," he wrote. It is the way in which the state is able to appear as natural and right and fair, the noncoercive way in which the state is able to gain consent for its project. Not surprisingly, perhaps, his own ongoing work in adult education underscores how education can happen in a broad theater beyond the classroom, in all the civil spaces where hegemony unfolds. In this sense, Gramsci's work in education becomes quite important—for example, his efforts to work on factory floors and in prisons.

There is a difference, however, between "education" and "schooling," and Gramsci also wrote more specifically about traditional schooling in his essay "On Education." Here, Gramsci wrestled with the competing roles of classical humanistic education, typically reserved for elites, and vocational education, typically reserved for subordinate groups.

Gramsci argued that a common humanistic education was important for all classes before going on to more specialized training:

> A common basic education imparting a general, humanistic formative culture; this would strike the right balance between development of the capacity for working manually (technically, industrially) and development of the capacities required for intellectual work. From this type of common schooling, via repeated experiments in vocational orientation, pupils would pass on to one of the specialized schools or to productive work. (1971, p. 27)

In certain respects, Gramsci's call for "common schooling" appears antidemocratic, as limiting choice in calling for a unified mode of education. But for Gramsci, real democracy can only come when everyone has the capacity to deliberate thoughtfully. For this reason, he resisted the proliferation of particular vocationally oriented schools for working people. This has led certain scholars in education to call him "conservative" (Entwistle, 1979), though others challenge this interpretation (Borg, Buttigieg, and Mayo, 2000).

Indeed, Harold Entwistle in *Antonio Gramsci: Conservative Schooling for Radical Politics*, argues that Gramsci was very conservative in his beliefs about schooling. For Entwistle, Gramsci believed in a firmly authoritarian education system. He "believed in an *active* teacher, transmitting the mainstream humanistic culture, enforcing linguistic discipline and accuracy" (1979, p. 28). Of course, all this was ultimately in service of his radical socialist politics. In contrast, many of the authors in the collection *Gramsci and Education* (2000) argue that this is a reductive reading of Gramsci. Many of these authors maintain that this appropriation takes Gramsci out of context. According to Borg and Mayo, these arguments make sense only if read against some of the currents of the time that tried to marginalize working-class youth by putting them in vocational education settings.

Gramsci's work has been extraordinarily influential in the field of education—for example, in the sociology of education and in critical pedagogy. In terms of the sociology of education, Michael Apple's work has wrestled with how political "power blocs" constitute and reconstitute themselves. Apple (2001) focuses on how the right has produced a certain kind of common sense that has drawn together various factions—Christian evangelicals, the new middle classes, cultural conservatives, and neoliberals—under a common umbrella. There has been an "accord" among these groups that has produced a certain kind of common sense about the role of education in the world.

In particular, sets of business logics have deeply lodged themselves in the popular imagination around education, expressed in vouchers, high-stakes testing, and related interventions.

Apple's is a classic Gramscian analysis. He is interested in how "accords" are built among different groups, and how new and emergent social movements are built, maintained, and sustained by invested actors in the realm of civil society. In this case, dominant interests have co-opted the concerns of marginalized groups and linked them to overarching conservative agendas. This is possible only because conservative groups are able to speak to the immediate needs and concerns of these marginalized groups. For example, neoliberals offer "vouchers" as a solution to poor African American families facing a crumbling public school system. The solution appears as a logical and even helpful one, though it plays into larger conservative agendas about the evacuation of the public sphere.

Related work in critical pedagogy has looked more closely at how educators can function as "organic intellectuals" across a wide range of pedagogical spaces. Giroux (2000) writes, "By emphasizing the educational force of culture, Gramsci explains the sphere of the political by pointing to those diverse spaces in which cultural practices are deployed, lived, and mobilized in the service of knowledge, power, and authority" (p. 132). For Gramsci (and Giroux), intellectuals have the imperative to engage this terrain, to abandon a narrow notion of pedagogy that stresses only the technical and administrative. "The questions that Gramsci raises about education, culture, and political struggle also have important ramifications for theorizing educators as public intellectuals and how they might challenge the institutional and cultural terrains through which dominant authority is secured and state power is legitimated" (Giroux, 2000, p. 133). Others have picked up and developed this idea of educators as organic intellectuals, particularly as it relates to teacher education and biography (Tickle, 2001).

Finally, with this more expansive notion of pedagogy, Gramsci's work has profoundly influenced the field of popular culture and education. As Nadine Dolby (2003) argues in the introduction to a special issue of *Harvard Educational Review* on "Popular Culture and Education," Gramsci's work has allowed theorists to get beyond a typical binary impasse—the idea that popular culture comes simply from either "above" (corporations) or "below" (the masses). Gramsci's notion of hegemony allows us to see popular culture as a terrain of struggle, where meanings are fought over and alliances are negotiated. It allows us to see popular culture texts as open and mutable, their meanings not dictated in advance. While popular culture is a site where consent is fought over, it is also a site where educators can intervene.

Further Reading
By Gramsci

1971. *Selections from Prison Notebooks*, translated by T. Q. Hoare and G. N. Smith. London: Lawrence and Wishart.

1992. *Prison Notebooks*. New York: Columbia University Press.

2000. "Hegemony, Intellectuals, and the State." In J. Storey, ed., *Cultural Theory and Popular Culture: A Reader*. Athens: University of Georgia Press.

About Gramsci / Relevance for Education

Apple, M. *Educating the "Right" Way*. New York: Routledge, 2001.

Borg, C., J. Buttigieg, and P. Mayo, eds. *Gramsci and Education*. Lanham, MD: Rowman and Littlefield, 2000.

Coben, D. *Radical Heroes: Gramsci, Freire, and the Politics of Adult Education*. New York: Garland, 1998.

Coben, D. "Revisiting Gramsci." *Studies in the Education of Adults* 27 (1995): 36-51.

Entwistle, H. *Antonio Gramsci: Conservative Schooling for Radical Politics*. London: Routledge, 1979.

*Giroux, H. "Radical Education and Culture in the Work of Antonio Gramsci." In *Stealing Innocence: Corporate Culture's War on Children*. New York: Palgrave, 2000.

Holst, J. *Social Movements, Civil Society, and Radical Adult Education*. New York: Bergin and Garvey, 2002.

Holst, J. "The Affinities of Lenin and Gramsci." *International Journal of Lifelong Education* 18 (1999): 407–421.

Ledwith, M. "Community Work as Critical Pedagogy: Re-envisioning Freire and Gramsci." *Community Development Journal* 36 (2001): 171–182.

*Mayo, P. *Gramsci, Freire, and Adult Education*. London: Zed, 2000.

Morgan, J. "Antonio Gramsci and Raymond Williams: Workers, Intellectuals, and Adult Education." *Convergence* 29 (1996): 61–74.

Mulenga, D. "Participatory Research for Radical Community Development." *Australian Journal of Adult and Community Education* 34 (1994): 253–261.

Schugurensky, D. "Adult Education and Social Transformation." *Comparative Education Review* 44 (2000): 515–522.

Tickle, L. "The Organic Intellectual Educator." *Cambridge Journal of Education* 31 (2001): 159–178.

STUART HALL

Key Concepts

- Marxism without guarantees
- ideology
- articulation
- "New Ethnicities"

Stuart Hall (b. 1932) was born and grew up in Jamaica in the West Indies, receiving a traditional colonial British education. However, Jamaica was moving toward postcolonial independence during this time, placing Hall at the center of the two distinct cultural pressures, those of the Caribbean and of England. He left for Bristol in 1951, eventually entering Oxford University. Here Hall was involved in various new Marxist movements, eventually helping to launch the journal *New Left Review*. In 1964 he joined Raymond WILLIAMS, Richard Hoggart, and E. P. Thompson at Birmingham University Center for Cultural Studies, where he played a prominent role, often serving as a kind of mediating group nucleus. Hall left this post to teach at the Open University in 1979. He retired in 1997.

Hall's work has been profoundly influenced by Karl MARX and Marxism. For Hall, Marxism is closely linked to the anticolonial struggles of less-developed countries like Jamaica. The key to emancipation for Jamaica and other Caribbean nations is economic liberation. Hall was thus profoundly influenced by so-called Third World Marxist movements of the later twentieth century, though he would not remain locked into their strictures. Hall's Marxism is a "**Marxism without guarantees.**" It does not assume an all-determining economic "base," nor that all history can be explained through a linear, progressive Marxist trajectory. Over the course of his almost fifty-year writing career, Hall would struggle with the implications of Marxism, though he would continually put it into dialogue with other bodies of thought and work, from his work on popular culture, to postmodernism, to postcolonialism.

Hall is centrally concerned with the question of **ideology**, though he did not draw on traditional Marxist doctrine here. For example, he grappled with what it meant that the conservative Thatcher regime in the United Kingdom was able to build wide public support, co-opting terms such as "freedom" and "equality" and linking them to the interests of new elites (Hall, 1988). A traditional approach to Marx and Marxism sometimes understands this in terms of "false consciousness," arguing that the sites of power have in some way "tricked" the masses into making decisions not in their own self-interest, by manipulating popular ideas. Drawing on the work of Antonio GRAMSCI, Hall was more concerned with the ways these popular "ideas" or "ideologies" have their own relative autonomy. As Hall wrote in his article "The Problem of Ideology: Marxism without Guarantees" (1986), ideology is "the mental frameworks—the languages, the concepts, categories, imagery of thought, and the systems of representation—which different classes and social groups deploy in order to make sense of, define, figure out and render intelligible the way society works" (p. 26). For Hall, these cannot be reduced merely to a function of class, though they have what he calls a "material force" (p. 27).

Important here is the notion of **articulation**. For Hall, articulation is the process by which different (and sometimes contradictory) ideas can be ideologically linked together "like cars on a lorry," in his phrase. This idea would resonate throughout his work. For Hall, articulation is "the form of the connection that can make a unity of two different elements, under certain conditions. It is a linkage which is not necessarily determined, absolute and essential for all time." These linkages create a unity of discourse that is "really the articulation of different, distinct elements which can be rearticulated in different ways because they have no necessary 'belongingness'" (1986, p. 53). They can and do arise at certain historical moments, though they are always the work of invested agents and actors.

Popular culture is particularly important here. One of Hall's earliest books is the sometimes overlooked *The Popular Arts* (1964, coauthored with Paddy Whannel), which deals with the complexities of popular culture and its multiple iterations and manifestations. Importantly, this book was rooted in Hall's experience as a teacher attempting to understand the range of cultural resources and influences young people bring to the classroom. For Hall and Whannel, popular culture is an important site for the young—in many ways, a more important site than traditional school settings. They wrote:

> Their symbols and fantasies have a strong hold upon the emotional commitment of the young at this stage in their development, and operate more powerfully in a situation where young people are tending to learn less from established institutions, such as the family, the school, the church and the immediate adult community, and more from one another. (1964, p. 276)

As the authors point out, popular culture is often treated as if it is a homogeneous or singular entity—as if it simply means one thing. In many respects, *The Popular Arts* is an attempt to create a more elaborate and baroque language to discuss the complexities of popular culture. Hall and Whannel argue for the importance of making internal distinctions within popular cultural forms, between forms that are "authentically a part of teenage culture" and those that are "provided for that culture by an adult and organized industry" (p. 67). Moreover, they urge expanding the range of ways these art forms are talked about, the distinction between commercial pop forms and jazz being the most notable example. Finally, they offer a set of resources for teachers in the concluding chapter entitled "The Curriculum and the Arts." Here, they offer lessons for students that look across different art forms thematically. Modules include "Society and the Hero," "Young People," and "The World of Pop."

Like many others associated with Birmingham's Center for Contemporary Cultural Studies, Hall was centrally concerned with youth and media culture more broadly. For example, his well-known book *Resistance through Ritual: Youth Subcultures in Post-War Britain* (1976, coedited with Tony Jefferson) discusses the range of youth subcultures that proliferated in England in the mid-twentieth century, including mods, skinheads, and Rastafarians. In addition, his important article "Encoding, Decoding" (1973) discusses the circuits or stages through which media (news) messages travel, from the production of media content where particular meanings are "encoded," through their reception where these meanings are "decoded." Each stage has its own relative autonomy. None of these stages fully determines any other, though none is simply free-floating. In another well-known article, "Deconstructing the Popular" (1980), Hall wrote about popular culture as an uncertain terrain of allegiance and common sense continually fought over. This article highlights the "continuous and necessarily uneven and unequal struggle, by the dominant culture, constantly to disorganize and reorganize popular culture; to enclose and confine its definitions and forms within a more inclusive range of dominant forms" (p. 447). It emphasizes, as well, points of resistance to this process, times when acceptance of such common sense is challenged. For Hall, this production of common sense largely serves the interests of capital. At the end of this article, he says that the goal for cultural critics is to look toward incipient forms of socialism. Otherwise, he says, he doesn't "give a damn about it" (p. 453).

Hall would continue to push these interests in questions of representation, though he would be increasingly influenced by postmodernism and postcolonialism. These concerns are pursued in several articles as well as in book-length collections such as *Representation: Cultural Representations and Signifying Practices* (1997). While capital and class analyses would remain central to his work, Hall increasingly decentered this notion to more closely consider notions of race. Characteristically, Hall's treatment of race is nuanced and complex. Here, too, he would destabilize any fixed notion of "blackness."

In his article "**New Ethnicities**" (1989), Hall discussed the so-called burden of representation facing blacks in England. According to him, political struggles around race have traditionally been linked to monolithic notions of "blackness" and the need for access to media forms in promoting messages of "racial upliftment." In this essay, Hall contested these notions on several levels, arguing that race is a socially constructed form open to multiple manifestations. He stressed "the recognition of the extraordinary diversity of subjective positions, social experiences and cultural identities which compose the category 'black'; that is, the recognition that 'black' is essentially a politically and culturally charged category, which cannot be grounded in a set of fixed trans-cultural or transcendental racial categories." Like class, struggles around race have "no guarantees in nature" (1989, p. 443). In this essay, Hall offered examples from the film *My Beautiful Laundrette* in exploring how notions of blackness are complicated—here, through sexuality—in dominant representational forms.

This notion is picked up and extended in his essay "What Is This Black in Black Popular Culture?" (1992), which asks similar such questions, including some concerning the "struggles around difference" that are endemic to contemporary cultural politics. For Hall, postmodernism has complicated any simple notion of "black" in "black popular culture," opening it up as a contested site or terrain that needs to be examined within and between these popular forms. Hall's move is complicated here. He both acknowledges the historical durability of expressive black forms (for example, around style and the body) in popular culture while eschewing any simple notion of authentic vs. inauthentic representation of a seemingly monolithic black community. For Hall, popular culture is a site where new and emergent forms of identity proliferate and are open to contestation.

Throughout his work, Hall has drawn on Gramsci's notion of hegemony to challenge simple notions of "class" and "race," exploring them as part of ongoing struggles with "no guarantees," particularly as they relate to culture in general and popular culture more specifically. Hall's work has been profoundly influential in education, particularly in cultural studies of education. As noted, one of his earliest projects, *The Popular Arts*, is explicitly pedagogical. In addition, Hall was later concerned with producing student-friendly readers that introduce students to key constructs in cultural studies. This work includes *Representation: Cultural Representations and Signifying Practices* (1997) as well as the coauthored *Doing Cultural Studies: The Story of the Sony Walkman* (1997) and the coedited *Formations of Modernity* (1992). Each case evidences the ways in which cultural studies has been a pedagogical project from the beginning.

More broadly, Hall has been critical for those in education working through questions of culture and representation, particularly around questions of race and popular culture. Henry Giroux, for example, has highlighted the ways in which Hall makes culture matter to educational researchers and critics. For Giroux, Hall makes the political pedagogical, "recognizing that how we come to learn and what we learn is immanently tied to strategies of understanding, representation, and disruption" (p. 166). Hall, says Giroux, offers a way to think about basic questions of equity and the distribution of resources, but he highlights how our understandings of these processes are culturally mediated. This is the space of the pedagogical, the work of culture. Hall also offers a way to come into public debates around the role of culture, looking beyond reductive positions of both the left and the right. As Giroux argues, both the left and the right have been complicit in the marginalization of culture. Those on the left often dismiss culture as mere entertainment, inconsequential to the realities of *Realpolitik*, while those on the right often assume that culture is not political at all, but a transcendental repository of everything timeless and good. Hall offers a way to think between and beyond these positions, a way to engage with the complexities of cultural politics more broadly. This engagement with "the popular" as a contested, pedagogical realm resonates throughout much work in the cultural studies of education (Dimitriadis and Carlson, 2003).

In addition, Hall's careful attention to questions of identity, difference, and culture allows us sharper purchase on the lived realities of young people today. Hall's foreword to Daniel Yon's ethnography *Elusive Culture: Schooling, Race, and Identity in Global Times* underscores this issue. Here, Hall highlights the limits of traditional multicultural approaches to education that assume a notion of culture that is "unitary, essentialist and all encompassing" (p. x). Rather, a close look at the lives of contemporary youth—including their connections with multiple forms of popular culture—gives us a different perspective on questions of difference. We find "a richly textured, more complex and 'elusive' sense of how culture works and how identity is produced when neither is fixed or stable" (p. x). All these insights promise to put us, as educators, closer to the lived realities of youth.

Further Reading

By Hall

1964 (with P. Whannel). *The Popular Arts*. New York: Pantheon.

1973. *"Encoding and Decoding in the Media Discourse." *Stenciled Paper 7*, Birmingham: University Center for Cultural Studies.

1976 (ed., with T. Jefferson). *Resistance through Rituals: Youth Subcultures in Post-war Britain*. London: Hutchinson.

1980. *"Notes on Deconstructing the Popular." In J. Storey, ed., *Cultural Theory and Popular Culture*. Athens: University of Georgia Press.

1986. "The Problem of Ideology: Marxism without Guarantees." Reprinted in D. Morley and K. Chen, eds., *Stuart Hall: Critical Dialogues in Cultural Studies*. New York: Routledge, 1996.

1986. "On Postmodernism and Articulation: An Interview with Stuart Hall." *Journal of Communication Inquiry* 10 (2): 5–27.

1988. *The Hard Road to Renewal: Thatcherism and the Crisis of the Left*. London: Verso.

1989. *"New Ethnicities." Reprinted in D. Morley and K. Chen, eds., *Stuart Hall: Critical Dialogues*.

1992. *"What Is This 'Black' in Black Popular Culture?" Reprinted in D. Morley and K. Chen, eds., *Stuart Hall: Critical Dialogues*.

1992 (ed., with B. Gieben). *Formations of Modernity*. Cambridge: Polity Press.

1997 (ed.). *Representation: Cultural Representations and Signifying Practices*. Thousand Oaks, CA: Sage.

2000. Foreword. In D. Yon, *Elusive Culture*. New York: SUNY Press.

About Hall / Relevance for Education

Dimitriadis, G., and D. Carlson, eds. *Promises To Keep*. New York: Routledge, 2003.

Gilroy, P., L. Grossberg, and A. McRobbie. *Without Guarantees: In Honour of Stuart Hall*. London: Verso, 2000.

Giroux, H. "Stuart Hall and the Politics of Education." In his *Stealing Innocence*. New York: Palgrave, 2000.

*Morley, D., and K. Chen, eds. *Stuart Hall: Critical Dialogues in Cultural Studies*. New York: Routledge, 1996.

BELL HOOKS

Key Concepts

- black feminist theory
- white supremacist capitalist patriarchy
- systems of representation
- engaged pedagogy
- multicultural pedagogy
- spirituality in education

The cultural critic bell hooks was born Gloria Watkins in Hopkinsville, Kentucky, in 1952. She received degrees from Stanford University (B.A., 1973) and the University of Wisconsin (M.A., 1976) before earning her Ph.D. in English in 1983 from the University of California, Santa Cruz. Her dissertation was on the work of the novelist Toni Morrison. She taught at Yale University and Oberlin College before becoming a Distinguished Professor of English at City College, New York, a position she later left to work as a freelance scholar, teacher, and writer. The scope and range of hooks's work is breathtaking. She has published theoretical studies of race, gender, and (more recently) class, and volumes on film and art. She has also written several memoirs of her childhood as well as books for children. She is the author of two widely read books on education that have helped bridge the concerns of black feminist theory and critical pedagogy in important and influential ways.

The earliest book by hooks (who distinctively writes her name without capital letters) is a volume of history and criticism entitled *Ain't I a Woman: Black Women and Feminism*. In this text, hooks discussed ways in which the specific experiences and struggles of black women have been marginalized in both race and gender struggles. She maintained that struggles for civil rights have typically stressed the particular experiences of black men. Similarly, the feminist movement had been almost wholly concerned with the struggles of white women. Opening up critical space for **black feminist theory**, hooks argued that the experiences and struggles of black women need to be looked at closely. As a key exemplar, she presented the experiences of black women slaves as unique, though often assumed to be similar to those of black male slaves. She wrote: "We cannot form an accurate picture of the status of black women by simply focusing on racial hierarchies" (1981, p. 12).

In the ensuing decades, hooks would pursue this project with several volumes of criticism extending her theoretical interest in the specificity of black female experiences and struggles. They include her first systematic exploration of black feminist theory, *Feminist Theory: From Margin to Center* (1984/2000). Throughout, it calls attention to the ways in which racism, capitalism, and patriarchy have devalued the lives of marginalized people. She has continually stressed the dominating power of **white supremacist capitalist patriarchy**—the interlocking ways in which race, class, and gender work to oppress marginalized groups in the United States and around the world. In all her work, she addresses the specificities of oppression.

For hooks, these systems of oppression are bigger than any one person. If one is to move beyond these oppressive, dominating notions of power, one must look not only to acquire power but also to transform it. This was one of the big problems with the early liberal notions of feminism. Texts like Betty Friedan's *The Feminine Mystique* spoke to the needs and concerns of largely middle-class women—in particular, their needs for satisfying employment outside the home. For hooks, such liberal notions of power do not aim to transform systems; instead, these white women wish to take part in a system that promotes white supremacy and capitalism. According to hooks, "If more feminist women had actively reconceptualized power, they would not have, consciously or unconsciously, shaped feminist movement using the class and race hierarchies that exist in the larger society" (2000, p. 88).

Later in her career, hooks took up questions of representation, asking how popular **systems of representation** help reproduce oppression. In her books *Black Looks: Race and Representation* (1992) and *Outlaw Culture: Resisting Representations* (1994), hooks powerfully examined power and representation. The latter book moves across several different kinds of popular texts—for example, the work of Madonna, gangsta rap, and Spike Lee's film *Malcolm X*. In each case, she discusses how these texts, which are often produced by marginalized groups, work to reproduce dominant cultural imperatives—for example, gangsta rap both foregrounds the voices of marginalized young black men and plays into brutal notions of patriarchy. These notions of patriarchy, for hooks, are not unique to rap. They have historically been a part of dominant culture. She has also looked at the ways in which Lee's *Malcolm X* depoliticized the Nation of Islam's leader, making him into a palpable figure for dominant mainstream American culture. For hooks, the film is conservative both in its content and in the "epic" film narrative that structures it. She resists the impulse to give the film a "pass" simply because the director is African American.

In performing this kind of ideological critique of popular texts, hooks contributes to a powerful line of work in cultural studies and education. Often associated with Henry Giroux, this line has looked at how popular media "educates" young people through the proliferation of ideologically conservative messages. Drawing on the work of GRAMSCI and others, these critics highlight the ways in which "culture" itself is a "terrain of struggle" where dominant culture fights to gain the consent of the people. Here hooks's contribution has been important, particularly in explicitly connecting these concerns to a black feminist agenda.

Other important connections with the field of education are found in hooks's work. She is the author of two important books on education: *Teaching To Transgress* (1994) and *Teaching Community* (2004). Each of these evocative and important books draws together key constructs from feminist pedagogy and critical pedagogy (specifically, the work of Paulo FREIRE) to reflect on her own educational experiences while thinking about the future. In *Teaching To Transgress*, hooks discusses her experiences in all-black elementary and middle schools as well as her transition to more integrated higher education institutions. She remembers her segregated schools fondly overall, calling her teachers caring people with high expectations. She recalls her transition to integrated schools as more painful: teachers who did not care for her, painful experiences in the classroom, and a markedly lower set of expectations. In general, she discusses her experiences as profoundly alienating.

Both feminist pedagogy and critical pedagogy provided a way to envision a more engaged kind of pedagogy. As hooks recounts, feminist pedagogy was one of the first areas where she encountered real ongoing critique of education as a male-dominated endeavor. Education, here, was political—connected to the ongoing struggles of women to resist ongoing gender domination. This was one of the first places where there was effort to make education empowering, and to experiment with modes of teaching. Yet, as hooks points out, like much of mainstream feminism, feminist pedagogy did not always interrogate its own limitations. In particular, it tended to focus on the needs and concerns of white women.

Work in critical pedagogy, and more specifically the work of Freire, proved important for hooks. Freire provided a way for her to think about education as a liberatory experience, as a socially engaged practice. In his critique of the "banking model of education"—in which teachers simply deposit information into students' heads—he provided a way to envision a more engaged and critical kind of education. Freire encouraged hooks to think about education as "praxis" or reflective practice, which always reflects on its own grounds. In fact, *Teaching To Transgress* includes a self-reflexive interview that hooks conducts with herself around the work of Freire. She discusses the ways in which Freire's work spoke to her and revitalized her own critical consciousness as a transformative intellectual. Though aware of the sexist bias of much of his work, hooks recounts a profound connection with his transformative social vision, rooted in communion with the poor of Brazil.

Nevertheless, hooks is also self-conscious about the limitations of both these bodies of work. Feminist pedagogy tends to ignore questions of race, while critical pedagogy is often uncritically masculinist. She argues for an **engaged pedagogy**, a joyful engagement of the whole person in a collective, community context. Looking beyond "objective minds" for a union of mind, body, and spirit, the goal is self-actualization and meaningful knowledge. This is often a "risky pedagogy," one that is open to the full range of political and social experiences students bring into the classroom. Indeed, hooks takes us to dangerous terrain in *Teaching To Transgress*, including that of "eros." For hooks, acknowledging eros in teaching means acknowledging that the classroom is a space where passionate bodies come together. This kind of passion, for hooks, is systematically squeezed out of teachers today. It is part of a move to convince us, in her words, "that love has no place in the classroom" (p.198).

This is at the heart of **multicultural pedagogy** for hooks. A fully engaged multicultural pedagogy would take us beyond basic questions of exclusion and inclusion within the existing system. A multicultural pedagogy would aim to transform those systems through individuals engaged in passionate communion. As she writes, the "recognition of difference" associated with multiculturalism means "a willingness to see the classroom change," allowing "for shifts in relations between students" (p. 30). Schools should be fully engaged spaces that challenge teachers and students alike to enact new, more democratic kinds of communities.

In a more recent book on education, *Teaching Community: A Pedagogy of Hope*, hooks draws on her later educative and teaching experiences. Building on the concerns of *Teaching To Transgress*, hooks details her decision to leave a prestigious academic position and devote her time to writing, workshops, and public lectures. More specifically, she discusses her efforts to redefine her own intellectual life, moving away from the strictures of formal academic institutions. She sums up, "Being an intellectual is not the same as being an academic" (2004, p. 22).

This means teaching and lecturing in informal settings to academic as well as nonacademic communities. In *Teaching Community*, hooks describes the importance of translating our words and ideas into other kinds of pedagogical spaces. This is often a great challenge to educators who have been socialized to speak in highly specialized ways from within narrowly defined spaces that they wholly control. As hooks writes, we must "learn to use the language that can speak to the heart of the matter in whatever teaching setting we find ourselves" (p. 43).

These meditations on teaching unfold against hooks's own growing alienation from formal education institutions, as well as from a growing backlash against the gains of programs such as African American studies, ethnic studies, and women's studies. She details the important gains that these programs and departments made beginning in the 1960s and 1970s, opening up space to contest the white male hegemony over the professoriate. While claiming to extend these concerns, hooks argues that recent gains in the area often called "cultural studies" have placed much institutional power back in the hands of white men.

In *Teaching Community*, hooks offers a more expansive notion of what it means to be a socially and politically invested teacher. While revisiting many of the themes of her earlier work, she gives particular attention here to **spirituality in education**. Education systems tend to disconnect us further from the world, one another, and ourselves, but hooks emphasizes the importance of finding a spiritual wholeness that we can bring to pedagogical encounters. She discusses the models of such spiritual wholeness she finds in Buddhism.

The work of bell hooks has been extremely important for introducing the ideas of critical pedagogy to wider audiences. A recent book, *bell hooks' Engaged Pedagogy: A Transgressive Education for Critical Consciousness* (1998) by Namulundah Florence, details her work and her connections with critical pedagogy. Other work has stressed the ways her pedagogy is in broader dialogue with the concerns of black feminist thinkers and writers, including Audre Lorde and Nikki Giovanni (Williams, 1996). In addition, like Paulo Freire, she has had resonance in the field of composition studies (Olson, 1994) as well as antiracist education (Lucal, 1996).

Further Reading

By hooks

1981. *Ain't I a Woman: Black Women and Feminism*. Boston: South End.

1990. *Yearning: Race, Gender, and Cultural Politics*. Boston: South End.

1992. *Black Looks: Race and Representation*. Boston: South End.

1993. *Sisters of the Yam: Black Women and Self Recovery*. Boston: South End.

1994. *Teaching To Transgress: Education in the Practice of Freedom*. New York: Routledge.

1994. *Outlaw Culture: Resisting Representations*. New York: Routledge.

1996. *Reel to Reel: Race, Sex, and Class at the Movies*. New York: Routledge.

2000 [1984]. *Feminist Theory: From Margin to Center*. 2nd ed. Boston: South End.

2004. *Teaching Community: A Pedagogy of Hope*. New York: Routledge.

About hooks / Relevance for Education

Florence, N. *bell hooks' Engaged Pedagogy: A Transgressive Education for Critical Consciousness*. Westport, CT: Bergin and Garvey, 1998.

Lucal, B. "Oppression and Privilege: Towards a Relational Conceptualization of Race." *Teaching Sociology* 24 (1996): 245–255.

Olson, G. *Philosophy, Rhetoric, Literacy Criticism: (Inter)views*. Carbondale: Southern Illinois University Press, 1994.

Williams, S. "Black Feminist Thought: Implications for a Transformative Women's Education." *Thresholds in Education* 22 (1996): 37–41.

JACQUES LACAN

Key Concepts

- symbolic order
- unconscious
- imaginary order
- order of the real
- mirror stage
- splitting
- desire
- entry into language
- phallus
- suture

Jacques Marie Émile Lacan (1901–1981) was born in Paris to a Catholic family. He trained as a medical doctor at the Faculté de Médecine de Paris and went on to become a psychiatrist. Lacan worked extensively with patients suffering from what psychiatrists then called "automatism" or *délires à deux*. This condition leads people to believe that their speech or writing is governed by an unseen but omnipotent force beyond their control. Often coupled with severe personality disorders and a history of familial conflict, the symptoms of automatism resemble certain aspects of the cases then being studied by the nascent psychoanalytic movement in France. Lacan pursued this connection between psychiatric medicine and psychoanalysis in his thesis for the *doctorat d'état* in psychiatry, *De la psychose paranoïaque dans ses rapports avec la personnalité* (1932).

Throughout his career, Lacan's relationship with mainstream psychoanalysis in Europe was always conflictual. As a result, he resigned from the Société Psychoanalytique de Paris in 1953, the same year he gave his famous lecture "The Function and Field of

Speech and Language" at the annual meeting of the International Psychoanalytic Association. In that same year Lacan inaugurated a weekly seminar for kindred intellectuals, which he continued to hold almost until his death. This seminar was the primary venue for disseminating Lacan's work, and it attracted crowds of "students," including Julia Kristeva and Luce Irigaray. Most of Lacan's published essays were originally given as papers in this seminar.

Becoming increasingly alienated from classical psychoanalysis, Lacan founded the École Freudienne de Paris (EFP) in 1963, a school much more devoted to theory and science than to clinical work. Eventually the EFP fell apart, largely owing to the rise of a parallel but more clinically oriented organization called Confrontations, which René Major and Jacques DERRIDA helped found. Confrontations harnessed much of the dissent that had emerged in the French psychoanalytic community in response to Lacan's devotion to theoretical (rather than clinical) aspects of psychoanalysis. The clinical emphasis of Confrontations drew in those less inclined toward issues they viewed as hermetically theoretical or philosophical. In the process, many questions were raised about the democratic nature of the EFP. During this time, Lacan became increasingly ill with colon cancer. A letter that included Lacan's signature was issued announcing the dissolution of the EFP. Because it was believed that his signature had been forged, the matter made newspaper headlines everywhere. Many scholars, including Louis Althusser, denounced the whole affair. In 1981, long before things were resolved, Lacan died.

By the time of his death, Lacan was one the most prominent and most controversial intellectual figures in the world. For more than fifty years, he had blended extensive clinical practice with speculative theoretical argument. Through extended close readings of Sigmund FREUD and his own clinical practice, Lacan pushed the boundaries of psychoanalysis to include insights from philosophy, linguistics, literature, and even mathematics. His work had influenced (and continues to influence) theory and research in fields as diverse as neuroscience, psychology, communication studies, literature, film, feminist studies, philosophy, religious studies, and education.

Lacan's career is often divided into four periods. In the first period, roughly from 1926 to 1953, he focused largely on clinical work but incorporated many psychoanalytic concepts into more conventional psychiatric practice. His publications from this period consist mostly of brief case studies. Beginning in the late 1930s, however, he began publishing longer, more academic articles that focused on the importance of the mirror stage in the development of a child's sense of self during the first two years of life. The mirror stage is discussed in detail below, but in brief, Lacan argued that the child's emergent sense of self was always formed in reference to some "other": the child's own image in a mirror, a sibling or friend, or other alternative models with which the child associated herself according to what Freud had termed "narcissistic identification."

In the second period of Lacan's work, roughly from 1953 to 1963, he focused primarily on structural linguistics and the role of signification in the work of Freud. He argued that Freud had understood that human psychology is based in language but had failed to theorize this adequately. Based on Ferdinand de SAUSSURE's vocabulary and structuralist concept of language as a system of differences, Lacan set out to redefine and correct many of Freud's basic insights and concepts. He began to argue, for example, that the unconscious is structured not by biological imperatives but rather like language, and that the unconscious is thus governed by the symbolic order (see discussion below). During this second period, Lacan also translated much of Martin Heidegger's work into French, and this work influenced his own thought in significant ways.

In the third period of his work, roughly from 1963 to 1974, Lacan departed even further from Freud and traditional psychoanalysis. He developed a unique style of discourse that we might call "Lacanian," which embodies his own neologisms and complex diagrams. He developed a view of the ego as the site of neurosis instead of the site of psychic integration, and he argued yet more strongly for subjectivity as an effect of the symbolic order. He still claimed to be continuing Freud's work. This claim led to his further alienation from mainstream psychoanalysis and psychoanalysts.

In the final period of his career, Lacan worked to create more precise, mathematically based versions of psychology and psychoanalysis. Among other things, he reinterpreted his earlier constructs of the real, the imaginary, and the symbolic according to mathematical topology and "mathemes" rather than natural language, claiming that "La mathématisation seule atteint ý un reel" ("Mathematization alone reaches reality"). From 1974 on, his thinking became more convoluted and opaque, confusing even his most strident followers and raising more questions than ever about whether his ideas could be effectively translated into clinical practice.

For Lacan there are three orders that govern human consciousness and the unconscious: the real, the imaginary, and the symbolic orders. Because it has the greatest significance in Lacan's theories, we begin with the **symbolic order**. This is constituted by meanings and exchanges of meanings, especially linguistic meanings. The symbolic order constructs desires and feelings according to particular kinds of representations. It exists *before* the subject and orders the subject *completely* within its preexistent system. That is, it comes from "outside" the subject and is said to alienate it.

Focused on the formation of the subject and the role of the unconscious, Lacan's work constitutes a radical reinterpretation of Freud and psychoanalysis in light of structuralism (especially the structural linguistics of Saussure and the structural anthropology of Claude Lévi-Strauss). Dissenting from the common conception that the ego or conscious self is autonomous, sovereign, and biologically determined, Lacan theorized that it was formed within a preexisting symbolic order. Far from being autonomous and sovereign, the subject emerges as an effect of that order.

The **unconscious**, then, is not a biologically determined realm of libidinal drives; rather, it is formed in tandem with the formation of ego. It is a side effect of the ego's subjection within the symbolic order. It is created as the excess, the surplus of self that does not fit within the subject as it is formed by the symbolic order. Thus the unconscious reveals the fact that we as subjects are always more and other than our social selves allow. The unconscious reveals our "too-much-ness," the fact that we are split selves. Far from being an autonomous, sovereign agent in the world, then, the ego is an illusion, a symbolically constructed selfhood whose excesses, splits, and gaps are revealed by the eruptions of the unconscious into conscious life. Lacan developed this understanding of ego formation and the unconscious vis-à-vis the structural linguistics of Saussure. For Lacan, the birth of subjectivity is one's entry into language, understood as a synchronic system of signs and social codes that generate meaning—that is, a symbolic order. It is this symbolic order that locates one, forms one, "subjects" one, thereby enabling one to become an acting subject. Before Lacan, most psychoanalysts believed that the development of the ego as the seat of consciousness was a biological phenomenon. Lacan argued that it was a linguistic-symbolic development. Birth into language is birth into subjectivity. As he famously pronounced, "Man speaks, then, but it is because the symbol has made him man" (1977, p. 65). And later in the same essay he wrote:

Symbols in fact envelop the life of man in a network so total that they join together, before he comes into the world, those who are going to engender him "by flesh and blood"; so total that they bring to his birth, along with the gifts of the stars, if not with the gifts of the fairies, the shape of his destiny; so total that they give the words that will make him faithful or renegade, the law of the acts that will follow him right to the very place where he is not yet and even beyond his death; and so total that through them his end finds its meaning in the last judgment, where the Word absolves his being or condemns it. (1977, p. 68)

The subject emerges from its nonindividuated, prelinguistic state of being not into unmediated reality but into a culturally constructed world of symbols, a symbolic order. The subject is culturally constructed through language, but the subject does not recognize itself as such. Instead, it experiences (or rather imagines) itself to be real, independent of any symbolic order.

A crucial stage in a child's development, according to Lacan, is his or her entry into the **imaginary order**, which is closely related to the mirror stage (see below). The imaginary order originates in the pre-Oedipal phase of development and thus precedes the child's entry into the symbolic order. Yet the imaginary order continues to operate along with the symbolic order and in tension with the real throughout one's life. The imaginary is the order according to which the child becomes aware of himself as an "I," a subject, among other subjects. During this time, the child yearns to fuse with what he or she perceives to be "other." The child confuses others with his or her own image, as seen in a mirror or a photograph. The imaginary order is thus the basic matrix of self and other. Because the self is experienced as a composite of self and others, it is a divided self. Within the imaginary order, individuals create fantasy images of both themselves and their ideal objects of desire. We will return to the origins and functions of imaginary when we discuss the mirror stage.

Throughout the remainder of one's life, the imaginary order governs the human imagination, especially aspects of the imagination that have to do with the incipient ego and its identifications. The imaginary seems to embody prelinguistic structures to some extent, but this does not mean that it is necessarily more original or authentic than the symbolic order. In other words, the imaginary is not a necessary precondition for language and the eventual dominance of the symbolic. It is a different, parallel order.

In many ways, the **order of the real** is the most difficult and elusive of all three orders to explain, largely because it can be discussed only by using the tools of the symbolic order. Lacan used the term "real" to refer to what people believe is out "there," or what they believe exists in the state of nature apart from its constitution within sign systems and their ordering of things. Importantly, the real is not synonymous with external reality. Instead, it is what is real for the subject. The real is also experienced as foundational—present rather than re-presented through language or some other sign system. (Note the similarities here between Lacan's argument with respect to the real and Derrida's critique of a metaphysics of presence.) Except for a brief period during infancy, the human subject, constituted in and through the symbolic order, is radically alienated from the real, the state of nature. Only as babies are humans close to this state of nature, a state in which there is nothing but need. Babies need and seek to satisfy those needs with no sense of separation between themselves and the external world or the world of others.

The **mirror stage** (roughly between six and eighteen months) is a developmental stage in which the young child begins to identify with her or his own image (what Lacan called the "ideal I" or "ideal ego"). At some point during this period, before the child can speak or even walk, he or she sees his or her image in a mirror. As the child looks at this mirror image, then at a real person (usually the mother), then back at the mirror image, he or she moves "from insufficiency to anticipation." The child moves from experiencing self as a "fragmented body" to an "orthopedic vision of its totality," to an inchoate sense of being a whole, integrated person. Lacan used the term "orthopedic" to characterize the mirror stage because this stage serves as a temporary scaffold on the way to experiencing true wholeness through the entry into the symbolic order.

Put another way, the child recognizes the self as an "I" during the mirror stage—not fully symbolically but in a "felt" sense. This act marks the primordial recognition of one's self as an object, although a somewhat undifferentiated object. It thus involves a misrecognition (*méconnaissance*) because it is a recognition of the self as other, an objectification of the self in an image whose point of view and position are outside the self. More specifically, this creation of an ideal version of the self gives preverbal impetus to the creation of narcissistic fantasies in the fully developed subject. That fantasy image of oneself can be filled in by others whom one may want to emulate in one's adult life, such as role models or anyone else one sets up as a mirror for oneself. In this regard, the mirror stage, which inaugurates the imaginary, may be seen as "one of those crises of alienation around which the Lacanian subject is organized, since to know oneself through an external image is to be defined through self-alienation" (Silverman, 1983, p. 158). As the subject continues to develop and constitutes social relationships through language, others will become elaborated within social and linguistic frameworks, and the subject will begin to define himself or herself through the abstract system of language rather than through external objects (mirror image or others). Although the mirror stage inaugurates the imaginary order, this order continues throughout one's life, exerting its influence on the subject long after the subject has entered the symbolic order.

Like Michel **Foucault**, Lacan aimed to deconstruct the notion of the unitary subject and to replace it with an account of the self wherein the subject is fundamentally decentered from consciousness. More important than this philosophical starting point, however, was Lacan's use of semiotics. For Lacan, the individual and the social are co-constituted in and through signification and signifying practices. Not only is the subject split from a world where the self/other distinction does not operate, but this very **splitting** is rooted in signifying practices. Subjectivity is conceived as "a continuous ordering of the 'subject' in specific moments and according to specific discourses and modes of interpellation" (Smith, 1988, p. 71). Interpellation is a term coined by Althusser to explain the ways in which ideologies recruit or "hail" subjects to become complicit with them. For example, advertisements for luxury cars or discourses of the benefits of home ownership recruit subjects to middle class ideologies to which they often subscribe or become explicit, and thus become subjects of (in the double sense of subjected to and consenting to) these ideologies. According to Althusser, this is the way that ideologies function and why they are so powerful. We voluntarily consent to validity or apparent "naturalness" of the ideologies that surround us and thus subject ourselves to them. Foucault's notion of governmentality is quite similar in this regard. Both interpellation and governmentality are effective primarily because a key function of ideologies or discourses (in Foucault's lexicon) is to recruit complicity.

Paradoxically, it is in identifying with signifiers and discourses that alienation occurs and an individual's production proceeds. The individual's identification with and alienation from the processes of the social begins with his or her accession to the symbolic—the point when the individual identifies with his name and the various pronouns used to refer to him. "It is being named in the father-mother dialogue that from being zero the subject becomes a 'he' or a 'she', but it is also by being designated as son or daughter—Akeem or Chela—by the parental word. The name is the best illustration of the paradox of the generation of one from zero" (Lemaire, 1977, p. 70). And the alienation central to this paradox is reduplicated thereafter in the myriad forms of social inscription of the individual experiences (for example, as friend, lover, mother, academic). In a cryptic passage, Lacan elaborates on this general noncoincidence of the individual with herself, which is grounded in discourse:

> The register of the signifier is established because a signifier represents a subject for another signifier. It is the structure of all the formations of the unconscious and it also explains the primal division of the subject. Being produced in the place of the Other (the symbolic), the signifier causes the subject to arise there, but at the cost of being fixed. What was ready to speak there disappears, being no longer any more than a signifier. (Lacan, cited in Lemaire, 1977, p. 71)

It is the entry into discourse that is the precondition for becoming aware of oneself as a distinct entity within the bounds of preexisting social relations and cultural laws. Moreover, Lacan argued that this process simultaneously founds the unconscious. The unconscious is continuously constituted by the discursive events and practices experienced by individuals throughout their lives. In this regard, the unconscious mediates between the subject and the social. Subjectivity is articulated in relation to discourse. Since discourse is, by definition, social, Lacan was able to bypass a biological conception of unconscious processes and replace it with a discursive one.

Based on this claim, Lacan argued that the discursive constitution of the unconscious is implicit in the psychoanalytic method itself, the talking cure. Moreover, he emphasized the concurrent transformation of needs into wishes and desires in the founding of the unconscious, something that he claimed is also consistent with Freud. This is especially important because it replaces the notion of the unconscious as a site of seething drives and instincts with a notion of the unconscious as a chain of signifiers or verbal-ideological perspectives. Biological sex is replaced by discourses of gender (as well as race, class, ethnicity, and so forth). Implicit in this account is the co-constitutive nature of the relationships between the self and the social. As a discursive process, the unconscious embodies social and ideological signs rooted in meanings and practices designed to maintain and reproduce particular forms of social power relations. The opening and closing of the unconscious in the activity of lived experience conjoins two domains: the individual and the social order. It exists between them as their fault line or boundary. The genesis of subjectivity through discursive processes is the central theme of Lacanian psychoanalysis. It is during the discursive activity at the dynamic break between being and social meaning that subjectivity gets articulated. The unconscious is a kind of way station for discourse on its way to the subject. Importantly, however, it is not a place where meanings get negotiated, but where signifiers intersect, overlap, and disrupt one another, thus offering up possibilities for being that may be taken up, transformed, or resisted.

Perhaps even more important than all his other insights is the centrality Lacan ascribed to the activity of **desire**. In Lacan's developmental philosophical anthropology, the child's **entry into language** as a subject coincides with his or her separation from the mother. The mother, therefore, is the child's first experience of lack—absence—which creates the condition of desire. The father intervenes in the mother–child relationship at a moment coinciding with the child's entry into the symbolic order and loss of union with the mother. As the child becomes a subject within the symbolic order, the father is identified with that order which constitutes and governs subjectivity. For this reason, Lacan sometimes called the symbolic order *le Nom-du-Père* ("the Name of the Father"), which in French is pronounced the same as *le Non-du-Père* ("the No of the Father"), thus signifying godlike authority and prohibition. Thus the child is subjected in both senses of the word: subjected to the law of the symbolic order (identified with patriarchal law/No of the Father), and constituted as an acting subject in the world. But, according to Lacan's developmental philosophical anthropology, · the workings of desire are far less classically psychoanalytic and far more complex than this. Desire itself is caught up in the discourse of the unconscious, and it is articulated by the processes of metaphor and metonymy. Lacan's transformed version of the classic Freudian Oedipal problematic provides a good illustration of this articulation. Oedipal conflict marks the first link in the chain of signifiers that constitute the unconscious. Whereas Freud's account, based on having or not having a penis, quickly reduces to biological differences between men and women, Lacan focused on the *sign* of the difference: the **phallus**. For him this stands for the "signifier of signifieds," or the ultimate difference that fixes meaning in discourse, which is itself regulated through the systems of power through which society is ordered. While problems with this account remain, notably its patriarchal premises that cast women as other, it marks an advance over Freud. And even if we deny the validity of Lacan's "signifier of signifieds," his insistence that the process of Oedipal resolution and all subsequent resolutions of social conflict are discursively mediated within and at the boundary of the unconscious remains an important contribution to conceiving subjectivity as multiple, contradictory, and resistant.

Briefly, the period of development known as the Oedipal stage marks the first step in the disjunctive process, the splitting or distancing that is fundamental to human consciousness and that lays the foundation for desire. In Lacan's account, the child uses his or her first words to establish an imaginary control over the object that gives satisfaction: the mother, an object which is not always readily available. As words displace the original object, the first steps in the process of repression that forms the unconscious occur. The entry into language inaugurates subjectivity and its fundamental alienation from the social (in the first moment, and from the object of satisfaction), and needs are transformed into desires. A gap appears between the object of satisfaction and the desired object that parallels the non-coincidence of the individual with herself. A key dimension of this process is the importance of the emotional investments made by individuals in their recursive positionings in discourses and relationships. In essence, this is at the heart of the issue of identification and is driven by the discursive dynamics of desire. The phenomenon of Oedipus and the phenomenon of being multiply constructed in the discourse of the unconscious converge to *ensure* that a child becomes conscious both of his autonomy as a subject and his being constituted in and through a network of social relations.

At the same time that need is transformed into desire, another very important process is set in motion: identification. For Lacan, as for Freud, the child identifies with the same-sexed parent and shares with this parent the object of desire. This is the initiating moment of the problematic of identity, which is regarded as fundamental in the development or production of subjectivity. This moment is reduplicated in various ways when people identify with other individuals and discursive formations and desire the objects and forms of life associated with them. Lacan referred to this process as the "suture," using the term to refer to the occlusion of multiple and contradictory subject positionings in the unconscious and the imaginary positing of a coherent "I." Playing on the similarity of the French verbs *séparer* ("to separate"), *se parer* ("to adorn oneself"), and *parer* ("to parry"), Lacan argued that subjectivity simultaneously separates itself from its construction in the social, deflects the effects of the unconscious, and constructs an aura of unity and coherence for itself. In other words, subjectivity resists some of its production in discourses and social formations and adopts others, thereby construing itself as coherent in language. The "I" fills in the gaps between the multiple "mes" of the discourses of the social. The unconscious seals off and/or integrates the dispersal of subjectivity in myriad symbolic formations. This idea is remarkably like Nietzsche's philosophical anthropology with its notion of eternal recurrence, wherein subjectivity desires itself and its whole life to be repeated just as they are and attempts to blend itself into a coherent whole of actions, dispositions, power relations, and resistances. Coherence is possible through the power of the imagination over the symbolic, which takes the risk of essence in order to increase the substantive efficacy of resistance. By the "risk of essence," Lacan is referring to the fact that, although the self is multiple and fragmented and really has no essence because it is constantly being produced through discourse, it must imagine and claim an essence (even if such an essence is an overdetermination) if it is to have any political viability or effectivity. Within this dynamic double process, subjectivity is continually forged and immediately called it into question.

Lacan's accounts of the unconscious as the source of a fragmented or "pastiche" subjectivity and of its partial negation through suturing processes ensures a conception of the subject that allows for both continuity and contradiction, and therefore for resistance. The composition of the unconscious—as a network of discourses regulated by the processes of metaphor and metonymy and originating in the child's "accession to the symbolic"—functions to render subjectivity not as singular and coherent but as multiple subject positions whose arrangement discloses no necessary relations or logics. The multiple and contradictory nature of subjectivity is revealed in two ways. First, the act of identifying with various discourses objectifies subjectivity and therefore alienates the subject from itself. Second, the metaphorical and metonymic processes within the unconscious index multiple and contradictory subject positions available to the individual. This unsettling multiplicity is counteracted in acts of suturing. A constant dialogue results that both discloses and forecloses upon the imaginal construction of subjective coherence and unity. By prioritizing the workings of signifying practices and by playing off the multiple positioning of subjectivity in relation to discourse practices and the suturing that occludes such multiple positioning—a process based on desire, emotional investment, and identity—Lacan arrived at a complex, process-oriented account of subjectivity as multiple, contradictory, and resistant. Importantly, all these processes are grounded in the historical development of signifying practices rather than in the intentional activity of an agent or in the monolithic production processes of social and ideological formations. Indeed, the complexity and paradoxicality of Lacan's account of subjectivity seems to mark an advance over accounts that either prioritize the unitary and cohesive subject, posit subjectivity simply as the internalization of social and ideological formations (e.g., Althusser, 1971; Berger and Luckman, 1966), or negate the possibility of subjectivity by prioritizing signs over practices (e.g., Derrida, 1982). Although it is patently psychological, implicit in Lacan's account of subjectivity is a recognition of the co-constitution of the self and the social, the psychic and the political. To make explicit this coarticulation, and therefore to enhance the usefulness of Lacan's account, we need to rethink these internal psychic processes in relation to individuals' appropriation, resistance, and rejection of actual discursive and material formations in their life histories.

The nature and functions of the phallus are closely related to desire. One of the first childhood experiences of sexual difference for the male child, according to Lacan as well as Freud, is the recognition that the mother does not have a penis. But for Lacan, what is most important is not the physical penis but the symbolic significance of the penis, a significance he emphasizes by consistently using the term "phallus." First, it signifies sexual difference. Second, insofar as the father (identified with the symbolic order) has a penis and the mother (identified with the prelinguistic state of bliss before entry into the symbolic order) does not, the phallus signifies lack/absence within the symbolic order. For Lacan, the phallus comes to signify both women's and men's lack, dependence, and subjective vulnerability within the symbolic order. The father may be identified with the symbolic by the child, but the father, too, was once a child, subjected to the same law and always inadequate and incomplete in relation to it, never in full possession of it. No one possesses the phallus; all are castrated in this symbolic sense. In this regard, for Lacan, there is nothing essential or "natural" about sexual difference itself. Woman, man, femininity, and masculinity are symbolic constructions, formed arbitrarily by a repressive system of meaning that masquerades as the real.

As we mentioned earlier, the unconscious is formed at the same time as the subject/ego. It is an effect of the repression that takes place during subjection. Ego formation requires repression of whatever does not fit within the symbolic order—whatever exceeds it. The unconscious is "the censored chapter" in the history of psychic life (Lacan, 1977,

p. 50). It is an otherness within (or in Freudian terms, the *unheimlich*, "not being/feeling at home with") that remains, closeted in the home of selfhood—manifesting itself in and through language, often as interruption, misspeakings, slips of the tongue, forgetting names, and so on. When the unconscious intrudes in these ways, it threatens the integrity and wholeness of subject and her world, potentially revealing the self's illusory nature. In other words, the break-in of the unconscious within conscious existence reveals the fact that the subject is a tentative construction, by no means entirely stable, permanent, or whole. In Lacan's words, "the unconscious is that part of the concrete discourse ... that is not at the disposal of the subject in re-establishing the continuity of his conscious discourse" (1977, p. 49). It is a breaking in that may open one's consciousness to the possibility that the real is elsewhere, lost beyond one's grasp.

Though perhaps not as broad as one might expect, Lacan's influence on education has run deep. Among other things, it has helped educational sociologists understand the ways in which schools function—largely through practices of linguistic and material surveillance—to produce particular kinds of citizens and thus to reproduce systems of social and economic stratification. Lacan's work has also helped educators and educational researchers realize the fundamental role of relationships between selves and others in effective teaching-learning interactions, as well as the importance of dialogue in collectively constructing knowledge that is comprehensive and "effective" in Foucault's (1984) sense of this term. Related to these issues, Lacan's work reveals that teaching and learning are largely a matter of fulfilling our psychological needs. His ideas can thus help teachers to understand the importance of psychological and emotional dimensions in teaching and learning and to work against the traditional assumptions that posit these processes as primarily cognitive or intellectual. They can also help educators and educational researchers become more self-reflexive, realizing that their actions and orientations may function more to serve their psychological needs than to promote the interests of their students or research participants. The primary purpose of teaching and learning is to help all people involved lead personally fulfilling and socially productive lives. We can achieve this goal only if we understand the complexity of subjectivity and the role of language in the constitution of this complexity, and Lacan's work is a rich resource for developing such understanding.

Further Reading

By Lacan

1968. *The Language of the Self: The Function of Language in Psychoanalysis*, translated by Anthony Wilden. Baltimore: Johns Hopkins University Press.

1977. *Écrits: A Selection*, translated by A. Sheridan. New York: W. W. Norton.

1978. *Four Fundamental Concepts of Psychoanalysis*, translated by A. Sheridan. New York: W. W. Norton.

About Lacan

Evans, D. *Introductory Dictionary of Lacanian Psychoanalysis*. New York: Routledge, 1996.

Grosz, E. *Jacques Lacan: A Feminist Introduction*. New York: Routledge, 1990.

*Lemaire, A. *Jacques Lacan*, translated by D. Macey. London: Routledge & Kegan Paul, 1977.

Rabaté, J-M., ed. *The Cambridge Companion to Lacan*. Cambridge, UK: Cambridge Univesity Press, 2003.

Roustang, F. *Dire Mastery: Discipleship from Freud to Lacan*, translated by N. Lukacher. Baltimore: Johns Hopkins University Press, 1999.

Silverman, K. *The Subject of Semiotics*. Oxford: Oxford University Press, 1983.

Relevance for Education

Aoki, D. S. "The Thing Never Speaks for Itself: Lacan and the Pedagogical Politics of Clarity." *Harvard Educational Review* 70 (2000): 347–369.

Bracher, M. *The Writing Cure: Psychoanalysis, Composition, and the Aims of Education*. Carbondale: Southern Illinois Press, 1999.

Briton, D. "The Teaching Imaginary: Collective Identity in the Global Age." Paper presented at the Graduate Student Research Conference, Edmonton, Alberta, Canada, 1997.

Greene, M. "Toward Possibility: Expanding the Range of Literacy." Paper presented at Annual Meeting of the American Educational Research Association, San Francisco, CA, 1986.

Lather, P. "Drawing the Lines at Angels: Working the Ruins of Feminist Ethnography." *Qualitative Studies in Education* 10 (1997): 285–304.

Luykx, A. *The Citizen Factory: Schooling and Cultural Production in Bolivia*. Albany: State Univesity of New York Press, 1999.

Mowrey, D. "The Phrase of the Phallic Pheminine: Beyond the 'Nurturing Mother' in Feminist Composition Pedagogy." Paper presented at Annual Meeting of the Conference on College Composition and Communication, San Diego, CA, 1993.

Mullin, A. "Crossing Over: Individualism and Social Construction in the Writing Center." Paper presented at Annual Meeting of the Conference on College Composition and Communication, Milwaukee, WI, 1996.

Palermo, J. *Postructuralist Readings of the Pedagogical Encounter*. New York: Peter Lang, 2002.

Other Readings

Althusser, L. *Lenin and Philosophy*. New York: Monthly Review Press, 1971.

Berger, P., and T. Luckmann. *The Social Construction of Reality: A Treatise in the Sociology of Knowledge*. New York: Doubleday, 1966.

Derrida, J. *Margins of Philosophy*, translated by A. Bass. Chicago: University of Chicago Press, 1982.

Foucault, M. "Truth and Power." In P. Rabinow, ed., *The Foucault Reader*. New York: Pantheon, 1984.

JEAN PIAGET

Key Concepts

- constructivism
- genetic epistemology
- assimilation
- accommodation
- developmental stages
- relations between thought and speech

Born in Neuchâtel, Switzerland, Jean Piaget (1896–1980) was a developmental psychologist, best known for his structuralist theory of cognitive development, in which development is organized into a series of sequential and invariant stages. His father, Arthur Piaget, was a professor of medieval literature with an interest in local history. His mother, Rebecca Jackson, was intelligent and energetic. Their first-born child, Piaget was independent and took an early interest in nature, especially collecting seashells. He published his first "paper" when he was ten, a one-page account of his sighting of an albino sparrow.

During high school, Piaget got a part-time job working for the director of Neuchâtel's Museum of Natural History. While working there, he published several papers on mollusks. His excellent work on mollusks became well known among European biologists, who assumed that Piaget was an adult. Later in adolescence, Piaget turned to more philosophical and psychological subjects. Encouraged by his mother to receive religious instruction, he found religious arguments puerile, but he became very interested in philosophy, especially logic. He blended this with his interest in science and began searching for biological explanations of cognition. Frustrated because the tools of philosophy were not helping him in this effort, Piaget began studying psychology.

After high school, Piaget attended the University of Neuchâtel. While studying and writing, he decided to develop a philosophy/biology of life and life forms, the centerpiece of which was the idea that all forms of life (organic, mental, and social) are organized as "totalities" that are greater than the sum of their parts, and that these totalities impose the organizing structure of the parts. This basic principle would guide almost all his future theory building, and it has served as the foundation for many other structuralist models, from gestalt psychology to various kinds of systems theory.

In 1918, Piaget received his doctorate in science from the University of Neuchâtel. He worked for a year at psychology laboratories in Zürich and at Eugen Bleuler's famous psychiatric clinic. During this period, he read the works of Sigmund FREUD, Carl Jung, and other psychoanalysts. In 1919, he got a job teaching psychology and philosophy at the Sorbonne in Paris, where he met Alfred Binet (co-inventor of the Simon-Binet Intelligence Quotient, or IQ) and began work on intelligence testing. He quickly lost interest in whether children generated right responses to test questions and became intrigued by their mistakes and their spontaneous talk about how to answer certain questions. Using his knowledge of psychiatric interviewing techniques, Piaget began asking participants questions about their reasoning. Over time, he developed an interviewing technique for probing reasoning and cognitive development, known as the Piagetian clinical interview.

In 1921, Piaget published his first article on the psychology of intelligence in the *Journal de Psychologie*. In the same year, he accepted a position at the Institut J. J. Rousseau in Geneva. Two years later he married Valentine Châtenay. They had a daughter in 1925, another in 1927, and a son in 1931. Both Jean and Valentine Piaget engaged in observing their children's behavior intensely, and Jean Piaget wrote about this work in several books, including *Language and Thought of the Child*. While at the Institut, Piaget also began studying the reasoning of elementary school children, and his research was published in five books on child psychology. Although he considered this work tentative and speculative, it met with strong public and scientific approval.

In 1929, Piaget began work as the director of the Bureau International Office de l'Education (BIE), in collaboration with UNESCO. The BIE was founded in 1925. Beginning in 1934, the BIE organized the International Conference on Public Eductation (now known as the International Conference on Education). From 1946 until the present day, this conference was convened together with UNESCO. In 1969, the BIE became an integral part of UNESCO, though it enjoys intellectual and functional autonomy from this organization.

Also, in 1929, Piaget became a professor of child psychology at the University of Geneva, a position he held for the rest of his life despite concurrently holding many other academic and public service positions. At the University of Geneva, Piaget began large-scale research with Bärbel Inhelder and several other psychologists. Over the years, Inhelder became his closest collaborator. (It is worth noting that Piaget was particularly committed to welcoming women into the field of experimental psychology and supporting their development.)

Piaget also worked as professor of psychology at the University of Lausanne from 1937 through 1954. In 1940, he became chairman of experimental psychology and president of the Swiss Society of Psychology. In 1942, during the Nazi occupation of France, he gave a series of lectures at the Collège de France, later published as *The Psychology of Intelligence*. At the end of the war, Piaget was named president of the Swiss Commission of UNESCO. In 1949 and 1950, he published a synthesis of his life's work, *Introduction to Genetic Epistemology*.

In 1952, Piaget became a professor at the Sorbonne, and in 1955, he created the International Center for Genetic Epistemology, where he served as director the rest of his life. A year later, he created the School of Sciences at the University of Geneva. He continued working until his death, largely at refining his theories of cognitive development based on emerging findings from biological and psychological research and theory building. He also remained a tireless public servant, largely as the Swiss delegate to UNESCO. By the end of his career, Piaget had written more than sixty books and several hundred articles. He died in Geneva, one of the most significant psychologists of the twentieth century.

Reacting to a long legacy dominated by behaviorist learning theories, Piaget proposed a dynamic, cognitive model of learning, now called **constructivism**, wherein learning is conceived to be a holistic, "bottom-up" process enacted by an active learner. In contrast to behaviorist learning theories, he proposed several new and radical themes: the individual learner is an active constructor of knowledge; developmental processes must precede learning through instruction; and language is an epiphenomenon of thought and not constitutive of thought. He called his theoretical orientation to the study of cognitive development "**genetic epistemology**." He noted, for example, that even infants seem to possess knowledge and skills in relation to objects in their world, and that this knowledge and these skills seem to get reorganized over time and as a function of experience. Piaget called the knowledge and skills possessed by individuals "schemas" (alternate plural, "schemata"), and he explained how they get reorganized with the concepts of assimilation, accommodation disequilibrium, and equilibrium, all of which are discussed below.

Piaget grounded his developmental learning theory in the individual learner and positioned children as active, intelligent, creative constructors of their own knowledge structures. The term often used to refer to this process is "psychogenesis," which is the idea that intellectual growth is most influenced by learner's own personal intellectual activities (Goodman, 1990). In essence, then, Piaget claimed that children learn primarily through their own actions on external objects of knowledge and construct their own categories of thought while they attempt to organize the world around them. Children are not only learning subjects but also knowing subjects, in that they are always acquiring new knowledge and skills as they constantly take in information and actively try to integrate that information into increasingly complex, coherent, and complete frameworks for understanding. This search for coherence drives children's propensity to build interpretive systems. These systems develop, according to Piaget, in ontogenetically ordered ways. Thus, the knowledge systems and structures children construct usually differ (both qualitatively and quantitatively) from those with which adults typically operate.

To eventually arrive at adult-like forms of understanding—or, in Piagetian terms, objective knowledge—children actively proceed through a spiral of stages in which they develop different hypotheses based on their experience and integrate these hypotheses into different naive theories for understanding and explaining the world around them. As they actively explore linguistic, mathematical, and scientific concepts, for example, children search for regularities and test their predictions and hypotheses about what they are exploring. In the process, they construct and reconstruct the nature and functions of these knowledge domains for themselves. Piaget's theory differs from behaviorist approaches in that it proposes that stimuli from the world do not simply act directly on children, molding them to think and act in specific ways. Instead, children's epistemologies about the world are continually transformed as they act in and on the world and reflect on the nature and effects of their actions.

Although this process all takes place within a social world, Piaget did not emphasize the influence of social input, but instead focused on the actions and reflections of the individual learner. In this regard, he posited that learning first occurs on an intrapsychological plane, with children's thinking at the center of things. Only later do development and learning become interpsychological, as children share their knowledge with others and negotiate conventional, adult-like forms of understanding. This position stands in sharp contrast to Lev VYGOTSKY's understanding of the role of social experiences in the development of individual knowledge.

For Piaget, learning occurs primarily through self-regulation. It involves a series of active constructions and adjustments on the part of the child in response to external perturbances. These constructions and adjustments are both retroactive (loop systems or feedbacks) and anticipatory. Together they form a permanent system of compensations, always seeking equilibrium. The compensations are accounted for primarily by assimilation and accommodation. **Assimilation** is a matter of making a new object or experience fit into an old schema. **Accommodation** is a matter of making an old schema fit a new object. Together, assimilation and accommodation account for children's continual adaptation to the world around them, which most people call "learning." Adaptation is typically motivated by the experience of disequilibrium, the uncomfortable sense that one's experience is at odds with one's capacity to understand and explain it. When individuals experience disequilibrium (for whatever reason), they engage in the dual processes of assimilation and accommodation until they reach a new state of equilibrium where they feel that they have developed good (or good enough) naive theories of experience and the world.

As already noted, children learn by developing, testing, and refining hypotheses and theories about the world. Even though Piaget claimed that children are active participants in the creation of knowledge, he also claimed that they progress through distinct **developmental stages**, each with its own specific kinds of knowledge and ways of organizing that knowledge, as well as specific behavioral characteristics. These stages include the sensorimotor stage, the preoperational stage, the concrete operational stage, and the formal operational stage. The first, the sensorimotor stage, occurs roughly between the birth and two years of age. During this stage, children explore things that can be seen, felt, and touched through their senses. This exploration helps them develop both gross and fine motor skills. Their knowledge during this stage is largely immediate, sensory, and concrete. Toward the end of this stage, children are able to develop stable and lasting mental representations and to engage in pretend play. They are also able to combine related mental acts such as putting down a toy to open a door or drink from a bottle.

The next stage, the preoperational, occurs roughly between the ages of two and seven years. During this stage, children's thinking is self-centered: they have difficulty taking the perspective of others or understanding transformations. Their thinking is more intuitive and concrete than logical and abstract. One of the best-known examples of preoperational children's centrism is their inability to imagine what an object looks like from another person's perspective. Another is their inability mentally to conserve liquid or volume. For example, if a child is shown a tall, narrow glass filled with milk and a short, stout glass filled with milk, she will insist that the tall, narrow glass holds more milk, even when the milk from the short, stout glass is transferred to the tall glass and overflows it.

Despite this centrism, preoperational children become adept at symbolic thinking, or thinking with and through symbols. They understand, for example, that a drawing of a dog or the written word "dog" represents or stands for a real dog. They also become adept at creative or symbolic play, such as using jar tops to represent plates or a cardboard box to represent a table. Along with being able to think symbolically comes an understanding of time: past, present, and future. For example, while a child in the sensorimotor stage might be inconsolable in the absence of her mother, a child in the preoperational stage may be consoled by being told her mother will return soon.

The third stage, concrete operations, occurs roughly between the ages of seven and eleven years. During this stage, children begin to understand numbers, space, and classification. They also begin to apply logical operations to concrete problems. "Concrete" is the key term here. Children are quite skilled at thinking logically, but only in the context of specific, concrete situations. They have difficulty thinking abstractly and forming generalizations based on particular experiences. Children also become able to conserve number, length, and liquid volume in this stage—to think through the fact that numbers of objects, lengths of objects, or volumes of liquids remain the same despite changes in appearance (for example, a particular number or marble is divided into three sets, or milk is poured from a tall, narrow glass into a short, stout one). They also develop the concept of reversibility during the concrete operations stage. "Reversibility" refers to such facts as that a ball of clay can be rolled out into a long cylinder or even broken up into five smaller balls and then rolled back into a ball of the original look, shape, and size. Children also learn classification and seriation in this stage. "Classification" refers to the ability to sort objects by features such as color, shape, and so on, and to make judgments such as whether there are more black squares than white squares in an array of black and white squares. "Seriation" refers to the ability to arrange objects in order and according to particular characteristics like size (from smallest to largest).

The final stage, formal operations, occurs roughly between the ages of eleven and fifteen years. During this stage, children develop the ability to view problems from multiple perspectives, to think abstractly, to form and test hypotheses intentionally, to generalize from the particular to the abstract, to engage in logical (deductive) reasoning, and to develop ideals. They can also solve abstract problems like syllogisms without getting caught up in the concrete specifics of the language used to express them. This is often called "hypothetical thinking," thinking *about* systems of knowledge and not just with and within those systems. Finally, children in the formal operations stage can engage in logical operations in the abstract. They understand, for example, the meanings of concepts such as conjunction, disjunction, implication, negation, reciprocity, and correlativity. Moreover, they can use their understanding of these concepts in problem-solving activities.

Although Piaget posited that these four stages are sequentially invariant, he also acknowledged that the ages when children pass through different stages are approximate, and that children sometimes move back and forth between stages during transitional developmental periods, a process he called "décalage." Along the path to learning, children make predictions and hypotheses that do not coincide with conventional knowledge. From a developmental perspective, these systematic errors are not viewed negatively but as approximations or constructive errors that reveal the knowledge systems that children have developed for making sense out of their world, and as potential sites of knowledge transformation. According to Piaget, to understand how children think, we must hear their words, follow their explanations, understand their frustrations, and listen to their logic, which again highlights the centrality of the learner within the learning process. As noted above, to make children's unconventional ways of thinking salient, Piaget used a particular form of questioning, the clinical interview. These questions facilitate dialogic interactions that expose children's thinking patterns. They also reveal conflicts and contradictions children encounter, and how children work out these conflicts and contradictions to develop new ways of thinking that increasingly approximate adult-like ways.

Because Piaget relied heavily on individual construction of knowledge in his theory, he privileged development over learning in the sense of change through instructional scaffolding. He posited that children's development will occur with or without instruction. Additionally, children must be developmentally "ready" for any form of instruction to be effective. In other words, development always runs ahead of learning, an idea that Vygotsky later turned on its head.

The **relations between thought and speech** in Piaget's theory of development are important. In the early stages of development, thought and language are not related, or at least not in theoretically important ways. More specifically, Piaget argued that language does not facilitate cognitive development. Cognition can develop normally without language acting as a mediational means. Additionally, he thought that although language is instrumental in sharing of knowledge, it is not a source of knowledge. Instead, for Piaget, thought development precedes language development. Language is simply a reflection of the thought. This claim seems rooted in Piaget's insistence that the individual learner is a little scientist, constantly constructing and reconstructing theories about the world and how it works. This perspective is controversial and was strongly opposed by Vygotsky and his followers.

Piaget also theorized changes in the relations between language and thought across developmental stages. He posited, for example, that children under six years of age are incapable of logical and inferential thought and speech. Rather, they possess illogical thought and egocentric speech because they are unable to decenter and consider another person's point of view. Egocentric speech is situated between autistic thought, which is individual, and directed thought, which is social. During the period when children's speech is egocentric, their thinking is syncretic. Syncretic thinking is concrete and functional rather than abstract and logical. When their thinking is syncretic, children absorb the gist of communicated messages and assimilate them into existing schemas, often confusing the meanings and logical flow of the messages. Therefore, children may make incorrect assumptions about message meanings, which may affect their verbal understanding. However, this does not seem to bother children most of the time. They seem perfectly happy with the ways in which they interpret the messages. They also seem unaware that their perspectives differ from those of other people. Whether correct or incorrect, Piaget's assumptions about the relations between children's thought and language fit with his general theory of development as an active constructive process within the minds of individuals, relatively independent of social and semiotic mediation.

As time goes on, children begin to focus less on their own idio-syncratic experiences and turn their attention more to the social world and the conventional meanings and theories that constitute that world. This shift is characterized by corresponding changes of children's thinking and language use. Children's language progresses from egocentric speech, with no communicative self-regulatory functions, to social speech, which is used primarily to communicate and negotiate understandings with others. From Piaget's perspective, until children's thought and language have developed sufficiently, communication and meaningful, intentional interactions cannot occur, because children are egocentrically focused on their own thoughts, speech, and related meanings, rather than on their communicative partners and the sometimes different ways in which these partners have constructed the world. For example, while playing side by side, two young children may voice their thoughts and opinions to each other, but neither will be actively listening or processing the other's speech because they are intently focused on their own actions and thoughts. Only later will the ideas and utterances of others be incorporated into children's active construction of knowledge and meaning. From this perspective, socialization and teaching is effective only after children have moved beyond syncretic thought and egocentric speech.

Piaget worked in education himself, exploring the implications of his theory for many aspects of intelligence, cognitive development, and moral reasoning, with most of his research focused on the development of mathematical and logical concepts. Besides his own contributions to educational theory and research, Piaget's work has made significant and long-lasting contributions to education. Indeed, much educational research and many educational innovations of the 1970s and 1980s were a direct result of the appropriation and use of Piagetian theories. These included the development of child-centered and discovery pedagogies based on Piaget's view of the child as an active constructive learner, the strategic use of cognitive conflict in delivering instruction based on his notions of assimilation and accommodation, and the development of readiness models and related pedagogies based on his stage theory of development.

To conclude, Piaget's theories of cognitive development effectively cornered the market in educational theory, research, and practice during the 1960s and 1970s, and they continue to make significant and powerful contributions to the work of educational researchers, teachers, and developmental psychologists alike. Indeed, Piaget's cognitive developmental theories are still probably better known in these professional domains than those of any other theorist, though Piaget's prominence is waning in the wake of the uptake of Vygotskian and neo-Vygotskian theories.

Further Reading

By Piaget

1929. *The Child's Conception of the World*, translated by J. & A. Tomlinson. New York: Harcourt, Brace, Jovanovich.

1932. *The Moral Judgment of the Child*, translated by M. Gabain. New York: Harcourt, Brace, Jovanovich.

1959. *The Language and Thought of the Child*. 3rd ed., translated by M. & R. Gabain. London: Routledge & Kegan Paul.

1967. *Six Psychological Studies*, translated by A. Tenzer, translation edited by D. Elkind. New York: Random House.

1969. *The Mechanisms of Perception*, translated by G. M. Seagrim. London: Routledge & Kegan Paul.

1969 [with B. Inhelder]. *The Psychology of the Child*, translated by H. Weaver. New York: Basic Books.

1970. *The Science of Education and the Psychology of the Child*, translated by D. Coltman. New York: Grossman.

1973 [with B. Inhelder]. *Memory and Intelligence*, translated by A. J. Pomeranz. New York: Basic Books.

About Piaget

Brainerd, C. *Piaget's Theory of Intelligence*. Englewood Cliffs, NJ: Prentice-Hall, 1978.

*Flavell, J. H. *The Developmental Psychology of Jean Piaget*. New York: Van Nostrand Reinhold, 1963.

Gallagher, J. M., and D. K. Reid. *The Learning Theory of Piaget and Inhelder*. Monterey, CA: Brooks/Cole, 1981.

*Opper, S., H. P. Ginsberg, and S. O. Brandt. *Piaget's Theory of Intellectual Development*. 3rd ed. Englewood Cliffs, NJ: Prentice-Hall, 1987.

Relevance for Education

Bissex, G. *GNYS AT WRK: A Child Learns How To Read and Write*. Cambridge, MA: Harvard University Press, 1980.

Brooks, J. G., and M. G. Brooks. *In Search of Understanding: The Case for Constructivist Classrooms*. Alexandria, VA: Association for Supervision and Curriculum Development, 1992.

Bybee, R. W., and R. B. Sund. *Piaget for Educators*. 2nd ed. Columbus, OH: Charles Merrill, 1982.

Ferreiro, E., and A. Teberosky. *Literacy before Schooling*. Portsmouth, NH: Heinemann, 1982.

Goodman, Y. M. *Print Awareness in Preschool Children: A Study of the Development of Literacy in Preschool Children*. Tucson: University of Arizona, Arizona Center for Research and Development, 1981.

Goodman, Y. M., ed. *How Children Construct Literacy: Piagetian Perspectives*. Newark, DE: International Reading Association, 1990.

Scribner, S., and M. Cole. *The Psychology of Literacy*. Cambridge, MA: Harvard University Press, 1981.

Siegler, R. S. *Children's Thinking*. 2nd ed. Englewood Cliffs, NJ: Prentice-Hall, 1991.

Wadsworth, B. *Piaget for the Classroom Teacher*. New York: Longman, 1978.

EDWARD W. SAID

Key Concepts

- postcolonial criticism
- colonial discourse
- Orientalism
- imperialism
- contrapuntal reading

Edward W. Said (1935–2003) was a postcolonial literary critic and the Parr Professor of English and Comparative Literature at Columbia University. He was born in Jerusalem; his Palestinian family became refugees in 1948 and moved to Egypt, where Said attended British schools. He also spent time during his youth in Lebanon and Jordan before immigrating to the United States. He earned his B.A. from Princeton University in 1957 and his Ph.D. in literature from Harvard University in 1964. He spent his entire academic career as a professor of English and comparative literature at Columbia University.

Said's work includes both intellectual and political pursuits. On the one hand, he is well known for his engagement with literary criticism and postcolonial theory, often drawing from theoretical perspectives and methods developed by Michel FOUCAULT. On the other hand, he was politically active as an advocate of Palestinian independence and human rights. Critical of U.S. foreign policy, especially in the Middle East, he also spoke out against corruption within Palestine.

Said's intellectual and political agendas address the ways in which white Europeans and North Americans fail to understand—or even to try to understand—differences between Western culture and non-Western cultures. His **postcolonial criticism** is particularly concerned with issues of discourse and representation in relation to the history of Western colonialism. Said asked questions about how colonized cultures are represented, about the power of these representations to shape and control other cultures, and about **colonial discourse**— that is, the discourse through which colonizer and colonized subject positions are constructed.

Following Foucault, Said understood discourse as systems of linguistic usage and codes—discursive formations, whether written or spoken—that produce knowledge and practice about particular conceptual fields, demarcating what can be known, said, or enacted in relation to this body of knowledge. For example, medical discourse establishes knowledge about such things as the hierarchical nature of the doctor/patient relationship, the identification and classification of diseases, and the distinction between physical and mental illness. It is through different discourses that we know about and categorize the world. For Foucault, there are significant ramifications to the discursive process. In any cultural setting, there are dominant groups that establish what can and cannot be said and done by others on the basis of the discursive knowledge they impose on others—the dominated. In the end, both dominant and dominated are made into subjects of this knowledge and live within the parameters that the discursive knowledge allows. This knowledge attains the status or appearance of an independent reality, and its origins as a social construction are forgotten. Discursive knowledge is invariably connected to power. Those in control of a particular discourse have control over what can be known, and hence power over others.

Discourse, as a form of knowledge that exerts power, is of particular importance in Said's articulation of the nature of **Orientalism**, Western discourse about the East that engenders the oppressor/oppressed relationship pertaining between colonizer and colonized (see especially *Orientalism* and *Culture and Imperialism*). Said focused on the ways in which discursive formations about the "Orient" exert power and control over those subjected to them. For Said, the concept of Orientalism has three dimensions: the discursive, the academic, and the imaginative. All three, though, are interconnected and should be understood as such. The *discursive* concerns the notion that "Orientalism can be discussed and analyzed as the corporate institution for dealing with the Orient—dealing with it by making statements about it, authorizing views of it, describing it, by teaching it, settling it, ruling over it: in short, Orientalism as a Western style for dominating, restructuring, and having authority over the Orient" (1978, p. 3). The *academic* refers to "[a]nyone who teaches, writes about, or researches the Orient—and this applies whether the person is an anthropologist, sociologist, historian, or philologist—either in its specific or its general aspects, is an Orientalist, and what he or she does is Orientalism" (1978, p. 2). Finally, the *imaginative* refers to the idea that "Orientalism is a style of thought based upon an ontological and epistemological distinction made between 'the Orient' and (most of the time) 'the Occident'" (1978, p. 2). Said referred to this culturally constructed space as an "imaginative geography" (1978, p. 54).

Orientalism (1978), Said's groundbreaking study that explores the intellectual history of European (particularly British and French) representations of the Arab Middle East, is an early example of postcolonial criticism. Indeed, Said's work on Orientalism cannot be understood without framing it within the larger concept of postcolonialism and the postcolonial theory that examines it. Postcolonial theory and criticism, which became prominent in the 1990s, are concerned with analyzing the relationship between culture and colonial power and exploring the cultural products of societies that were once under colonial rule. Postcolonial Indian and African literature, for instance, addresses such issues as the lingering effects of colonialism on identity, nationality, and the nature of resistance to colonial power.

One goal of postcolonial theory is to question universal humanist claims that cultural products can contain timeless and culturally transcendent ideas and values. When, for instance, colonizing nations make universal claims—claiming to make judgments on the basis of some universal standard—the colonized, other culture is by default seen as tentative and provisional. These other cultures are somehow "less than" the colonial power. Victorian British literature often claimed to represent the universal human condition. In so doing, it depicted Indian culture, whether consciously or unconsciously, as misrepresenting the truth or reality discoverable in the world by those with the ability to do so. Postcolonial theory refutes this universalizing impulse and instead seeks to give voice to local practices, ideas, and values. Eurocentrism, which places Europe at the center and relegates non-European culture to the margins, is seen as a hegemonic characteristic that must be resisted. A problematic side effect of colonialism is that in a postcolonial culture a people have to locate strategies for reclaiming their cultural past and prizing its value.

The nature of colonial discourse and the ways in which it was used to wield power and control over the colonized are therefore central to Said's thesis in *Orientalism*. This volume explicates ways in which Western colonizers constructed the colonized as "other." Ways in which colonizers represented the colonized also created a social hierarchy and hegemonic power over the colonized. Said's analysis focuses especially on the Middle East as "Orient," but his thesis can be extended to other cultural contexts where colonization occurred (and is still occurring).

Said critiqued Eurocentric universalism for its setting up a binary opposition of the superiority of Western cultures and the inferiority of colonized, non-Western cultures. Said identified this perspective as a central aspect of Orientalism. This view sees the Middle East—and by extension, Africa and South, Southeast, and East Asia—as the "Orient," an "other" inferior to Western culture. Said pointed out that Orientalist discourse has the pernicious effect of treating the colonized as if they were all the same. Thus, "Orientals" are perceived not as freely choosing, autonomous individuals, but rather as homogeneous, faceless people who are known by their commonality of values, emotions, and personality traits. They are, in effect, essentialized to a few stereotypical, often negative characteristics and rendered as lacking individual personalities. A strong racist tendency is also operating in such views. Said provided numerous accounts of colonial administrators and travelers who described and represented Arabs in dehumanizing ways. After citing one such example, he remarked: "In such statements as these, we note immediately that 'the Arab' or 'Arabs' have an aura of apartness, definiteness, and collective self-consistency such as to wipe out any traces of individual Arabs with narratable life histories" (1978, p. 229).

Orientalist discourse, wrote Said, makes possible "the enormous systematic discipline by which European culture was able to manage—and even produce—the Orient politically, sociologically, militarily, ideologically, scientifically, and imaginatively during the post-Enlightenment period" (1978, p. 3). Said is less interested in refuting some notion that this discourse is "true" in some essential, transcendent way than in marking out the ground on which colonial discourse acted on the objects of its knowledge claims. He asserted: "The Orient was almost a European invention, and had been since antiquity a place of romance, exotic beings, haunting memories and landscapes, remarkable experiences" (1978, p. 1). For Said, the issue is not whether this European representation is true, but rather its effects in the world.

If colonial discourse oppressed the colonized subject, it also worked its effects on those who wielded this language in the first place. Orientalism delineates a relationship between "Europe" and the "Orient." For instance, the concept of "the Orient has helped to define Europe (or the West) as its contrasting image, idea, personality, experience" (1978, pp. 1–2). Thus, European identity is framed in terms of what it is—or, more likely, is not—in relation to a constructed "Orient." Concepts of the Orient also create a self-identity for Europe. "Europe" is as much a fiction as is the Orient, if by "Europe" we mean some homogeneous entity that is known by a set of essential "European" characteristics.

In a later study, *Culture and Imperialism* (1993), Said drew a distinction between **imperialism** and colonialism. For Said, "'imperialism' means the practice, the theory, and the attitudes of a dominating metropolitan center ruling a distant territory; 'colonialism,' which is almost always a consequence of imperialism, is the implanting of settlements on distant territory" (1993, p. 9). Imperialism is embedded in colonial discourse and serves as an important tool for creating the colonized subject. Said argued that any discourse that comments on a colonized culture cannot remain neutral or stand outside of a consideration of imperialism, because all such discourses are invested in how the view of the other is constructed. One need only consult the literature, history, and other cultural products of a colonizing nation that are directed at the colonized to find the colonized equated with the "other."

The history of colonialism and Orientalism is deeply entangled with the history of religion in the West, and Said has been extremely important to efforts to draw attention to this fact within the field of religious studies. How might one tease out from a religious text those aspects of colonial discourse that may be embedded therein? Said's notion of **contrapuntal reading** is particularly suggestive. Borrowing the concept of counterpoint from music, Said (who also wrote on music) described a strategy for reading that exposes the colonial discourses hidden within a text. Contrapuntal reading not only unveils the colonial perspective, but it also tries to read for nuances of resistance ("counterpoints") that may also be lurking within the narrative. Said argues that we need to "read the great canonical texts, and perhaps the entire archive of modern and pre-modern European and American culture, with an effort to draw out, extend, give emphasis and voice to what is silent or marginally present or ideologically represented" (1993, p. 66). In practice, reading contrapuntally "means reading a text with an understanding of what is involved when an author shows, for instance, that a colonial sugar plantation is seen as important to the process of maintaining a particular style of life in England" (1993, p. 66).

Said has modeled powerful notions of intellectual activity and freedom. In his important book *Representations of the Intellectual*, he distinguished between teachers as functionaries, those who are charged with preserving and transferring the parameters of existing systems, and intellectuals as outsiders. For Said, intellectuals should stand at the borders of dominant institutions; they should be outsiders in their own homes, never too comfortable being co-opted. Intellectuals should create new knowledge as they face new challenges. Intellectuals are always socially, culturally, and historically situated. For Henry Giroux and others, Said modeled this notion of an organic, border intellectual, particularly in his combination of academic and political work.

Further Reading
By Said

1978. *Orientalism*. New York: Pantheon.

1983. *The World, the Text, and the Critic*. Cambridge: Harvard University Press.

1993. *Culture and Imperialism*. New York: Alfred A. Knopf.

1994. *Representations of the Intellectual*. New York: Pantheon.

About Said / Relevance for Education

Ashcroft, B., and P. Ahluwalia. *Edward Said*. London and New York: Routledge, 2001.

Giroux, H. "Edward Said and the Politics of Worldliness: Towards a 'Rendezvous of Victory.'" *Cultural Studies/Critical Methodologies* 4 (2004): 339–349.

King, R. *Orientalism and Religion: Postcolonial Theory, India and "the Mystic East."* London and New York: Routledge, 1999.

Lopez, D. S., Jr. "Belief." In *Critical Terms for Religious Studies*, ed. Mark C. Taylor. Chicago: University of Chicago Press, 1998.

Lopez, D. S., Jr., ed. *Curators of the Buddha: The Study of Buddhism Under Colonialism*. Chicago: University of Chicago Press, 1995.

McCarthy, C. *The Uses of Culture*. New York: Routledge, 1998.

Moore, S. D. "Postcolonialism." In *Handbook of Postmodern Biblical Interpretation*, ed. A. K. M. Adam. St. Louis: Chalice Press, 2000.

Viswanathan, G. *Masks of Conquest*. New York: Columbia University Press, 1988.

GAYATRI CHAKRAVORTY SPIVAK

Key Concepts

- subaltern
- othering
- worlding
- strategic essentialism

Gayatri Chakravorty Spivak (b. 1942) is a Bengali cultural and literary critic. Born in Calcutta, India, to a middle-class family during the waning years of British colonial rule, she attended Presidency College of the University of Calcutta, graduating in 1959 with a degree in English literature. She came to the United States in 1962 and attended graduate school at Cornell University, where she received her Ph.D. in comparative literature under the direction of Paul de Man, who introduced her to the work of Jacques DERRIDA. Her 1977 translation of Derrida's *Of Grammatology* (1967) into English made Derrida's work available to a wider audience. Her outstanding introduction to that work quickly brought her recognition among English-speaking academics seeking help in understanding Derrida's text. Spivak was named Avalon Foundation Professor in the Humanities at Columbia University.

Spivak operates at the intersection of postcolonial theory, feminism, deconstruction, and Marxism. She rigorously interrogates the binary oppositions that animate both postcolonial and feminist discourse. She further questions concepts found in the imperialist language of colonizers, including concepts of nationhood, fixed identity, and the Third World. The numerous articles and interviews that comprise Spivak's scholarly production have been compiled into several books. *In Other Worlds: Essays in Cultural Politics* (1987) is a collection of essays on a wide range of topics, from Virginia Woolf's *To the Lighthouse*, to French feminism, to the concept of "value." *The Post-Colonial Critic: Interviews, Strategies, Dialogues* (1990) is a compilation of interviews that present Spivak's often difficult thinking in a reader-friendly format. *Outside in the Teaching Machine* (1993) brings together her writings on higher education and globalization. *A Critique of Postcolonial Reason: Toward a History of the Vanishing Present* (1999) both expands on her studies of the postcolonial—she explores, for instance, the idea of the "native informant"—and reconsiders and revises some of her earlier work.

Fundamental to Spivak's work is the concept of the **subaltern**. "Subaltern" means "of inferior rank." Spivak borrows the term from Antonio GRAMSCI, who used it to refer to social groups under the hegemonic control of the ruling elite. In this sense, the term can refer to any group that is collectively subordinated or disenfranchised, whether on the basis of race, ethnicity, sex, religion, or any other category of identity. Spivak, however, uses this term specifically to refer to the colonized and peripheral subject, especially with reference to those oppressed by British colonialism, such as segments of the Indian population prior to national independence. Spivak emphasizes the fact that the female subaltern subject is even more peripheral and marginalized than the male. In "Can the Subaltern Speak?" (first published in 1985), Spivak observes: "If in the context of colonial production, the subaltern has no history, and cannot speak, the subaltern as female is even more deeply in shadow" (1995, p. 28). Spivak's notion of the subaltern is thus also implicated in feminist concerns. She discusses ways that colonialism—and its patriarchy—silences subaltern voices to the extent that they have no conceptual space from which they can speak and be heard, unless, perhaps, they assume the discourse of the oppressing colonizer. The original version of "Can the Subaltern Speak?" discussed here has been enormously influential in postcolonial theoretical circles. Spivak has, however, revised aspects of her theory of the subaltern in *A Critique of Postcolonial Reason* (1999, see especially pp. 306–311).

Another aspect of Western colonialism explored by Spivak is the way that colonial discourse participates in a process she refers to as "**othering**." Othering—a term derived from a whole corpus of texts by Hegel, Jacques LACAN, Sartre, and others—is an ideological process that isolates groups that are seen as different from the norm of the colonizers. For Spivak, othering is the way in which imperial discourse creates colonized, subaltern subjects. Like Edward SAID, she views othering dialectically: the colonizing subject is created in the same moment as the subaltern subject. In this sense, othering expresses a hierarchical, unequal relationship. In her research into this process, Spivak utilizes British Colonial Office dispatches to reveal othering in historical context. Yet she makes clear that othering is embedded in the discourse of various forms of colonial narrative, fiction as well as nonfiction.

Spivak's concept of **worlding**, derived from Heidegger, is closely related to the dynamics of othering in colonial discourse. Worlding is the process whereby a colonized space is made present in and present to a world crafted by colonial discourse. She states, "If ... we concentrated on documenting and theorizing the itinerary of the consolidation of Europe as sovereign subject, indeed sovereign and subject, then we would produce an alternative historical narrative of the 'worlding' of what is today called 'the Third World'" (1985, p. 247). A worlding narrative of a colonized space operates to inscribe colonial discourse and hegemony on that space. This is a social construct because it is a "worlding of the world on uninscribed earth" (1985, p. 253). A central way in which the practice of worlding occurs is through mapmaking, but there are ideological aspects as well. For instance, Spivak cites the example of an early nineteenth century British soldier traveling across India, surveying the land and people: "He is actually engaged in consolidating the self of Europe by obliging the native to cathect the space of the Other on his home ground. He is worlding *their own world*, which is far from mere uninscribed earth, anew, by obliging *them* to domesticate the alien as Master" (1985, p. 253). In effect, the colonized are made to experience their own land as belonging to the colonizer. Worlding and othering, then, are not simply carried out as matters of impersonal national policy, but are enacted by colonizers in local ways, such as the soldier traveling through the countryside.

Spivak often refers to the highly problematic nature of terms like "Third World," "Orient," and "Indian." For her, as for Said, these terms are essentialist categories whose meanings hinge on binary oppositions that are of dubious usefulness because of their history and arbitrary nature. Essentialist perspectives stress the idea that conceptual categories name eternal, unchangeable characteristics or identities really existing in the external world. Hence, a category like "Orient" becomes essentialist when it is seen as naming a real place inhabited by people with the same characteristics and personality traits that are eternal and unchanging, and, by extension, inescapable because they are "naturally" possessed. Classic essentialist categories include masculine/feminine and civilized/uncivilized. But essentialist categories are unstable because they are social constructions, not universal names for "real" entities in the world. Further, the categories Spivak discusses were constructed by a colonial discourse whose usage had significant hegemonic and ideological implications and effects. A label like "savage Indian" literally "others" its subject. That is, it forces the colonized into a subaltern subject position not of their own choosing. Once located in a particular subject position, the colonizing power can treat them accordingly, and the subjects often assume this role.

In her 1985 essay "Subaltern Studies: Deconstructing Historiography," Spivak argues that although essentialism is highly problematic for the knowledge it creates about an other, there is sometimes a political and social need for what she calls **strategic essentialism**. By this she means a "*strategic* use of positivist essentialism in a scrupulously visible political interest" (1987, p. 205). She argues that it is necessary to assume an essentialist stand—for instance, speaking as a woman or speaking as an Asian—so that the hegemony of patriarchal colonial discourse can be disrupted and questioned. Spivak acknowledges that the application of essentialist categories can have a salutary effect on struggles against oppression and hegemonic power despite the problems inherent in essentialist discourse: "I think it's absolutely on target to take a stand against the discourses of essentialism … [b]ut *strategically* we cannot" (1990, p. 11). Spivak is arguing that strategic essentialism is expedient, if only in the short term, because it can aid in the process of revitalizing the sense of personal and cultural worth and value of the dominated. One example of this occurs when postcolonial cultures essentialize their precolonial past in order to find a usable cultural identity.

The intersection of theory and social activism is a tension that runs throughout Spivak's work. For instance, she has been criticized for her view of strategic essentialism on the grounds that she has given in to the very essentialist, universalist language to which she seems to be so adamantly opposed. For Spivak, however, the strategic use of essentialist categories is not a matter of violating some notion of theoretical "purity," but rather is necessary from the perspective of social and political exigencies—and identity politics—that require, among other things, certain kinds of discursive tools in order to counter oppression and other ills. Spivak is also critical of Western feminists for sometimes ignoring the plight of women of color and, contrarily, for sometimes presuming to speak for non-Western women on issues about which Western feminists have no direct knowledge or experience. In the latter instance, speaking for non-Western women is once again to mute the voices of the women that Western feminists are trying to assist. Such Western feminist discourse creates non-Western women as subaltern subjects and subverts their attempts to speak for themselves.

Spivak has made several important interventions in the field of education. *Outside the Teaching Machine* takes up questions of higher education and globalization. In particular, Spivak intervenes in debates around the literary canon, arguing that a new, reconceptualized curriculum must avoid falling into a new kind of "Orientalism" that reifies and makes static evolving global identities. In addition, Spivak underscores how English departments have historically been complicit with making the "other" exotic, and thus with imperialism. *Death of a Discipline* (2003) takes up the efficacy of "area studies" programs for the contemporary study of difference, arguing for a rapprochement between these programs and departments of comparative literature. All this highlights the importance of literature as a pedagogical tool that "teaches" us about the world and our place in it.

While Spivak has brought her work to bear on higher education, others have picked her up in critical pedagogy more broadly. As Henry Giroux (1993) makes clear, Spivak has contributed important insights about the critical nature of intellectual work today. She has modeled a kind of critical disposition that is concerned not with acquiring "skills" but with thinking about questions of difference and location in reflective and complex ways. Like other postcolonial intellectuals, Spivak moves us away from simple binary oppositions to more nuanced and complex spaces. Critical pedagogues have claimed her work as part of a general project of redefining intellectual activity and life.

Further Reading

By Spivak

1985a. *"The Rani of Sirmur: An Essay in Reading the Archives." *History and Theory* 24: 247–272.

1985b. "Three Women's Texts and a Critique of Imperialism." *Critical Inquiry* 12: 243–261.

1987. *In Other Worlds: Essays in Cultural Politics*. New York: Methuen. Includes "Subaltern Studies: Deconstructing Historiography."

1990. "Criticism, Feminism, and the Institution." In S. Harasym, ed., *The Post-Colonial Critic: Interviews, Strategies, Dialogues*. New York and London: Routledge.

1993. *Outside in the Teaching Machine*. London and New York: Routledge.

1995. *"Can the Subaltern Speak?" In B. Ashcroft, G. Griffiths, and H. Tiffin, eds., *The Post-colonial Studies Reader*. London and New York: Routledge.

1996. *The Spivak Reader: Selected Works of Gayatri Chakravorty Spivak*, edited by D. Landry and G. MacLean. New York and London: Routledge.

1999. *A Critique of Postcolonial Reason: Toward a History of the Vanishing Present*. Cambridge: Harvard University Press.

2003. *Death of a Discipline*. New York: Columbia University Press.

About Spivak / Relevance for Education

Giroux, H. *Border Crossings: Cultural Workers and the Politics of Education*. 2nd ed. New York: Routledge, 2004.

*Morton, S. *Gayatri Chakravorty Spivak*. London and New York: Routledge, 2003.

Young, R. "Spivak: Decolonization, Deconstruction." In *White Mythologies: Writing History and the West*. London and New York: Routledge, 1990.

LEV SEMENOVICH VYGOTSKY

Key Concepts

- social and semiotic mediation
- learning and development
- internalization
- thought–language relations
- conceptual and development
- zone of proximal development

Lev Semenovich Vygotsky (1896–1934) was born in Orsha, in present-day Belarus. His father was a department chief in a bank; although his mother was trained as a teacher, she worked at home raising eight children. The Vygotsky household was stern, intellectually rich, and cultured. Vygotsky studied law, philology, and literature at the University of Moscow and was awarded a law degree. Before devoting his attention to psychology, he worked at a teachers' college in Gomel, an experience that brought him in contact with children who suffered from congenital birth defects such as blindness, deafness, and mental retardation. Propelled by a desire to understand and help these children, Vygotsky began to study academic psychology.

In 1924 Vygotsky was invited to the Second Psychoneurological Congress in Leningrad to help create a psychology and an educational system built on Marxist foundations. He worked for the next decade or so in the areas of developmental psychology, education, and psychopathology until his untimely death from tuberculosis.

Vygotsky's scientific contemporaries included many behaviorists such as Ivan Petrovich Pavlov and John B. Watson, as well as founders of the Gestalt psychology movement such as Max Wertheimer, Wolfgang Kohler, Kurt Koffka, and Kurt Levin. However, Vygotsky was unique among his peers in developing theories of learning and development that pivoted on the roles of **social and semiotic mediation**. Specifically, through culture children acquire much of the content of their thinking. The surrounding culture also provides children with the mediational means for their thinking (language and other sign systems).

During his brief career, Vygotsky acquired vast knowledge not only of psychology but also of the social sciences, philosophy, linguistics, and literature. For various reasons, including the political relationship between the United States and the Soviet Union, Vygotsky remained unknown in the Americas for decades. When the Cold War ended, the wealth of Vygotsky's work began to be translated into English. In the early twenty-first century, it is nearly impossible to find any serious discussion of learning that does not foreground Vygotsky's ideas and perspectives.

Whereas Jean PIAGET developed constructivist theories of learning, Vygotsky developed social constructivist theories. "It is through others that we develop into ourselves," he argued. "Development does not proceed toward socialization but toward the conversion of social relations into mental functions" (1981, pp. 161–165). What is constant in his theories is the important relationship between learning and the child's social and cultural worlds. What changes is how the relationships and forms of mediation are defined and viewed. Vygotsky had a plethora of intellectual roots and research interests. Despite the extraordinary range of his knowledge, three core themes run throughout his theories on most subjects, especially his theories of learning. First, he insisted on a genetic or developmental method. Second, he claimed that higher mental processes in the individual have their origins in social processes. Third, he believed that mental processes can be understood only if we first understand the social and semiotic instruments that mediate them. Looking at the second theme more closely provides an example of Vygotsky's theory and its implications for learning and education.

According to Vygotsky, biology accounts only for very basic elements of human development, and the social environment accounts almost entirely for the development of higher-level cognitive processes such as language, memory, and abstract thinking. Unlike the theories posited by Piaget in which biology and development lead learning, Vygotsky's theories foreground social mediation and insist that learning pulls development along. The zone of proximal development (ZPD; discussed below) is perhaps the most central construct within the theories Vygotsky developed to explain this process.

Contra Piaget, Vygotsky asserted that all fundamental cognitive activities have social foundations and remain quasi-social forever. Vygotsky posited that **learning and development** always occur on two distinct yet mutually constitutive planes: the social and the psychological. Learning is first mediated within an interpsychological plane, between the child and more knowledgeable others, and only later moves into the intrapsychological plane through a process that Vygotsky called "**internalization.**" Internalization is "the process whereby the individual, through participation in interpersonal interaction in which cultural ways of thinking are demonstrated in action, is able to appropriate them so they become transformed from being social phenomena to being part of his or her own intrapersonal mental functioning" (Cole, 1985, cited in Rogoff, 1990). This is not a simple one-way transmission from the more knowledgeable other to the learner, but an appropriation in which information is taken in to use and manage the new skills in different ways for later application. For example, as toddlers participate in many book-sharing activities with their parents, they begin to appropriate the routines and actions necessary for such participation. As time goes on, toddlers gain control of these routines and actions and can use their knowledge to participate in book-reading experiences in new and different ways. Eventually, children internalize these routines and actions so fully that they can read independently. As children move toward self-regulation and independence, they appropriate not only conceptual knowledge but also social values of interacting with family members and the cultural values of using literacy in their daily lives.

Fundamental to the nature and effectiveness of social interaction for Vygotsky was the idea of semiotic mediation: the mediation of activity through semiotic tools such as language. Sign systems, especially language, account for the internalization of interpsychological activity, and "internalization transforms the process itself and changes its structures and functions.... [Thus], the process of internalization is not the transferal of an external activity to a preexisting, internal 'plane of consciousness': it is the process by which the plane is formed" (Vygotsky, 1981, p. 163). Language and other semiotic tools (for example, gestures, pictures) function as "mediational means" (Wertsch, 1985) within the context of social experience. Because specific forms of semiotic mediation vary from one social group to another, the nature and content of learning varies across these groups. In other words, learning is socially and culturally specific more than universal largely because social and cultural tools vary across social and cultural contexts.

Although the extent to which Marxist thought influenced Vygotsky is often debated, some Marxist insights seem clearly evident in his work. For example, he extended Friedrich Engels's basic insights about instrumental mediation to include psychological or cultural tools as well as technical/material tools, arguing that the former fundamentally transform higher mental processes such as memory, concept development, and creativity. Indeed, he viewed the development of such processes as neither incremental nor stagelike, but as a series of qualitative transformations or revolutions associated with mediation by specific cultural tools. In other words, major developmental accomplishments are always associated with new forms of semiotic mediation. Importantly, psychological (or cultural) tools are social and historical and not individual in nature. They develop as a function of social needs and are used at particular historical times for specific social functions, and then they sediment as "natural" components of social and cultural life.

Although semiotic mediation may involve any sign or sign system, Vygotsky viewed language as the most important semiotic system in human activity. The phrase "semiotic mediation" has thus come to stand for mediation by linguistic signs. Vygotsky's privileging of linguistic signs seems to be related to his belief that, of all the semiotic systems, only language is capable of being reflexive, classifying reality, construing communicable human experience, and articulating the many voices of a culture with equal facility. These qualities of language are key to its capacity to function as a mediational means, especially in the cognitive development of children.

How Vygotsky theorized the **thought–language relations** is perhaps most obvious in his critique of Piaget. Piaget claimed that the early activity of the child is egocentric and that social understanding develops late. According to Piaget, the young child at first talks mostly about himself and only himself, with little or no concern for communicating with others in his immediate surroundings. The intersubjectivity central to normal adult discourse is not part of the young child's language practice. Vygotsky could not have disagreed more:

> The primary function of speech, in both children and adults, is communication, social contact. The earliest speech of the child is therefore essentially social. At a certain stage the social speech of the child is quite sharply divided into egocentric and communicative speech....

Egocentric speech emerges when the child transfers social collaborative forms of behavior to the sphere of inner-personal psychic functions.... When circumstances force him to stop and think, he is likely to think aloud. Egocentric speech, splintered off from general social speech, in time leads to inner speech, which serves both autistic and logical thinking. (1962, p. 19)

Vygotsky devoted considerable research to understanding how thinking and speech develop in children. He argued that the thought and speech of young children, between approximately birth and two years old, vary in nature and function depending on the development of the child. Yet he acknowledged that both function as instruments for planning and carrying out actions in the world. As a whole, language is used to navigate social situations, develop concepts, and regulate thinking.

Conceptual development was another area in which Vygotsky did much theorizing and research. Importantly, he defined conceptual development as the development of the functional use of semiotic tools (signs) as a means of focusing one's attention, selecting distinctive features, and analyzing and synthesizing them. In developing concepts, children bring their experiences and language together to create new meanings and contexts. Learning and development were conceived by Vygotsky in terms of repertoire theories rather than stage theories. Children (and adults) have repertoires of ways to organize their worlds conceptually, and which ways they use varies as a function of the task and goal structures of particular activities. He viewed concept development as an iterative and dynamic process: "A concept emerges and takes shape in the course of a complex operation aimed at the solution of some problem.... A concept is not an isolated, ossified, and changeless formation, but an active part of the intellectual process, constantly engaged in serving communication, understanding, and problem solving" (1962, p. x). Learning and development are thus characterized as revolutions or transformations that are effects of particular forms of social and semiotic mediation. They are not characterized as linear and incremental, and their trajectories are certainly not invariant and sequential but display unpredictable leaps and regressions.

Though not a stage theorist, Vygotsky did outline the general trajectory of learning. He posited that children's initial concepts are spontaneous and characterized as unorganized or loosely juxtaposed meanings and ideas, or what Vygotsky called "incoherent coherence." Only gradually do children develop the capacity to think more logically, eventually becoming able to understand and use abstract or scientific concepts.

He also argued convincingly that spontaneous concepts and scientific concepts are mutually constitutive. Each helps the other develop. Whereas spontaneous concepts begin in concrete experiences, scientific concepts begin with abstract linguistic definitions. "Scientific concepts grow downward through spontaneous concepts; spontaneous concepts grow upward through scientific concepts" (1962, p. 194). The development of spontaneous concepts is required to facilitate (or anchor) the absorption of scientific concepts. In turn, scientific concepts provide the theoretical frameworks that facilitate new understandings that change the structure and organization of spontaneous concepts.

Vygotsky's theories about conceptual development thus mark a shift from the traditional developmental models of learning and development toward understanding individual mental functioning as situated within social and cultural activities. The primary unit of analysis of such a view is the person in a context engaged in a task with a goal. Vygotsky used the term "learning" to describe the important shifts in growth and behavior of learners, while Piaget relied on the term "development." This different terminology indexes an important shift in thinking. From a Piagetian perspective, development is a prerequisite for learning. From a Vygotskian perspective, development does not necessarily precede learning. Instead, socially and semiotically mediated learning allows for the possibility of future development. In other words, learning propels development. Importantly, Vygotsky considered the capacity to teach and to benefit from instruction as fundamental attributes of human beings.

The **zone of proximal development** (ZPD) is probably the construct from Vygotsky's work that is most familiar to scholars of developmental psychology and education. Teachers and teacher educators often discuss the ZPD with great interest. Vygotsky developed the construct of the ZPD to investigate and understand "those functions that have not yet matured but are in the process of maturation, functions that will mature tomorrow but are currently in an embryonic state. These functions could be termed the 'buds' or 'flowers' of development rather than the 'fruits of development" (1978, p. 86). Vygotsky went on to define the ZPD as *"the distance between the actual developmental level as determined by independent problem solving and the level of potential development as determined through problem solving under adult guidance or in collaboration with more capable peers"* (p. 86; italics in original). The ZPD, according to Vygotsky, embodies three key aspects or themes. First, it represents the joint effort of the consciousnesses of the participants engaged in dialogue. It is thus a construct about dyads, not individuals. Second, both participants play active instrumental roles. Third, the interaction between participants is organized in a dynamic, dialectical fashion.

According to Vygotsky, the most effective forms of teaching-learning processes occur within the ZPD. Since learning involves moving beyond current levels of competence, scaffolding should function to move learners into the nearest reaches of their incompetence (not too far) and should help them become competent there. As learning continues, the leading edge of the reaches of incompetence keeps moving on. Teachers and learners must both map the limits of competence and strive together to move just beyond it.

The ZPD provides a model for intellectual growth that has been utilized by teachers and others to explain how they should organize learning experiences. Moll, for example, describes the ZPD as follows:

> a "connecting" concept in Vygotsky's theory, it embodies or integrates key elements of the theory: the emphasis on social activity and cultural practices as sources of thinking, the importance of mediation in human psychological functioning, the centrality of pedagogy in development, and the inseparability of the individual from the social. (1990, p. 15)

The ZPD does not contain finite boundaries of learning or development. Instead, it should be viewed as a dynamic and fluid social space within which individuals move about as the content, learning contexts, and learner characteristics change.

Because Vygotsky's theory foregrounds the social, the theoretical importance of the ZPD is that it is situated within the context of the specific social and cultural environments with which the child or learner is involved. These environments are constructed in a web of social interactions and relations, and so learning in the ZPD leads not only to the development of concepts and knowledge but also to the development of culturally appropriate practices.

Vygotsky was indeed a genius who crossed disciplinary boundaries, drawing together key ideas from biology, philosophy, psychology, literary criticism, poetics, social theory, linguistics, and ethnology. He transformed our thinking about learning and development in children. He helped us more fully understand the nature and functions of many human activities such as social speech, private speech, tool use, and sign use. Even more than Piaget, he showed how children's learning is complex, dynamic, socially based, and semiotically mediated. His unique approach to the study of human learning disrupted the traditional idea that individuals are separate from the sociocultural settings in which they function. He replaced traditional theories with a theory that explains how the individual and the social are co-constitutive. Despite his brief life, there is probably no major thinker, except perhaps DEWEY, who has exerted more influence on educational research and practice than Lev Semenovich Vygotsky.

Further Reading

By Vygotsky

1962. *Thought and Language,* translated by E. Hanfemann and G. Vakar. Cambridge, MA: MIT Press.

1978. *Mind in Society: The Development of Higher Psychological Processes,* edited by M. Cole, V. John-Steiner, S. Scribner, and E. Souberman. Cambridge, MA: MIT Press.

1981. "The Genesis of Higher Mental Functions." In J. V. Wertsch, ed., *The Concept of Activity in Soviet Psychology.* Armonk, NY: M. E. Sharpe.

About Vygotsky

Daniels, H. *Vygotsky and Pedagogy.* London: Falmer, 2001.

*Dixon-Krauss, L. *Vygotsky in the Classroom.* Boston: Allyn and Bacon, 1995.

*Kozulin, A. *Vygotsky's Psychology: A Biography of Ideas.* Cambridge, MA: Harvard University Press, 1995.

Wertsch, J. V. *Vygotsky and the Social Formation of Mind.* Cambridge, MA: Harvard University Press, 1985.

Wertsch, J. V. *Voices of the Mind: A Sociocultural Approach to Mediated Action.* Cambridge, MA: Harvard University Press, 1991.

Relevance for Education

Bruner, J. *Acts of Meaning.* Cambridge, MA: Harvard University Press, 1990.

Bullowa, M. *Before Speech: The Beginnings of Interpersonal Communication.* Cambridge, UK: Cambridge University Press, 1979.

Clay, M. *Reading Recovery: A Guidebook for Teachers in Training.* Portsmouth, NH: Heinemann, 1993.

Cobb, P., T. Wood, and E. Yackel. "A Constructivist Approach to Second-Grade Mathematics." In E. von Glasersfeld, ed., *Constructivism in Mathematics Education.* Dordrecht: Kluwer, 1991.

Edwards, C., L. Gandini, and E. Foreman. *The Hundred Languages of Children: The Reggio Emilia Approach — Advanced Reflections.* Greenwich, CT: Ablex, 1998.

Gallimore, R., and R. Tharpe. "Teaching Mind in Society: Teaching, Schooling, and Literate Discourse." In L. C. Moll, ed., *Vygotsky and Education.* Cambridge, UK: Cambridge University Press, 1990.

Katz, L., and S. Chard. *Engaging Children's Minds: The Project Approach*. Stamford, CT: Ablex, 2000.

Krashen, S. D. *Second Language Acquisition and Second Language Learning*. Upper Saddle River, NJ: Prentice-Hall, 1988.

Lindfors, J. W. *Children's Inquiry: Using Language To Make Sense Of The World*. New York: Teachers College Press, and Urbana, IL: NCTE, 1999.

Luria, A. R. *The Mind of the Mnemonist*, translated by L. Solotoroff. Cambridge, MA: Harvard University Press, 1968.

Luria, A. R. *Selected Writings of A. R. Luria*. Armonk, NY: M. E. Sharpe, 1979.

Moll, L. C., ed. *Vygotsky and Education: Instructional Implications and Applications of Sociohistorical Psychology*. New York: Oxford University Press, 1990.

Moll, L., N. Gonzalez, and M. Civil, eds. *Funds of Knowledge for Teaching*. Final report submitted to the National Center for Research on Cultural Diversity and Second Language Learning. Tucson, AZ: College of Education and Bureau of Applied Research in Anthropology, University of Arizona, 1995.

Palinscar, A. S., and A. L. Brown. "Reciprocal Teaching of Comprehension Fostering and Comprehension-Monitoring Activities." *Cognition and Instruction* 1 (1984): 117–175.

Purcell-Gates, V. *Other People's Words: The Cycle of Low Literacy*. Cambridge, MA: Harvard University Press, 1995.

Rogoff, B. *Apprenticeship in Thinking: Cognitive Development in a Social Context*. New York: Oxford University Press, 1990.

Rowe, D. W. *Preschoolers as Authors: Literacy Learning in the Social World of the Classroom*. Creskill, NJ: Hampton, 1994.

Trevarthen, C. "Descriptive Analyses of Infant Communicative Behavior." In H. R. Schaffer, ed., *Studies in Mother-Infant Interaction*. London: Academic Press, 1977.

Wells, G. *Dialogic Inquiry: Towards a Sociocultural Practice and Theory of Education*. New York: Cambridge University Press, 1999.

Wells, G., and G. L. Chang-Wells. *Constructing Knowledge Together*. Portsmouth, NH: Heinemann, 1992.

RAYMOND WILLIAMS

Key Concepts

- Culture versus culture
- cultural studies
- ideal, documentary, and social culture
- the structure of feeling
- dominant, residual, and emergent aspects of history

Raymond Williams (1921–1988) was a British literary theorist, a novelist, a leading Marxist, and one of the founders of cultural studies. He was born in Wales and raised in a working-class family; his mother was a housewife, and his father a railway signalman. In 1939 he entered Cambridge University on a scholarship. There he studied literature and was a member of the Cambridge University Socialist Club. His studies were interrupted in 1942 when he was called to military duty, serving as a tank commander. After the war, Williams returned to Cambridge to finish his degree.

After graduating from Cambridge, Williams worked in the Adult Education Department at Oxford University for fifteen years; during that time he wrote two major works, *Culture and Society, 1780–1950* (1958) and *The Long Revolution* (1961). He joined the faculty at Cambridge University as a lecturer in English and drama in 1961 and remained there for the rest of his career.

Williams approached literature from an interdisciplinary Marxist perspective. He explored ways in which social class hierarchy is expressed in literature, usually to the advantage of the upper classes. He was also interested in how modes of communication are connected to the material conditions of a society. His theories, especially those on culture, have affected other intellectual currents, such as the New Historicism, and are often associated with Hayden White's concept of metahistory and his focus on historiography as a form of interpretive narrative that is never disinterested with regard to matters of social power.

Williams's ideas about culture are foundational for the field now known as cultural studies. In *The Long Revolution*, his second major theoretical work, he explored conceptual issues connected with the term "culture." He distinguished between **Culture** (with a capital "C") and **culture** (with lowercase "c"). The former is a moral and aesthetic term originally conceived by English writers such as the Victorian poet and humanist Matthew Arnold and the twentieth-century literary critic F. R. Leavis. In their discourse, "Culture" means "high culture," the sum total of civilization's greatest moral and aesthetic achievements. The not-so-hidden agenda of this idea of Culture is to assert and maintain social class—"high culture" and "high class" are synonymous. Against this view, Williams developed a concept of "culture" (lowercase) in terms of the social. This culture is not comprised exclusively of those ideas and achievements deemed to be the high points of civilization. Rather, culture includes all products of human activity, including language, social, political, and religious ideas and institutions, and other expressions, both conceptual and material. In other words, culture in this sense comprises all that humans create and enact in order to make sense of their existence.

It is this concept of culture that is the focal point of Williams's literary-cultural studies. By arguing that the concept of culture is not reducible to the products of an elite class, Williams helped create a new academic field—**cultural studies**—which examines the everyday life of non-elite groups, among other topics.

This conception of culture as social is for Williams one of "three general categories in the definition of culture" (1961, p. 57): the ideal, the documentary, and the social. **Ideal culture** refers to the concept of culture as a "state or process of human perfection" measured by absolute or universal standards. In this instance, cultural analysis "is essentially the discovery and description, in lives and works, of those values which can be seen to compose a timeless order, or to have permanent reference to the universal human condition" (1961, p. 57). **Documentary culture** approaches culture as a documentary record, a repository for the artifacts of cultural achievements, including literature, arts, and philosophy. Here, "culture is the body of intellectual and imaginative work, in which, in a detailed way, human thought and experience are variously recorded" (1961, p. 57). Finally, **social culture** focuses on culture not simply in terms of the artifacts and achievements of high, elite culture, but in terms of all the many ways that people conceive and enact their lives. Thus, culture encompasses the political, the religious, and the economic, as well as all modes of thought and practice by which people live in the world.

For Williams, thinking of culture in terms of this third definitional category, as social culture, breaks down distinctions between elite culture and the "popular" culture of the masses. Social culture claims that the products of elite culture are not to be valorized over the products of popular culture. All cultural products count as culture. Culture is not static but instead is a process that on the one hand always asserts itself and acts on humans, and on the other hand is constantly produced and changed by them. Cultural process flows both toward us and away from us. The idea of culture as social is meant to express this dynamism.

These three categories or definitions are to be understood, said Williams, as a whole and in terms of the interactions and relationships existing between these three aspects of culture: "However difficult it may be in practice, we have to try to see the process as a whole, and to relate our particular studies … to the actual and complex organization" (1961, p. 60). One of the byproducts of Williams's egalitarian, nonelitist view of culture was that he laid a foundation for the study of popular culture. Because all human products and practices are considered valuable and available for cultural analysis, forms of what we now refer to as "popular" culture—such as television, film, pop and rock music, sports, and weblogs—are arguably more revealing about the nature of culture because it is in these aspects of culture that lived experiences of the non-elite are expressed. The products of high culture tell us only about elites; popular culture tells much more because of its inclusivity. Williams studied popular culture in later works such as *Television: Technology and Cultural Form* (1974).

In his examination of culture, Williams paid considerable attention to what he called "**the structure of feeling**." A structure of feeling is the particular character and quality of a shared cultural sense. In general, Williams's notion of the structure of feeling refers to the lived experience of a people—or a generation of people—within particular cultural contexts. The lived experience includes the interaction between "official" culture—laws, religious doctrine, and other formal aspects of a culture—and the way that people live in their cultural context. The structure of feeling is what imbues a people with a specific "sense of life" and experience of community. It is comprised of the set of particular cultural commonalities shared by a culture despite the individual differences within it. As Williams noted, the sense of commonality is not necessarily shared throughout a culture but is most likely the feeling of the dominant social group. This cultural feeling is not typically expressed in any verbal, rational mode of discourse, though it can often be located in literary texts that reveal it only indirectly. Cultural analysis of the structure of feeling aims at uncovering how these shared feelings and values operate to help people make sense of their lives and the different situations in which the structure of feeling arises.

In *Marxism and Literature* (1977), Williams examined historiographical issues, arguing that the cultural analyst must recognize the complex interactions that occur within historical contexts and be careful to avoid privileging those dominant, empowered voices within it. In other words, rather than viewing history as a progression of nameable cultural periods, in which each period determines the one that follows, Williams wanted to look at history through the lens of cultural struggle and resistance. To this end, he posited three terms "which recognize not only 'stages' and 'variations' but the internal dynamic relations of any actual process" (1977, p. 121). These are the "dominant," "residual," and "emergent" aspects of historical periods.

The **dominant** aspects of a historical period are the systems of thought and practice that dictate, or try to dictate, what can be thought and what can be done—that is, the assertion of dominant values, morality, and meanings. For Williams, the concept of the dominant is related to the concept of hegemony. The dominant is hegemonic, rigorously promoting the interests of the empowered and suppressing the interests of others, but it does not stand uncontested. Williams reminds us that within any cultural context, the "effective dominant culture" is always under siege by alternative values, meanings, and practices that are not part of it. These alternatives and oppositions to the dominant culture can be found in "residual" and "emergent" forms.

The **residual** aspects of a historical period are past cultural formations. These old values and meanings may have been dominant once but have now been supplanted by the present dominant power. Aspects of these older cultural forms may still be active in the present, exerting pressure on the dominant forms, although they are generally subordinate to the dominant. In short, the residual can both be incorporated into the dominant culture and also have aspects that stand in opposition or as an alternative to that culture. Williams cited by way of example the residual nature of organized religion in contemporary English culture.

The **emergent** aspects of a historical period are those newly emerging values, meanings, and practices that adumbrate future cultural directions and put pressure on the existing dominant culture. Cultural forms can never be frozen by the dominant culture. Dominant culture is always undergoing opposition by these new cultural forms that threaten to replace the dominant.

Williams views these three relations of cultural process as the ground where struggles over dominance and resistance to hegemony are waged. Further, this tripartite view of historical process requires us to view culture as dynamic rather than static, and to be mindful of the interactions and cross-fertilization of these three aspects of cultural movement and change.

Williams's work has been important for many who wish to reclaim the pedagogical roots of cultural studies. Cultural studies has been a widely popular project in several different disciplines, but Karl Maton and Handel Wright (2002), among others, have stressed the importance of this project's origins in everyday material practices of working people. In fact, many have tried to reclaim Williams's roots in adult education and his efforts to draw on the everyday lives of working people, especially women, in forging a relevant humanities curricula. The influence of Williams's work in adult education has been picked up and developed by several different scholars (e.g., Fieldhouse, 1990; McIllroy, 1993).

Further Reading

By Williams

1958. *Culture and Society, 1780–1950*. New York: Columbia University Press.

1966. *The Long Revolution*. New York: Columbia University Press.

1977. *Marxism and Literature*. New York: Oxford University Press.

1980. *Problems in Materialism and Culture: Selected Essays*. London and New York: Verso.

1983. *Keywords: A Vocabulary of Culture and Society*. New York: Oxford University Press.

2001. *The Raymond Williams Reader*, edited by J. Higgins. Oxford: Blackwell.

About Williams / Relevance for Education

Apple, M. Series Editor's Introduction. In Dworkin and Roman, eds., 1993.

Apple, M. *Official Knowledge*. New York: Routledge, 1993.

Dimitriadis, G., and D. Carlson, eds. *Promises To Keep: Cultural Studies, Democratic Education, and Public Life*. New York: Routledge, 2003.

Dworkin, D., and L. Roman, eds. *Views beyond the Border Country: Raymond Williams and Cultural Politics*. New York: Routledge, 1993.

Eagleton, T., ed. *Raymond Williams: Critical Perspectives*. Boston: Northeastern University Press, 1989.

Eldridge, J. E. T. *Raymond Williams: Making Connections*. London and New York: Routledge, 1994.

Fieldhouse, R. "Oxford and Adult Education." In Morgan and Preseton, eds., 1993.

Higgins, J. *Raymond Williams: Literature, Marxism, and Cultural Materialism*. London and New York: Routledge, 1999.

*Inglis, F. *Raymond Williams*. New York: Routledge, 1995.

Maton, K., and H. Wright. "Returning Cultural Studies to Education." *International Journal of Cultural Studies* 5 (2002): 379–392.

McCarthy, C. *The Uses of Culture*. New York: Routledge, 1998.

McIlroy, J. "Teacher, Critic, Explorer." In Morgan and Preseton, eds., 1993.

Morgan, J., and P. Preseton, eds. *Raymond Williams: Politics, Education, Letters*. New York: St. Martins, 1993.

Prendergast, C., ed. *Cultural Materialism: On Raymond Williams*. Minneapolis: University of Minnesota Press, 1995.

Whitty, G. *Sociology and School Knowledge: Curriculum Theory, Research, and Politics*. London: Methuen, 1985.